WRITERS ON WRITING

A BREAD LOAF ANTHOLOGY

WRITERS

*The Bread Loaf Anthology of
Contemporary American Poetry,
edited by Robert Pack, Sydney
Lea, and Jay Parini, 1985.*

*The Bread Loaf Anthology of
Contemporary American Short
Stories, edited by Robert Pack
and Jay Parini, 1987.*

*The Bread Loaf Anthology of
Contemporary American Essays,
edited by Robert Pack and
Jay Parini, 1989.*

*Writers on Writing, edited by
Robert Pack and Jay Parini, 1991.*

EDITED BY

Robert Pack

Jay Parini

on WRITING

MIDDLEBURY COLLEGE PRESS

Published by University Press of New England

Hanover and London

MIDDLEBURY COLLEGE PRESS

Published by University Press of New England, Hanover, NH 03755

© 1991 by the President and Fellows of Middlebury College
Printed in the United States of America 5 4 3 2 1

CIP data appear at the end of the book

Acknowledgments for previously published material appear on p. 295

CONTENTS

vi   *Contents*

FOREWORD

It seems odd that so many books about writing, including books of criticism as well as "how to" books for both poets and fiction writers, are written by people who have never written a poem or a story. Nevertheless, much of the best criticism and most of the useful practical advice about writing has come from writers. It's no accident that in virtually every age the dominant poets were also the dominant critics, from Ben Jonson and Dryden, to Coleridge and T. S. Eliot. Today, of course, with the proliferation of academic criticism, writers of poetry and fiction are outnumbered by critics by a considerable margin. And a further wrinkle has been added in that the language of criticism has become so technical, even jargon-ridden, that writers of poetry and fiction often can't or, more usually, won't stoop to conquer. As a result, the domain of criticism—and writing about writing—has been given over to "experts," many of whom are far more interested in the theoretical aspects of literature (in itself a good thing) than in the process and techniques of writing.

"Pay no attention to the criticism of men who have never themselves written a notable work," says Ezra Pound with characteristic force in a well-known essay. This states the case rather extremely and fails to take into account the fact that a piece of criticism can itself be deemed a "notable work" (or that women as well as men might take up the pen!). Yet Pound's cannonball of a remark is still hurtling through space, and it calls attention to the fact that one should pay special attention to what writers have to say about writing—about past and present authors, about their own works, about their craft in general.

In the same essay quoted above, Pound continued: "My pawing over the ancients and semi-ancients has been one struggle to find out what has been done, once for all, better than it can ever be done again, and to find out what remains for us to do." While this, once again, puts the case too narrowly, Pound reminds us that writers have a vested interest in criticism of a particular kind; the writer-as-critic is, like Captain Morgan on the Spanish Main, a pirate of sorts, taking what he or she can where it is available. In many respects, the essays contained in the current anthology are classic examples of writerly criticism: essays in the root-sense of the term (*essai*), which connotes exploration, an expedition into unknown waters. They were not written to a "thesis," not written with any particular theoretical slant. Their bias is always individual, even idiosyncratic, and their critical presuppositions are those of a given writer's imaginary universe.

The writers included here are all seasoned practitioners, poets and fictionists, and these particular pieces have never been published before in book form. They are all spin-offs of the writers' private literary workshops, and they reflect the various preoccupations of the individual imaginations that set them into motion. As in the essays by Richard Ford, Rosellen Brown, Francine Prose, and Nicholas Delbanco, the writer's focus is commonly on another writer. Some of the essays deal more generally with thematic aspects of writing—as in John Irving's practical guide to beginning a story and Nancy Willard's reflections on narrative. William Matthews's necessarily brief essay, "The Soul of Brevity," takes a close look at what it means to write succinctly, whereas T. R. Hummer examines the central trope of all writing—metaphor—concluding that "if we come to see everything double, in a precise and disciplined way, then we may hope to hold the terrible paradoxes of our situation before ourselves, and truly know them." Bob Pack's essay deals with word choice. Jay Parini writes about the complex relation between literary productivity and quality in "On Being Prolific," while in "The Prose Sublime," Donald Justice examines the aesthetic effects in prose that one more commonly associates with poetry, "a sort of transport, a *frisson*, a thrilled recognition, which, 'flashing forth at the right moment,' as Longinus has it, 'scatters everything before it like a thunderbolt. . . .'"
A few of the essays, such as those by David Huddle, Donald Justice, Ellen Bryant Voigt, Hilma Wolitzer, Tim O'Brien, Stanley Elkin, Lynne Sharon Schwartz, and Marvin Bell, appear at times to have come directly out of the experience of teaching writing; they are pedagogically rich and full of the wisdom that comes from many years of work as writers and teachers. A number of these pieces, including those by Paul Mariani, Erica Jong, Linda Pastan, Joyce Carol Oates, Gail Godwin, and Sydney Lea, can be thought of as autobiographical writing in which the subject

becomes, finally, writing itself—a brand of essayistic excursion with deep roots in our culture. "Part of the Problem" by Philip Levine stands on its own as a marvelous adventure in polemical criticism, one likely to raise hackles in various academic quarters.

Writers on Writing is, finally, a book for writers about writing. It should be of use to apprentice writers—students of writing—as well as more experienced writers. In the spirit of the Writers' Conference on Bread Loaf Mountain in Vermont (where many of the contributors to this volume have studied and taught), the essays all reveal an underlying commitment to writing as a craft, something that can be passed on from generation to generation of writers, and to the notion of literature as a place where values are tested, where ideas are bodied forth, where the only limits are those enforced by the limits of a writer's own imagination: limits that, by the paradox of art, make that production possible.

ROBERT PACK
JAY PARINI

WRITERS ON WRITING

Three Propositions:
Hooey, Dewey, and Loony

I have brought something along to serve as prologue. It's an article by Bob Thomas of the Associated Press in which Thomas is interviewing William Shatner about the movie *Star Trek V: The Final Frontier.* This is not the first occasion William Shatner, better known as Captain Kirk of the Starship *Enterprise,* has spoken for me. You may remember that in *Star Trek IV: The Voyage Home* Captain Kirk and his crew return to Earth in our time. Kirk is eating pizza in a joint in San Francisco with a woman whose help he will need, when he decides to 'fess up about who he is and where he has come from. The camera circles the room, then homes in on Kirk and his companion as she bursts out with, *"You mean you're from outer space!"* "No," says Kirk, "I'm from Iowa. I only *work* in outer space."

That was the first time that the captain spoke for me. The second time occurs in this article. Trying to explain the popularity of Star Trek, Kirk—I mean Shatner—says, "Is it possible that we're creating a mythology? . . . The more I read and the more I think about it, I wonder if the key to Star Trek is not all the wonderful stuff we talk about: the character interplay, the sci-fi, action and adventure, and all those good things that seem to be on the surface. Somewhere underneath, the chemistry and the concept touch upon a mythological need in modern culture. That's my real thought." And then he backs up just like an artist and says, "I don't quite know what I mean. It would take a far more intelligent and perceptive person to divine what I mean."

Since we are free in the imagination to begin anywhere, let me begin with three propositions about poets. The first is an analysis in the form of a prediction, the second is an explanation, and the third is a testimonial. Here are the three propositions: (1) The future belongs to the helpless; (2) We all think we are frauds but none of us is rich enough to say so in public; and (3) The rain is too heavy a whistle for the certainty of charity.

First, "the future belongs to the helpless." I phrased it thus to echo the confidence with which the Russian poet, Yevgeny Yevtushenko, proclaimed some years ago that in poetry the future belonged to those poets who could jump the farthest, those who could freely associate most wildly. Although at the time Russian and East European writers often spoke about politics in unpolitical metaphors—hence, a Polish pencil might stand for a Polish bureaucrat—the "free association" to which Yevtushenko was referring was not the coming liberalism of *perestroika*, but that of juxtaposition, which, it can be argued, may be poetry's most constant and visible technique.

But what does one mean by a constant, visible technique? First, we have to make some gesture toward defining a playing field where any technique might matter. So here is today's definition of poetry. It has occurred to me, during the ongoing game—and it is only a game: artificial in conception, justified by assumptions, dependent on tacit cooperation, and well forgotten afterward—the game of defining poetry, vis-à-vis prose, that we might say that prose is prose because of what it includes while poetry is poetry because of what it leaves out.

Juxtaposition is a form of leaving out. Pound wanted more of it, demonstrating its strength in his broad editing of *The Waste Land*. In its simplest manifestation, it means leaving out the transitions. The practice overlaps the classroom advice to "Show, don't tell," it reiterates by example Archibald MacLeish's well-known line, "A poem should not mean, but be," and it reaffirms Billie Holliday's "Don't explain."

Why should a poem be effective, even "poetic," because it leaves things out? Shouldn't a reader—intelligent, practical, demanding, sensible, reasonable—want to secure a path through the poem at first glance? Whoa! I have imagined a reader who isn't necessarily a reader of poetry. A reader of poetry is not, at the moment of reading, practical, but indulgent; not demanding, but attentive; not sensible, but audacious; not reasonable, but imaginative; not even so much intelligent as simply aware. For poetry, like beauty, is in the eye of the beholder. One cannot make an unwilling reader see the unflowering life of a poem when he or she has something else to do, such as proving a point.

The action of poetry requires a reader. The writer, having found his or her way from the first word of the poem to the last, leaves it to the reader to find the route for himself or herself. Each rereading is a fresh start. As for the Emily Dickinsons of this world, publishing little or not at all during their lifetimes, they must be their own and perhaps only readers, but so are we all as we write and then first see what it is we have written.

Poetry is unparaphrasable. We repeat this maxim, we shove it in the faces of critics, we use it to escape the responsibility of the classroom, and we are allowed to because, yes, it is true. The Imagist credo: A new cadence is a new idea. Robert Creeley, as quoted by Charles Olson: "Form is never more than an extension of content." Frank Lloyd Wright: "Form follows function." How a poem says what it says *is* what it says. We all know this. Of course no word expresses what another word expresses, we all know this too (there are no absolute synonyms), and this truth is promoted by the phrase and further by the sentence and so is true of all language. In poetry, however, it is true with a vengeance. To apprehend the full expression that is a poem, we have to read between the lines, go outside the borders, engage in metaphor, hear the silences, change direction in the interludes, and, often most important, be ready to think many things at once.

In the classroom, despite the best of intentions, this has proven almost impossible. Graduates of what we call our "educational *system*," and the academics thereof whose professional standing depends on research into what can only be called, with gross naiveté, "the facts" of literature, often make a poor audience for the poetry in poems. They want to find out what a poem means and how to use it, rather than how to follow and experience it. They have been schooled in getting to the gist of things and moving on, and so they approach poetry as if it were content covered up by words.

I take a backseat to no one in my appreciation of poetry as an occasion for conversation. But there is something overlooked in most of the conversation that surrounds poems, and that something, I have come to believe, is the poetry.

American poetry sometimes seems to be a playground of contesting ideologues, promoting themselves as narrative poets, neoformalists, language poets, class poets, and so forth. Insofar as the techniques and manners of poetry may serve many motives, some contradictory to one another, and insofar as poetic license is not obtained from any authority other than the expressive self, I suppose that they must be, all of them, in some sense correct, no matter what they say. I think to add only this little epistemological alert: Where all things are correct, it is equally true that none are.

So. Helplessness. We are, all of us, trained not to be helpless. We are schooled in what we do, as well as how, when, where, and why to do it.

We become purposeful, reasonable, civic, deliberate, and . . . predictable and programmable. After all that, art becomes, more and more, the refuge of our helplessness: our purposeless, unreasonable, personal or private, accidental, unpredictable selves. It is where we have a chance to experience the helpless "Yes!" of life, to experience nature and artifice, inner and outer, as if life itself were what there is to life.

As if life is what it is, nothing more. I want to be careful to respect that feeling some have, out of faith or partial research, that there is a life hereafter. Nonetheless, it seems to me that poetry springs from the need and the wish to express what this life feels like. Even when it sings of another life or another world, it sings it in the frequencies of this one.

It is good to recall, in first classes, these four lines by the Spanish poet, Antonio Machado: "People possess four things / that are no good at sea: / anchor, rudder, oars, and / the fear of going down." Poetry is an abandonment of position (or anchor), an abandonment of the deliberate course (or rudder), an utter nonchalance about propulsion (or oars), and, perhaps scarily, a relinquishing of the fear of going down. Good-bye, known ports of call; good-bye, mapped interstates; good-bye, teacher with one finger held aloft; good-bye, sophisticated schooler of privilege; farewell, burden of right, the lists in the pocket.

The poet comes to his or her helplessness, and to its value, by way of the helplessness of others—and much of that masquerading as help*ful*ness. See if any of you recognize the usual poetry workshop in this description: The poet reads aloud his or her poem, hurrying through it fearfully as if it were prose garbage, and as if the greatest vulnerability is to be seen with one's mouth open. Then the discussion begins. One person says we just can't use a certain word in a poem—it's archaic, or it's crude, or it's fancy, or—God forbid—its meaning has to be looked up in the dictionary. Another thinks the poem should be shorter, or longer, or should start later, or end sooner. The group gradually cuts out all the "bad" lines, leaving, if anything remains, a smaller poem ostensibly of "good" lines. In the end, the group, if it is a smart one, has produced another publishable poem in imitation of a great many other already published poems.

Little artistic growth can come from such talk. First off, one learns nothing from other's bad work, only from one's own. Let me repeat that because I think it may imply a way of life: One learns nothing from other's bad work, only from one's own. Would we attempt to learn to sing by listening to the tone-deaf? Do we imagine we could learn to fly by imitating the labors of a kangaroo? To fly, study the eagle or the sparrow—as you prefer. To know the richness of language, read—well, it's obvious, isn't it?

Second, the growth of a poet does not rest in what he or she can do already. It rests in what he or she cannot do yet. In other words, the worst part of a poem may contain the seeds of what will become the next poem and, beyond that, bigger and better poems by that writer.

Behind each poem brought to group discussion may lie a ghost poem, a poem that is bigger (not necessarily longer), more complex (not necessarily more complicated), deeper, richer, more enveloping. To disdain the raw, unrealized portion of such a poem is to relegate the writer to the role of good scout on the trail of the acceptable. I realize that one comes to a writers' conference not simply to listen, even to writers who are willing teachers, and that there is a nurturing, supportive element to any purposeful group. The truth is, nonetheless, that most of those one sees on the platforms of writers' conferences are those of us who were too ornery to listen to the crowd, too helpless to take good advice. We were the lucky examples of Blake's dictum, "If the fool persist in his (or her) folly, he (or she) shall become wise."

Ask yourself not if you are smart enough and clever enough and diligent enough to write the poetry to which you aspire, but if you are dumb enough, bullish enough, helpless enough to get through.

Poems are written not from intelligence but from ignorance. The stores are endless, the paths not yet taken innumerable. For every real poet finds a new way with each poem by which to lose him- or herself. One loses oneself to find oneself, if you will. One walks away from the path—the road marked by reasonable men and women who are expecting one at the other end—and creates a new path as one goes, eventually unto finding its direction, which may or may not rejoin the others where they have built what they call a civilization.

The future belongs to the helpless. I am often presented that irresistible question asked by the beginning poet: "Do you think I am any good?" I have learned to reply with a question: "If I say no, are you going to quit?" Because life offers any of us many excuses to quit. If you are going to quit now, you are almost certainly going to quit later. But I have concluded that writers are people who you cannot stop from writing. They are helpless to stop it.

One final note about helplessness. We see now what pride and planning have brought the so-called civilized world. The seeds of our destruction were always present in the language of our successes. The same language that enabled us to pass along the uses of fire also allows that double-talk by which mankind creates, permits, and endorses nuclear dump sites, trickle-down economics, and the knee-jerk justifications and falsehoods of every lobby from the gun nuts to the cancer farmers. No other creature tortures; none destroys its homeland with such recklessness. Mankind is God's curse on Nature. In a world that inevitably uses language not primarily to make art or note fact but for lies, evasions, and distortions—all of these fed by convention and prejudice—it seems to me not only more interesting, but more useful and, yes, even virtuous—one might say moral—for serious writing to leave at every turn the path of the willful, to fly from the calcified spine of urbanity, and to get its boots muddy.

Besides, do you really want to succeed by doing it the way you were taught? Ten years, twenty years from now, after you have published that book or books of poetry or prose, will the writing have made a difference to you? I would think it a great pleasure to be able to look in the mirror and know that you followed your instincts and that you did it your way.

Now to the issue of "fraud." I put it as I did because I was quoting a friend: Frank DiGangi, a potter. Recently, while two potters, two painters, and your humble servant were sitting around in the midst of art talk, amused by the distance between what artists know about the making of art and what the world of culture says about it, he said, "We all think we are frauds, but none of us is rich enough to say so in public." Of course, it was a joke, dependent on a sophisticated point of view and a large dose of irony. *We* are not the frauds. The frauds are those who teach poetry as if it were more schooling, another viewing area on the way to some invisible heaven of total understanding where we won't have to be bothered any longer by all this confusion, this ambiguity, this ambivalence, this disorder, this—this—this . . . *life!*

Thus, in the classroom poems are presented as if they were etched in stone by writers who had, above all, a Plan. "Why does the poet say this and why does she say that?" we are asked. A better question is, "What is the *effect* of this or that?" And an even better question may be, "How do you imagine the poet happened on this or that?"

William Stafford has noted that "writing poems is easy, like swimming into a fish net," but that explaining how poems are written is difficult, "like swimming out of a fish net." This is not to deny that many writers have made the act of writing sheer hell for themselves. We have all heard how one writes by sitting in a room with a piece of paper until droplets of blood appear on one's forehead, and the one about writing being one-tenth inspiration and nine-tenths perspiration.

But it is equally true that, while ordinary trumpet players trying to play high C above the staff may turn red and threaten to go all the way to blue from the pressure, the virtuoso trumpeter, Rafael Mendez, could do it on a horn suspended by a string, with his hands behind his back.

I believe that for each of us there is a way of writing we can do with one hand behind our back, in a world where the telephone rings, children cry, and sometimes the doctor has bad news. If we are writers, eventually we may have the good luck to find that way. Then, we will understand the true ease of the writer, that ease that seems to give him or her the powers of a medicine man or priest or psychic, and that threatens those self-proclaimed arbiters of their own temporal preferences, which of course they call standards but which time clearly shows to be nothing more than opinions.

The difficulty of writing lies in turning from our reasonable, pragmatic selves long enough to idle our way into the imagination. Once there, however, the creative engine runs smoothly and time flies past. Poets know the experience of starting a piece just before bedtime because one has a line or two, and then finding that it is three hours later. On the other hand, one has also labored over poems of substance that would not breathe or dance or fly, no matter how hard one worked to give them life, only to have a poem emerge suddenly all of a piece; it needs little revision afterward, only a bit of correction, yet it puts the other poem to shame by its richness and vitality.

About creative writing, there are some things to admit to ourself. Curmudgeons cannot admit these things, and they will not want you to admit them either. They do not understand Kierkegaard's remark that laughter is a kind of prayer. They have no sense of humor. They do not want you to be freer than they are. They worry about what the critics of the *New Amsterdam Times* or the *New Amsterdammer* will think.

Like the members of a closed guild, they do not want the truth to be known. For the truth is that writing poetry is first a matter of getting into motion in the presence of words; that the accidental, the random, and the spontaneous are of more value to the imagination than any plan; and that it is more valuable to be able to write badly than to write well, for writing well always involves some imitation of the routine while writing badly always involves something original and raw. This is as true for formalists as for informalists and antiformalists.

So we are all frauds, if it is fraudulent not to know what you are doing until you have done it. The truth about writing is so simple that no one can win a teaching job by admitting it. It is more and more necessary to surround such simple truths as relativity and overlap in the use of language with theories such as "structuralism" and "deconstruction." Theories are pretzel-benders. They tie us in knots.

Perhaps you have heard the saying, "He's so dumb he couldn't empty piss out of a boot if the instructions were written on the heel."

My third proposal is, "The rain is too heavy a whistle for the certainty of charity." That sentence is two lines of poetry I wrote more than twenty-two years ago. I knew then that they might not make a lot of sense to many readers, but to me they contained the essence of naturalism, metaphysics, and morality—and, thus, poetry. While I went on writing what I could, these lines stayed with me, suggesting a kind of poem I was not yet prepared to write.

In the beginning, I had tried to go forward from those two lines in this way:

> The rain
> is too heavy a whistle for the certainty of charity.
> The moon
> throws us off the sense.
> The wind
> happens at night before you drop off.
> The mountains
> on them sufferance blisters its skin of paint.
> The oceans
> in which this happens.
> The ash
> of which we are made.

Later, I used some of the lines in a poem about a home-sewn pillow. The pillow, which supported me for years, is finally shedding its cover and spilling its guts, while these twelve lines of poetry remain pristine and withholding.

But not unapproachable. For while I have not yet written the rest of the poem, I feel that I am now closer to it. I understand now—no, I *feel* now—its mix of external and internal, of reaching and reticence. If I have had anything on my mind over the years of writing, beyond each single poem as it came into being, if I have hoped for more than a momentary illumination, it has been for this. So much comes to mind in relation to that ideal that I cannot tell you all of it. On the low side of specificity, there are the many other examples I have found and cared for: this one, for example, by Theodore Roethke, the start of an elegy: "Is that dance slowing in the mind of man / That made him think the universe could hum?" And on the high side of the general, there is Pound's quotation from De Quincey or Coleridge (he is not himself sure which) to the effect that "The character of a great poet is everywhere present yet nowhere visible as a distinct excitement."

And where did I find, other than in living day to day, the sense of the complex that made such sense to me? I found it in poems other people did not care about, in the raw language of journals and letters, and in poetry in translation.

More and more I want my poetry raw or abstract. In the words of an old song, I "don't want to mess with Mr. In Between."

Listen to this report by a therapist, written after a session with someone called Robin:

"I used to call him the Hound of Hell, that's how bad he was. Now he talks. He says, 'When I walk into that house it's like the air has fists.' A mean place he's from. I may be the first who ever held his tears. 'I've been reading Gertrude Stein in the way that you instructed me, just listening to the sounds,' he said, and once he said the word *henceforth*. Nearly fell off my rocker that day. He wrote me a letter, he wrote, 'Amazing how quickly snow disappears.' He wrote he would like to be an athlete or Thomas Mann, he loves that guy. He wrote he thinks I would like his dog better than him. He brought in a book about a boy who thought spiders had ears in their legs which he wanted to discuss instead of his father who shouted Shut Up before he even opened his mouth. 'How does poetry enter the mind,' he asks. 'Gee, and then sometimes it just packs up and leaves.' People grow to love what is repeated, who said that? Today before he goes he makes a kiss and bats it to me, then says, 'Dead writers are best. They stay the same so long.'"

Or how about this helpless, shockingly innocent journal entry from a junior at a high school in Georgia:

"Yesterday I messed around with everything and goofed off all day. I gave away five of my bulldog pups yesterday. Eddie Burgess got three and Lynn Beck and Romeo got two. I went over to Ma's about dark and ate supper. Then I went home.

"I have been writing about my life and I have realized that you don't understand some things. I will explain. I live by myself. I live about a mile and a half from my ma. I used to be married. I was married to Terri Metts. She was five months pregnant. I had a 1966 Chevy Chevelle it had a nice white paint job and rally wheels. It had a 350 4-bolt mane with a four-speed transmission and a 4:11 rear end. Terri never drove it. I let her drive it one day to the Handy Corner in Dawson County. On the way back she wrecked. She lost the baby. She was in the Hospital three months and I never went to see her. I loved my car. She died. I now have a 69 roadrunner it is black and gold with a 440 plus 6 and a 4 speed and high speed rear end, a 77 Ford Ranger, 351 Cleveland and 3 speed on column with a spicer rear end. It is painted black. I also have two motorcycles a Yamaha maxim and Yamaha 360. I dig graves for a living that is how I afford my vehicles."

By the way, I was deliberately exaggerating when I said a moment ago that I wanted my poetry, if not raw, to be abstract. Truly, what attracts me in poetry other than the raw is not abstraction itself, but the quality of abstraction that comes out of the generalized. And what connects the generalized to the abstract is metaphor, with its peculiar ability to contain a thing without it being the thing itself.

Remember, if you will, that, while modern poetry may begin somewhere back in, say, Baudelaire, where the image became the repository for a mixture of the objective and the subjective all at once (that mix came to be the essence of modernism, even a formula for it), something else we might as well call "contemporary poetry" begins in the previously unknown contemporary knowledge of the general condition of man and the universe. Some people might say it begins with "the Bomb," but the Bomb of the fifties was only a localized blot on the Malthusian landscape. After that, we came to know much more.

Some artists brag about not watching television, not reading newspapers, and the like. One understands their brand of escapism. Some people can sense a totality in private. I will say, however, that I think generalized knowledge, rather than the particularity of book learning—what used to be called wisdom as distinct from intelligence—is one of the signs of contemporary art.

So. I come back to the water and the singing string of charity. I feel with a strength I have not felt earlier the rightness of any second line. When the Exxon-*Valdez* layered Prince William Sound with oil, the story floated all the way down to the lower Forty-eight. And there on a day when we fed the marmot and then the deer, breaking the rules, with a study of pulp mills just about to be released in a new report on cancer, Chinese armor poised to roll over the student rebellion, and everywhere in the world something else, the DiGangis were celebrating their thirtieth wedding anniversary all year long, so that, feeling the impulse to dance as much as to run, we all knew that, when we talk about poetry, we are talking about a perfect vacancy, resonant and responsive to whomever takes up residence and stays.

Stay up half the night for a week and write one hundred poems. Write badly, rawly, smoothly, accidentally, irrationally . . . join the disparate. Make the like unlike and the unlike like. When you can't write, read. Use the word "window" in every line. Write about colors. Set out to write a poem "like a sweater." It makes no difference. The coherence is already within you. Afterward, you will have learned more about writing than an entire semester of classes can teach you.

In writing, as in the imagination, as in dreams, there is no right way, and there is no one way. Thus, one does not require a compass, just a good supply of nourishment and a push.

At this point, I am going to strengthen or weaken my case with a bit more testimony. First, I will use a poem to illustrate some implications of believing that there is no one way and no right way. This poem is not reproduced here for praise but for attention. The illustration and testimony I offer is that of a common reader.

Lawn Sprawled Out like a Dog

When the peacock screams out at night, do you think it knows
its cry makes a man look at himself to see if he is suffering?
Perhaps the peacock and all birds realize
the effect of their voices. They carry a musical score in their bones,

which are so thin—toothpicks, really—their only defenses
are the gluttony that puffs them up, the edges of their songs and cries
and the flimsy handkerchiefs on struts
they wave as they fly or run from grass to grass.

Even the tiny mosquito, most blood-thirsty of God's creations,
considering the brevity of its life, must sense the communion to come
when, shivering and wild,
with nothing to eat, she sings us to the wood like Circe.

Forgive me, I mixed up the horrible little mosquito, an insect,
with the eagle, the loon and the brave, little sparrow.
Forgive me, I only recently learned
to slap down the gnats that hover near the shores of human swans!

In the reading of poetry, it sometimes seems that one encounters example after example of willful misunderstanding. I would like to propose an opposing attitude: that of willful *under*standing. From such small acts of sympathy, great rewards may follow.

Hence, lacking any attribution to the contrary, one could perhaps imagine this poem to have been written in a language other than English and then translated. I rather like that quality myself. Perhaps Spanish, given the surreal quality of the title and last line. Or Russian—Russian writers, we believe, are free with sentiment and such words as "suffering." Or perhaps the poem was translated from one of the languages of eastern Europe, given the satiric bent of the last two lines, a turn on social expectation and civilized blindness. It could even be British, if I hear the tone of voice correctly in the phrase "toothpicks, really" and sense the exacting attitude that turns bird wings into flimsy handkerchiefs.

All of this interests me. As does the bizarre sympathy in stanza 3 of the speaker (or poet?) for the mosquito. Who among us has considered a blood bank for mosquitos?

Who is being addressed? We don't know. *I* don't know. Could be it is the reader who is asked to imagine the knowledge, or awareness, possessed by other animals. Easy to do, or at least to think about, perhaps (there's that "perhaps" again), when it's the peacock crying out in the dark with that all-too-human voice. Easy to move from there to bird song at large. There is much less to a bird than we are led to believe by our wishes, our fancy, and its own skillful song. But even if we are made to concentrate, still the eagle is noble; the loon, elegant and mysterious; and the common sparrow, brave beyond number. But the mosquito?

I lean forward as a reader when I come upon, first, a title so imbued—for me, that is—imbued with a suddenness of imagination encircling ordinary things, and, second, quickly thereafter an initial sentence that mixes location and involvement and raises the stakes in a hurry. In leaning into the poem, I get caught up by what might be called a "narrative of mind." In this case, the poem plays off the self-serving distinctions we make between ourselves and other sentient beings. This is the sort of theme that engages me when it is left to simmer underneath everything else, because I don't believe in crystal power, I don't think aliens are coming to save us, channelers are frauds, a sucker is born every minute, and the truth will set you free.

In the end, I have to go back to the title, the strangest phrase in the poem. I can make more sense of it than I could before I read the lines that follow it. I see that it combines distance (I hear the echo of the phrase "a sprawling lawn") and locus (I see a sprawled-out dog). I see, when I linger on it, that the image is an amalgamation of nature and animal, and that it now parallels the last image in the poem in which animal and human are likewise combined in "the necks of human swans." Of course, swans are swans and humans are humans. Aren't they?

I do not think this poem shies from its human role or refuses its guilty survival. I do see that it questions conventional distinctions within a somewhat bizarre frame and that it handles notions of suffering and survival.

I like this poem because of its "Russian" sentimentality, its "Spanish" imagery, its "East European" irony, its "British" nuances, its strangeness, the elasticity of its line, and other things as well. I like it because I have paid enough attention to it as a reader to have been rewarded. And of course I like it because—and I recommend this reason to all of you—I like it because, yes, because I wrote it. However, I am not employing it here today because of who wrote it, but because of how it was written.

"In actual fact," like they say, I wrote it during a gathering in Fairbanks, Alaska, as part of a week's testimonial. I wanted to show my students that I meant it when I recommended that they write more, starting with whatever was at hand and daring to be odd. And so I wrote a poem a day. And at the end included them in a public reading. This is the one I kept. The title is a line reported as having come up in another class that was looking for a starting point for an assignment. It had been mentioned during a panel discussion at the start of the week. Later I realized that, because the line is unconventional, unsocialized, it required of me a human definition. And the human definition, in turn, led into a brief meditation on the human condition. And so it goes.

I want to refer back to the moment when I realized this essay had to have a title. It is sometimes bad to write with a title in mind. With a title in mind, that practical fellow or gal each of us can be sticks to the subject. If I had one minute to tell you a single piece of advice for writing poetry, and if I wanted to be certain your poetry would surprise you and others, and if above all I hoped your poetry would not be simply that kind of writing that goes gently to its end in the interest of soporific culture—if I had but one minute to say one thing, I would say, Don't stick to the subject. (The second thing I would say is, Listen!)

Afterward—the title comes afterward. Well, I had three items in mind at the beginning, so "Three Propositions" seemed seductively syllogistic. But those kinds of propositions are not so much fun, so I added three names: Hooey, Dewey, and Loony. If this seems silly, may I remind you that T. S. Eliot and Groucho Marx entered into a correspondence, including an exchange of photographs of themselves, and that, when Marx at last went to dinner at the Eliots, brushing up on "Macbeth" so that he might have the intellectual nourishment he craved, Eliot wanted only to talk about *Duck Soup*.

"Hooey," because most of what is said about writing poetry, after the event—often by critics, reviewers, and theorists, but sometimes by the poets themselves—is just that: hooooeeee! "Dewey," because as a schoolboy I had a fond spot for the so-called practical philosopher, John Dewey, who among other things suggested that classroom chairs should not be bolted down. And "Loony," because after all, by any reasonable standard of society at large, anyone who writes what some of us have written, or—heaven forfend—suggests that there might be utter clarity in the lines, "The rain / is too heavy a whistle for the certainty of charity," must certainly be loony.

So let us go then, you and I, when the evening is spread out against the sky like a pigeon poised upon a nickel. Let us not get into a pickle. Or, finding ourselves already deep in the briny pickly flesh, let us find there the seeds of our poetry. What rough beast, its hour come round at last, slouches toward Bethlehem to be born? No one knows. Is this a dish for fat lips? Roethke wasn't sure. Is that dance slowing in the mind of man that made him think the universe could hum? Yes, it is.

Don't Just Sit There: Writing as a Polymorphous Perverse Pleasure

Sometimes it's a good thing—like reflecting on the kind of adult you thought you'd become when you were a child, when thinking wasn't yet complicated by knowledge—for a writer to remember what writing felt like when you were back at the beginning.

This is probably most useful to those who were, like me, resolved to be writers at an early age. I was nine when words began to serve their extraordinary purposes for me. I was lonely and they kept me company, they materialized whenever and wherever I called on them, without an argument or a competitive leer. No one knew or judged how well I did them, this was not jumping in as the two ropes turned and came whipping down like a great moving parenthesis around me and slapped the ground and snarled my feet. This was not trying to connect the broad side of the bat with a ball that got miraculously smaller as it approached the scuff of dirt we called the plate. The words were purely mine at first, a secret transaction between inner and outer, between silence and speech, between what I knew—or *knew* that I knew—and what I didn't recognize as knowing, but that I could bring up like a brimming pail from a deep unlighted well.

What I wrote as a child I wrote for comfort, for invisible power, for the astonished pleasure of the *feel* of the letters—for their look, which was shape and color: every letter had a color for me, *E* yellow-orange and *K* and *P* blue and purple, like shadows on snow, *W* brown; *I* transparent as ice. There was a private *ad hoc* physics at work in the form those letters took; and sound, the fricatives and glottals and aspirates as satisfying to move around, for me, as tin soldiers or matchbox cars for someone who liked to wage different kinds of fantasy wars. This was a time of polymorphous perverse pleasure in language, with no end outside the moment, no end outside myself.

So I wrote murder mysteries: My first, whose plot (because even then I was no good at plotting) lifted in part from a Sherlock Holmes Classic Comic, was called "Murder Stalks at Midnight," which I thought marvelously original until my brother, a musician, showed me a record—Ray McKinley or Lionel Hampton, I can't remember whose—called "Celery Stalks at Midnight." I enacted dreams beyond achieving, namely ownership of a black horse with a perfect white star on its forehead, and a stint at boarding school with girls whose names—Ashley du Lac and Cynthia Weatheringham—came from the trickle-down of debutante lists I'd seen in the newspaper and English gothic novels I hadn't read. I wrote rhyming doggerel—"In the wonderful land of Rin-Tin-Tin"—We lived in Los Angeles at the time, just up the block from Hollywood, but I had never gotten the word that Rin-Tin-Tin was a *dog*: the sound of the name, its syllables that drummed like rain on the roof, conjured up a misty fantasy kingdom to me, and reality was nothing but intrusion.

But I had entered phase two of the writer's life by then—the power of words deployed on the page for my own delight had inevitably asserted itself in public, in school. Like a talent for numbers, only more ubiquitous, a talent for words will eventually come to someone's attention, and then, having blown your cover, you find you have happened upon a skill that is, as they say, marketable; that can serve to disarm, to amuse, to make itself pragmatically useful in the communal intercourse of children. *You're* the one who does slogans, news stories, yearbook jingles, class shows, petitions—you're available and you're unbeatable at all the odd lots of verbal communication most people lack the grace to execute easily or well. It is, in fact, the area in which, quite possibly, all your panache puddles, and your élan, and whatever other French nouns have never been used in your direction. You've got rhythm, you've got dash and dazzle, you've got a voice that cuts like a sharp beam through the fogs of verbal confusion, you've got something almost like a sixth sense about organization and metaphor that operates somewhere between your tongue and your hand that is not quite art, not yet, but (unless you abandon it, and even then it's persistent) will someday perhaps *become* art.

I was recently reading a 1934 essay by E. B. White about the St. Nicholas League, a group of children across America "who wrote poems and prose, took snapshots with box cameras, drew pictures at random and solved puzzles." They submitted the results of their fervor, White wrote, to the League, which was a permanent competition sponsored by *St. Nicholas Magazine,* and the lucky winners pocketed the Gold or the Silver Badge of extreme merit: this was clearly the point at which the young artists-in-potentia had reached phase two, the moment at which they realized their secret ardor could buy them respect and even local fame. "We were an industrious and fiendishly competitive band of tots," White says. "And if some of us, in the intervening years of careless living, have lost or mislaid our silver badge, we still remember the day it came in the mail: the intensity of victory, the sweetness of young fame. . . ." In the first few years of this century, Edna St. Vincent Millay won all the trophies the judges had to give; Robert Benchley and Elinor Wylie excelled at drawing, Conrad Aiken and Babette Deutsch wrote poems. Ring Lardner won his laurels for verse and puzzles. Cornelia Otis Skinner wrote a poem; Janet Flanner, famous later for her essays dispatched from Paris, won for a drawing, and Vita Sackville-West sent a rather immodest though matter-of-fact little essay about the house she lived in, which had once belonged to Queen Elizabeth—that's the first Queen Elizabeth—and possessed 365 rooms, fifty-two staircases, and an altar in the chapel that was given by Mary Queen of Scots before she was executed. A huge number of the contributors to the magazine have familiar names, though they may not be so to this generation of readers. Most of them put those as-yet-unnotable names on record in the great access of nonspecific energy of creative children—they were talented at just about everything solitary and crafty and made of ink, undoubtedly the kinds of children whose mothers tried to get them outside on sunny days to play with kids on the block. Half a century later I recognized the loose rules of the club: had it still been around, surely I'd have wanted to join it.

But to return to ourselves. Phase three in the life of the young writer-to-be commences when your academic essays begin to bring home superlatives. Your teacher has her eye on you. You write without outlines, your ideas just line up in neat formation, at times the elegance of your style is a camouflage under which huddle insufficiencies of fact and comprehension and you write a paper on an economic theory you don't understand or an analysis of *The Golden Bowl* which you actually didn't finish reading *but it doesn't show,* and you get an A, and then you do a book report that debones an inferior author and holds his little spine up before the class to be laughed at for its puniness and insufficiency and you realize, a little sheepishly, that this thing you drive has a lot more power than the family car you're not yet allowed to take out alone and, if you're decent and honest, you'd better be careful with it.

Unless you are unnaturally shy and not academically and personally ambitious and you keep this skill hidden like a weapon, then you become the quasi-public commodity called the Class Writer. Your secret pleasure, like a terrific voice or face or even body, has become negotiable currency.

There is one thing I want to say about all this writing: the small child's innocent self-delighting scrawl and the cynical college student's paper on the Regressive Tax and Its Effects on the National Debt. They were committed to paper, all of them, but especially the child's. You had no commitment to a style, to an attitude nor—least of all—to a genre. At nine, like the versatile members of the St. Nicholas League, I was not a poet or a short-story writer or, God forbid, a novelist. (Though at twelve I admit I delivered up in three secretarial notebooks a huge opus about Mickey Mantle, in which Mickey was Mickey but I was his preliberation love, a ponytailed, saddle-shoed fan who had broken through the membrane of his fame like a girl leaping out of a cake and, having brought myself flamboyantly to his attention, now reaped the reward of his grateful love. "With you I can be just plain *me* again," he said as he took me in his muscular arms. I repeat, this writing business brought a lot of power in its wake. Illusory power but satisfying nonetheless.)

One of the things that separates the child writer, whose only interest is in pleasurable discovery, from the adult, aside from our entry into the lists of competition or the need for mastery, for patience and energy and for an outside source of income, is that most writers have, like kids on the ballfield, chosen up sides. Give or take a shockingly small number of writers, most of us are poets or fiction writers, subspecies short-story writers or novelists or playwrights. With the hard-won expertise that allows us to do only one thing well, and that if we're lucky, has come a sort of tightness of the muscles that makes it hard and maybe even makes it feel unnecessary to adapt from one form to another, and I think it's a shame and a loss.

Because with versatility come a lot of benefits, chief of which is a constant openness to possibility and its sister, serendipity. To revert to my first love, Mickey Mantle, you can face a lot more pitchers comfortably and go for a lot more kinds of pitches if you can swing from both sides. You stay closer to a memory of the sources of your writing, the sheer improvisatory joy of it, if you can remember that first you were writing the way you swam or sang or roller-skated, just because it felt good to do so.

Let me assume some of you know all this and are now, or are getting ready to be, working in more than one genre. Let me assume the rest of you have to be coerced. Here is a miscellany of observations, caveats, threats, promises, and speculations arranged for you by the writer who made the list of the best and worst post-office kissers in fifth grade, the official grievances of a seventh-grade class abused by a malicious teacher, and, latterly, of questions I *really* wanted to see answered by my college class for our thirtieth reunion. I have never given up my love of lists: I even published a story called "All This" that dumps out the contents of a particular woman's mind as if it were her purse overturned on a desk-top. I recommend the form to you. Here are the confessions and caveats of a switch-hitter.

1. *Steal from yourself.* Cannibalize your own work. Handel stole from himself constantly: you aren't given so many terrific melodies that you can afford to waste any. If you have been writing out of an obsessive interest in something, say, in the form of poems—I remember, for example, a spell of guilty motherhood, full of fears and doubts—do not hesitate to use those poems somewhat but not wholly altered in a prose piece, in a story or a pastische of prose and poetry that makes its own rules. My own witch-mother poems surfaced, revised, in a story about a hyperactive child who was nothing like my own; thus they were considerably distanced by the time they found their most effective setting. But their rhythm was compact, their imagery arresting. Their intensity, in other words, was a poet's, not a prose writer's, and what they enriched was not story but an interior landscape. It is a fact that sounds more cynical than it is that a so-so line of poetry, journeyman stuff, can make a lovely line of prose. It is a fact, however sad, that readers do not expect prose to be "written"—by which I mean *wrought*, with an attention to sound, to syllabic weight and echo, to varying sentence length and phrase length, which are the fundamentals in the armament of poetry. You also have at your disposal, as a poet, an appreciation for silences, ellipses, leaps in the narrative, and a talent for compression that can make an interestingly spare superstructure for certain kinds of prose. E. L. Doctorow, discussing his impatience with the realistic novel, quotes Marcel Duchamp at a point when he seemed to have given up painting. "Someone said, 'Marcel, why have you stopped painting?' and he said, 'Because too much of it was "filling in." ' " If you can play fast and loose with the rhythms and strategies of another genre you will be that much less likely to spend your time filling in or, as Virginia Woolf called it, padding out your work with the "cotton-batting" of everyday activity.

I recently came upon two references in Raymond Carver's miscellany, *Fires*, to the basic situation in his well-known story, "Why Won't You

Dance?" That story begins: "In the kitchen, he poured another drink and looked at the bedroom suite in his front yard. The mattress was stripped and the candy-striped sheets lay beside two pillows on the chiffonier. Except for that, things looked much the way they had in the bedroom—nightstand and reading lamp on his side of the bed, nightstand and reading lamp on her side." In *Fires*, there is a poem called "Distress Sale":

> Early one Saturday morning everything outside—
> the child's canopy bed and vanity table,
> the sofa, end tables and lamps, boxes
> of assorted books and records. We carried out
> kitchen items, a clock radio, hanging
> clothes, a big easy chair
> with them from the beginning
> and which they called Uncle.
> Lastly, we brought out the kitchen table itself
> and they set up around that to do business . . .
> I slept on that canopy bed last night. . . .

In the same book, in his interview with the *Paris Review*, Carver tells this story, or rather anecdote: "I was visiting some writer friends in Missoula back in the mid-seventies. We were all sitting around drinking and someone told a story about a barmaid named Linda who got drunk with her boyfriend one night and decided to move all of her bedroom furnishings into the backyard. They did it, too, right down to the carpet and the bedroom lamp, the bed, the nightstand, everything. There were about four or five writers in the room, and after the guy finished telling the story, someone said, 'Well, who's going to write it?' I don't know who else might have written it, but I wrote it. Not then, but later. About four or five years later, I think." And wrote it, apparently—this is me, not Carver—as a poem, not a particularly noteworthy one but as evidence of the idea in process, working at him, before it became one of his most characteristic stories of suppressed hostility and loss, the kind that is almost a play, all that furniture on the sidewalk a little clot of props, oddly, almost luridly back-lit, set up in isolation on what feels like a stage facing an audience of tranced onlookers.

Writers are, as this might illustrate, a peculiar hybrid: we are half obsessives who can't get those melodies out of our heads, and half—to change the metaphor mid-sentence—half frugal housewives, practical cooks and seamstresses who will find a way to use a turnip or carrot or leftover end of meat to make a stew or cotton to sew a pillow cover rather than let it go to waste. Just as every experience is useful to a writer, joy and misery included, so is every intuition of a usable situation if you've got the craft to bend it to your will. It's worth checking our pockets from time to time to see what's lurking in the corners, still to be aired and used. And it's necessary to be comfortable in many genres so that we don't have to pass on it, let it go, or give it away to someone else.

I remember when I was a young writer, a poet and nothing but a poet, and I lived in Mississippi in the mid-sixties—exciting times. Quite frequently something fascinating would happen, either violent or contradictory or otherwise too complex for the kind of poetry I knew how to write. And I would utter, without recognizing its stupidity and lack of resourcefulness, the most helpless of all sentences: "If only I knew how to write stories"—and sigh and pass up a priceless opportunity because I thought I had a license that limited me to poetry, like the code on my driver's license that allowed me a car but specifically forbade me to drive a motorcycle.

2. If you have written something you like and it doesn't work in its original form, you are hereby enjoined to borrow or invent a form to contain it. Play fast and loose with definitions and categories. We write in an age that has lost a lot of the old comforts and courtesies of form but what we have in their place is a wonderfully fluid, fanciful sense of form that makes few rigid demands of us. Consider books like Bruce Chatwin's *Songlines*, poetry like Frank Bidart's monologues, Phillip Lopate's personal essays that read like fiction, Max Frisch's unique series of notations in *Man in the Holocene*, including many from the encyclopedia; pseudo-historical fiction like Doctorow's *Ragtime* or *Billy Bathgate*. The list of works that use old forms with new license is endless. My own first book of prose, the stories in *Street Games*, began as a set of vignettes that I published as what I thought of as an essay called "Mainlanders." The magazine in which the essay appeared forgot, that quarter, to differentiate in their index between fiction and essays and the story won third prize in the *O. Henry Prize Stories for 1973*. I didn't argue. Instead I went on to take apart the pieces of "Mainlanders" and make them into fuller, more conventional stories, add new ones to the mix, and there was a whole book of interrelated narratives. Back to my first rule: steal from yourself relentlessly.

Another time I sent around a story I was calling "Justice of the Peace" that concerned a woman I knew in Mississippi in the mid-sixties who had tried to become the first black justice of the peace of her little Delta town. (This is a woman—my daughter's godmother, in fact—who makes appearances, though in different situations and different language, in a poem I wrote in the sixties and a novel I wrote in the eighties.) But in the case of the story, it was not being published and, I suspected, it was not being read with an appreciation for its tone, which, though it wasn't exactly didactic, might have been called exemplary: it was an angry little tale about small town politics, jealousy, vote-buying and the defeat of modest ideals—half politics, half art. In frustration, to clarify its intent, I renamed it (re-aimed it, in a sense) "Justice of the Peace: An Essay in the Form of a Story" and immediately sold it to a good little magazine. I could almost hear *those* readers saying "Ohhh, in *that* case . . ."

3. Ask yourself nervy questions, such as: Must I really use this hunk of subject matter, or this intriguing character, or this haunting atmosphere or glimmer of emotional insight *whole*, or might I use a slice or a chip of it, cast it in a form that can absorb it or enlarge it, shrink it, spaces, blanks, unknowns and all? Let me give you some examples by way of elucidation. One is the suite of poems. Take Margaret Atwood's *Journals of Susannah Moody* or Ruth Whitman's *A Woman's Journey*, her poems about Tamsen Donner and the Donner party, or her recent book of poems about the World War II resistance martyr Hannah Senesh. Or Carole Oles's book-length poem *Nightwatches*, which introduces us to the astronomer Maria Mitchell. What is gained and what lost that these are not full prose biographies? That, of course, is not where their authors' talents or interests lie, they aren't researchers or scholars. Whitman, I know, actually traveled the path of the Donner party to its ill-fated end of the road en route to California, and she went to Israel and to Hungary to meet the family of Senesh: treated her subject, in other words, with the fullness of attention that might have issued in a factual book. But she wanted to distill an essence other than factual from all that study and especially in the Tamsen Donner poems she has made a moving elegy, part specific, part generic, to a woman who, in a very different time in America, did what she had to do, and died of it.

I have two instances of my own that I think are instructive for those who are saying, But why? If you write prose, why turn to poetry? For the first few years after I moved to New Hampshire I had promised myself that I'd write about a neighbor born and raised right on our small town road. She was a good friend who fascinated me partly for her differentness from anyone I'd known growing up and I thought I'd write something about the two of us, contrasting neighbors. But, blessedly, I had to come to terms with how little I really knew about her life—knew of its dark close-up places—and, lacking a story I wanted to tell, how little I could find to say about that life. What I really wanted was not exhaustive but rather a glancing impression. Not a superficial one but not a fully circumstantial one either. My friend was worth more than a single glimpse to me. Thus *Cora Fry*, eighty-four spare little syllabic poems that work like a mosaic to compose a modest life out of tiny pieces of experience. There is as much missing here as there is present, as much empty space as there is speech. But a picture emerges and even a bit of a story that illuminates the character. My challenge, especially because it came after I'd finished my first very wordy novel, was to see how few words I could use in the composition of that face and figure, town and time. I could not have done that in any prose I know.

A corollary to command (3): Find a form to contain the little you know without lying. Prose fiction, especially the novel but even the story, is an accretion of fact, knowledge, insight, observation. Poetry can be a quick hit, a fast high, a light touch. I was in the Soviet Union for a short while a few years ago; I wouldn't have *dared* make fiction or even an essay out of that trip, but ah, my pathetic pallet of a bed in a once-grand hotel in Leningrad yielded a poem, and so did my confrontation with the ghost of Anna Karenina beside the train track, and so did dozens of other small moments, experiences, visions, and the dreams they engendered. Taken together they work like mirrors to expand and reflect an experience too meager and, really, too incoherent to make lucid statements, let alone characters, out of.

If you, a fiction writer, are not prepared to make a set of poems out of your stalled novel, have you considered any of the other "odd lots and broken sizes" of form that are, these days, so enticingly available to you? In his small book *Little Lives*, Richard Elman, writing under the name Spuyker, composed a whole small town, like a prose-bound Edgar Lee Masters, as a cemetery full of ghosts speaking their audacious headstones. In *Flaubert's Parrot*, the British novelist Julian Barnes creates a character, a doctor named Geoffrey Braithwaite, who deconstructs Flaubert's life with an attention to fact and probability so obsessive and inventive that he traces every clue *ad absurdum*—for one example, the effect of railway travel on Flaubert's affair with Louise Colet. Braithwaite includes a short Dictionary of Accepted Ideas to parallel Flaubert's own, thus reminding us that the "father of Realism" had a few playful bones in his own staid body. Barnes has invented, or at least made use of, a form halfway between biography and antibiography—if there's such a thing as the antinovel there ought to be antibiography—that reminds us in turn of Nabokov's *Pale Fire*, which played fast and loose with poetic form as seriocomic case history.

A second corollary: If it begins to feel too easy to do something, change forms. Make yourself an amateur in a new genre. Professionalism is something we want in airplane pilots and plumbers. But writers should always be doing something new and therefore dangerous, putting their feet down carefully the first time, feeling themselves walking over an abyss, or leaping into space without any idea where they'll come down.

A few years ago I ran headlong into a story—I should say a plot—that was so perfect I felt as if I'd already written the novel about it. So I'm writing a play to surprise myself. Half the play—the only half I've written—was performed in Houston. There was an audience there right before my eyes. There were actors who couldn't say certain lines and sound human. There was a whole new conception of acceptable, not to say engaging, action. The old virtues would not serve. Good conversation wasn't enough, in fact it was a blight because, contrary to a lot of people's understanding, conversation is not what theater is about. I learned so much so fast about play-making my teeth ached. I may turn out a good play, more likely I'll turn out a bad one, but I won't feel that I've danced the same old steps, which would have been the novel that was coming to me preshrunk to fit the idea and prematurely softened up, like stone-washed jeans.

4. When you've worked for a long time in a long form, your stomach will stretch, or your muscles, or whatever part of your body you care to locate the hard work in. When I'm caught in the intricate and slow-grinding machinery of a novel I begin to long, understandably, for the speed with which a story can be written, the fact that it can be finished during the same calendar year in which I began it. For its streamlined elegance, its canny capacity to do so many things at once. Just before I'd got sprung from my newest novel I looked at a list of Pushcart Prize winners, for which I hadn't been eligible because I'd published nothing that year while the large and deformed body of my novel hulked over me like Quasimodo's shadow, and, deprived of the pleasures of variety and visibility, murmured to myself self-pityingly, "I used to be a writer, but now I'm a *novelist*."

But when I was set free to return to those lost lamented forms, I remembered from the last time: they feel puny. They feel inadequate. Eventually, if you blow on them long enough, or read enough good ones by other people, they take on size and vitality again. But it's always hard and you have to expect that. You get used to the slow cumulative movement of the novel, the way your effects gather at their leisure from all the words you've laid down; the structure is broad and carefully articulated; you have flow-charts that tell you how recently certain characters have been heard from and which chapters hang together to make part I or part IV. But the story is bare, and time in it rushes by with a hummingbird flash. The play, after a novel, snaps like new elastic—wham. So few words. Nothing on the page, but on the stage space filled with tension, potentiality. You can write four scenes in a morning, a whole act on a good day. Then you can revise on another morning. And when you get onto the stage itself you can wipe another quarter of the words away—superfluous. It isn't any easier to write a play, not one bit, but it certainly is quicker.

Consider, though, how great the odds that as a fiction writer, especially a novelist, plump with narrative flab, you'll ever write a really good play: almost none have ever done so. Henry James and Thomas Wolfe wanted more than anything to write plays. Using those two baggy monsters as examples you might say ruins my argument that we should be conversant with all the available use of words, but in fact it doesn't. It only underlines the fact that, without free movement across the borders of genres, all of us could be stuck where we accidentally began. The Israeli novelist A. B. Yehoshua began as a playwright and somewhere along the way realized that he could take the form of the dramatic monologue into the novel with him: thus his two spectacularly interesting books, *The Lover* and *A Late Divorce*, which were almost all confidences, speech to an audience. ("It was the *stage* through which I moved from short stories to the novel," he said in an interview. "I wanted to get out from under the first person, the 'I,' the one character who dominated the short story and move to other characters without putting all the extra stuff around them. I just let them speak, as in a play, and eventually from these speeches came the novel.") Once inside the capacious house of the novel, Yehoshua says it occurred to him that there were other rooms as well. His newest novel, *Molkho*, called *The Fifth Season* in English, is a more formally conventional book. He has walked through a door I am trying to walk out of, each of us in search of the right size and shape of vessel, not so much to contain new matter as to make the old new, thus transforming it for ourselves.

5. In the eyes of others you have something called a Career. Certain people, should you be lucky enough to have them, like your agent or your editor, will hasten to tell you that what you need now for that career is another novel or another book of the same kind of poems that everyone loved last time. It is very difficult to ignore the practical exhortations of such parental figures in your life, but if you can afford to, you ought to ignore them with a gleeful sense of relief. The voice of responsibility can all too easily shout down the small shaky voice of your orig-

inality and your need to find another way, a road that you, at least, have not yet traveled. And your need, if necessary, to fail at it.

It doesn't need saying that the world is not set up to honor your as-yet-unfulfilled hopes. It tends to reward what is called a track record, implying that it is all a foot-race with winners, losers and also-rans, and a race with a clock, a race around a narrow unchanging track. Not only is your reputation at stake when you walk off attending to a distant voice, like Ferdinand the Bull who wanted to sit pacifically under a cork tree rather than fight, but every time you ask some foundation or writer's colony or whatever to buy into your uncertain future, of course all they can expect to go on is past work and project description. To answer truthfully at a moment of change would be like a suitor for someone's hand in marriage answering the inevitable question about career prospects by saying "I think I'm going to walk barefoot across America" or "I'm going to spend my time developing a blue rose." We shouldn't be surprised if our patrons are too dismayed simply to hand over the purse full of cash— we are declaring ourselves subject to a master other than nurturance of career, following a vagrant singer into the wild. Sometimes it leads us out the other side resplendent, sometimes we're never heard from again. And so we tend to perjure ourselves and say, "More of the same."

Needless to say, your internal doubts are by far the hardest to deal with. To make yourself an amateur is painful, it is like hitting the keyboard with gloves on. Why abandon what you do well? Why allow a long interruption in your visible output? Why take the chance, perhaps a long chance, that you'll *become* a good poet or whatever is the new skill needed? Why all this uncertainty? Each writer has to answer the question for herself, himself. But the writing child I was never thought much about habit or ease, and certainly not about career. She thought about how to use the word *cascade* as often as possible, or to find a place for *halcyon*, or wondered why there was no English rhyme for *orange*.

6. Have a bag of miscellaneous stop-gap ideas for the days when nothing "important" will come, or when there isn't time for a project with much heft to it. Retell old stories, fairy tales, myths, in new forms. Translate; translate from a language you don't know—I've seen fantastic poems bloom from intentional mistranslation. Make a list of all the things you know: how to make fudge, how to give the Heimlich maneuver, how to get from New York to Miami on five dollars. You will have a new respect for all you have mastered and all you might write out of. Make a list of all the things you'd like to know: How many of them can you learn, how many might you fake with a book or two and an on-site visit or a consultation with an expert?

Read Jamaica Kincaid's marvelous little story, "Girl," which is essentially a list of the wisdom her mother passed on to her, cynical and insulting, loving and necessary. Can you do the same? Better, can you adapt the idea of the list, with its secret order and shapeliness, to your own obsessions? Write a scene for impossible characters: Biblical. Comic strip. TV anchormen. Government officials. Recast one of your stories as a play. Eavesdrop and write it down from memory. Lorrie Moore wrote her wonderful book *Self-Help* as if she were constructing a manual for the proper use of the machinery of our emotions. Lydia Davis, in her odd and beguiling book *Break It Down*, demonstrates how you can create something as unlikely as a murder mystery in the form of a French lesson, in which the newly mastered but rudimentary words end up describing a scene of carnage.

Walk through a graveyard, meeting the people beneath the stones. I did a project with a photographer in which I wrote alternative stories, two apiece, for every suggestive gravestone he had photographed. Collaborate. The most pleasure I've ever had from my writing was a musical I wrote from a children's book. It made writing alone, after all those people who had shared my passion (director, actors, set and costume and lighting designers) the loneliest thing I had ever done.

Take a written line you love or a line you don't understand, someone else's, and write from it. Take a minimalist poem or story and convert it to maximalism, at least in style; fill in the blanks, like a detail of a painting enlarged. Find something old and terrible that you abandoned without hope. Recast it, preferably in a different genre. If you've never written a poem, take a list of interesting words—wildflowers, car parts, names of cities in Albania—and arrange them in their best-sounding order, listening to them in juxtaposition. If you've never written a novel, think about it. What would it demand of you to take your favorite, or your least favorite, story and make it into a two-hundred-page book? Would you kill it or cure it?

Unless you are in desperate need of a fallow period, a period of passivity, don't just sit there. Think of your words as molecules in constant movement, hot to cold, cold to hot. Religious Jews on the sabbath, when they, and presumably the whole universe, are enjoined from doing work, do nothing that will encourage anything to change form. They are not to use hard soap because it becomes bubbles, they are not to make steam or tear paper, any kind, not even toilet paper. They recognize that a change of form entails an exchange of energy. It is work.

But it is also play. It is the best exercise to forestall the hardening postures of middle age. It raises the adrenalin level. Gabriel García Márquez is possibly the world's most stunning proponent of change and flexibility at the moment. He has just, for example, written six screenplays from his own stories; he likens the imagination to a car battery: "When you leave it inactive," he says, "is when it runs down." One of his directors calls him "an amphibian" who moves easily between the written story and the film. "I have a lot of stories that occur to me," he says casually, "but when I am in the middle of working on them, I realize that they are not suited to literature, that they are more visual. So I have to tell myself that this one is good for a novel, this one for a story, this for a movie and this for television. . . . I'm a storyteller," García Márquez concludes. "It doesn't matter to me if the stories are written, shown on a screen, over television, or passed from mouth to mouth. The important thing is that they be told."

I, who can't tell his kind of story for love or money but who can tell my own kind, agree. Whether essence precedes existence or the other way around I surely can't say. But I know that *words precede the form that contains them,* and all of us, if we want to, can reach elbow-deep into the world of syllables and syntax and pull up a generous handful and arrange it to satisfy ourselves. We can do so exactly as we did when we first learned how to write words down and, in the silence of our own concentration, read them back to ourselves.

Judgment: An Essay

Ford Madox Ford is known today as the author of "the best French novel in the English language," *The Good Soldier*. Much praised, he has been little read. He produced eighty-one books. Ford's devotees—this writer among them—revere his tetralogy of war novels, *Parade's End*, and trilogy of historical novels, *The Fifth Queen*. He composed idiosyncratic books of biography, several splendid volumes of autobiography and travel. He wrote poems, essays, fairy tales, speculative prose. But whatever one makes of Ford's stature as author, there can be little doubt of his eye and ear as editor, his standing at the very center of this century's cluster of talent. He served as expert witness to its literary life. As editor, with the possible exception of Ezra Pound—whom Ford also helped and who performed much the same service for poets—he was nonpareil.

The first issue of his magazine, *The English Review*, appeared in December 1908. It contained a W. H. Hudson essay on Stonehenge and the first installment of Joseph Conrad's memoirs. It offered an installment of H. G. Wells's *Tono-Bungay* and a Constance Garnett translation of Tolstoy. Shorter fiction included a story by Henry James, "The Jolly Corner," and "A Fisher of Men" by John Galsworthy. Ford's taste astonishes; his judgment was first-rate. This was no proleptic *Norton Anthology*, a selection of survivors, but rather opinion rendered in the hurly-burly of the work itself. And when someone asked him how he managed to *read* as well as *write* so much, Ford made memorable answer. He spoke with difficulty; he had been mustard-gassed in the first World War. A great walrus of a man by then, he wheezed out his reply (I have it from the questioner). "It's easy," Ford averred. "It only takes a line."

Some called him a liar; all agree he took a lover's license with truth.

He embroidered; he worked for effect. He liked to call himself, after Basho, "an old man mad about writing," and at times his pursuit of the fictive could undermine mere fact. So it probably took him a paragraph. But I want to start this essay with an extract from Ford's memoir on discovery—and the process of judgment.

"In the year when my eyes first fell on words written by Norman Douglas, G. H. Tomlinson, Wyndham Lewis, Ezra Pound and others . . . upon a day I received a letter from a young schoolteacher in Nottingham. I can still see the handwriting—as if drawn with sepia rather than written in ink, on grey-blue notepaper. It said that the writer knew a young man who wrote, as she thought, admirably but was too shy to send his work to editors. Would I care to see some of his writing?

"In that way I came to read the first words of a new author:

The small locomotive engine, Number 4, came clanking, stumbling down from Selston with seven full waggons. It appeared round the corner with loud threats of speed, but the colt that it startled from among the gorse which still flickered indistinctly in the raw afternoon, outdistanced it in a canter. A woman walking up the railway line to Underwood, held her basket aside and watched the footplate of the engine advancing.

"I was reading in the twilight in the long eighteenth-century room that was at once the office of The English Review and my drawing room. My eyes were tired; I had been reading all day so I did not go any further with the story. It was called 'Odour of Chrysanthemums.' I laid it in the basket for accepted manuscripts. My secretary looked up and said:

" 'You've got another genius?'

"I answered, 'It's a big one this time,' and went upstairs to dress. . . ."

Ford then proceeds to analyze the first paragraph of D. H. Lawrence's first published story. His reading strikes me as a paradigm of judgment, worth reproducing at length.

"The very title makes an impact on the mind. You get at once the knowledge that this is not, whatever else it may turn out, either a frivolous or even a gay, springtime story. Chrysanthemums are not only flowers of the autumn: they are the autumn itself. And the presumption is that the author is observant. The majority of people do not even know that chrysanthemums have an odour. I have had it flatly denied to me that they have. . . .

"Titles as a rule do not matter much. Very good authors break down when it comes to the effort of choosing a title. But one like Odour of Chrysanthemums is at once a challenge and an indication. The author seems to say: Take it or leave it. You know at once that you are not going to read a comic story about someone's butler's omniscience. The man who sent you this has, then, character, the courage of his convictions, a power of observation. All these presumptions flit through your mind. At once you read:

" 'The small locomotive engine, Number 4, came clanking, stumbling down from Selston,' and at once you know that this fellow with the power of observation is going to write of whatever he writes about from the inside. The 'Number 4' shows that. He will be the sort of fellow who knows that for the sort of people who work about engines, engines have a sort of individuality. He had to give the engine the personality of a number ... 'With seven full waggons' ... The 'seven' is good. The ordinary careless writer would say, 'some small waggons.' This man knows what he writes. He sees the scene of his story exactly. He has an authoritative mind.

" 'It appeared round the corner with loud threats of speed.' ... Good writing; slightly, but not *too* arresting ... 'But the colt that it startled from among the gorse ... outdistanced it at a canter.' Good again. This fellow does not 'state.' He doesn't say, 'It was coming slowly,' or—what would have been a little better—'at seven miles an hour.' Because even 'seven miles an hour' means nothing definite for the untrained mind. It might mean something for a trainer of pedestrian racers. The imaginative writer writes for all humanity; he does not limit his desired readers to specialists ... But anyone knows that an engine that makes a great deal of noise and yet cannot overtake a colt at a canter must be a ludicrously ineffective machine. We know then that this fellow knows his job.

" 'The gorse still flickered indistinctly in the raw afternoon....' Good, too, distinctly good. This is the just-sufficient observation of nature that gives you, in a single phrase, landscape, time of day, weather, season. It is a raw afternoon in autumn in a rather accented countryside. The engine would not come round a bend if there were not some obstacle to a straight course—a water-course, a chain of hills. Hills, probably, because gorse grows on dry, broken-up waste country. They won't also be mountains or anything spectacular or the writer would have mentioned them. It is, then, just 'country.'

"Your mind does all this for you without any ratiocination on your part. You are not, I mean, purposedly sleuthing. The engine and the trucks are there, with the white smoke blowing away over hummocks of gorse. Yet there has been practically none of the tiresome thing called descriptive nature, of which the English writer is as a rule so lugubriously lavish. . . . And then the woman comes in, carrying her basket. That indicates her status in life. She does not belong to the comfortable classes. Nor, since the engine is small, with trucks on a dud line, will the story be one of the Kipling-engineering type, with gleaming rails, and gadgets, and the smell of oil warmed by the bearings, and all the other tiresomeness.

"You are, then, for as long as the story lasts, to be in one of those untidy, unfinished landscapes where locomotives wander innocuously amongst women with baskets. That is to say, you are going to learn how what we used to call 'the other half'—though we might as well have said, the other ninety-nine hundredths—lives. And if you are an editor and that is what you are after, you know that you have got what you want and you can pitch the story straight away into your wicker tray with the few accepted manuscripts and go on to some other occupation . . . Because this man knows. He knows how to open a story with a sentence of the right cadence for holding the attention. He knows how to construct a paragraph. He knows the life he is writing about in a landscape just sufficiently constructed with a casual word here and there. You can trust him for the rest" (From the *Bodley Head Ford Madox Ford*, vol. 5).

As indicated above, I revere Ford this side of idolatry. The passage demonstrates his informed and alerted response, his gift of split-second discernment. It's an articulated version of the process we engage in every day—the decision to *start* a story, *finish* an article, *buy* the book. Except in our role as teacher or friend, we enter into no contract to read—to fully read—a text; such judgment calls are continual. The "In" tray, the "Out" tray are with us wherever we go. And as anyone who has engaged in the process professionally can attest, the "Out" tray is much the more full.

Recently, however, I've come to question Ford. First of all, and though the memoir may be accurate, I have no doubt he finished the piece later on. He would have winnowed it for closer reading, might have shown it to his second-in-command. Had Lawrence not been printed here, he would no doubt have found another sponsor soon or late. And the first paragraph may well be the most successful of "Odour of Chrysanthemums"; what follows is Lawrence the tubthumper, the preacher.

Any such judgment, no matter how it purports to objectivity, cannot be absolute. It is subject to caprice. (One's eyes grow tired; one looks forward to dinner; the daily fare has been lean.) On that threshing floor for winnowed chaff, the next shift's custodian may pick out grain; after the judgment chamber, there comes a court of appeal. It is a piece of extraordinary arrogance, after all, to decide on the basis of a single line: thumbs up or down. And any set of judges will likely disagree.

The house of fiction has, as Henry James informed us, many rooms. The novel is as changeable a genre as can plausibly be labeled by a single name; so too with the short story. It is a convention, merely, or a laziness of language that causes us to classify the work of Jane Austen and William Burroughs by a common category; so too with the brief fictions of Chekhov and Davenport. This may prove the labeler's despair, but it is the reader's delight.

That art is descriptive is clear; that it is prescriptive is to be desired; that it should be proscriptive strikes me as inane. Dangerous, too, since that way lies censorship. . . . The virtue of the marketplace lies in its competitive jumble, its contradictory standards, its multiplicity of wares. So how do we go about choosing—in the forum of the classroom or the conference, the office of Simon & Schuster, or the drawing room that doubled as the editorial boardroom of Ford's *The English Review*?

De gustibus non est disputandum is a dictum accepted by all. There is no arguing—or at least no instructive disagreement—as to taste. Yet all of us, it seems to me, who spend our lives as teachers—as writers surely also—attempt to ensure the reverse. We have, however unverifiable, our own sense of gossamer truth, our conviction that *this* matters, *that* does not. We have, however hazily conceived or haphazardly constructed, our sense of value, achievement, of what is worth the celebration and what not. Few hierarchical systems are more of a muddle than that of aesthetics; how explain why *Moby Dick* is a better book than *Jaws*? As judge—whether anointed or self-appointed—we are constantly adjudicating this very question: rank.

The term itself is its own oxymoron. "Rank" suggests both the condition of hierarchy, the level of attainment, and its rancid concomitant, decay. "Oh my offense is rank," says Claudius, implying both at once. "Judgment" too is a word full of shadings—a word as impartial as the ideal practitioner thereof. The Last Judgment, for instance, conveys the threatful possibility of failure as well as eternal success; "Judge not, lest ye be judged." Think of Augustine's great conundrum: "Do not despair; one of the thieves was saved. Do not presume; one of the thieves was damned."

To be thrown into the "hoosegow" is to have been judged. "I was *juzgado*," the cowboys would say, when south of the border they landed in jail: hoosegowed. Even the judgment of Paris, so happy a circumstance—the first recorded beauty contest—is fraught with peril, risk; whichever goddess the lucky lover chooses (she daintily taking his hand, accepting the roses, weeping becomingly, smudging her mascara, smiling at the audience, her bosom swelling with emotion, showing the right length of leg while she curtseys) leaves two disgruntled also-rans. And then the Trojan War . . .

Too, our standards of beauty can change. Indeed they should, or we're likely to be accused of arrested development; think of the sixty-year-old who lusts only and repeatedly for the sixteen-year-old's shape. One changes one's opinion over time. Certain books that meant a great deal to me ten years ago now seem transient, fleeting in appeal; the hallmark of one's youth is not inevitably the benchmark of one's middle or old age. The very structure of instruction has to do with discernment, with learning how to see what had been hidden before. Think of all those fables where the young man chooses lead, not gold, and discovers its true value; think of those fairy tales where the ancient crone kissed becomes a princess, faithful forever, a boon to the bed. Don't judge a book by its cover, we say, but which of us would truly wish to have a cover so repellent as to forestall judgment or to have it predisposed? Nor is it always self-evident that the relation of outer to inner is inverse; an ugly cover—lead, the crone—does not guarantee the contents will prove beautiful. Kiss the frog if you so choose, but don't assume it must posthaste transmogrify to prince.

For judgment, too, shifts locus. It's not as if a single individual has a single standard and bears it aloft throughout a career. Though a writer's work is more like his or her own other work than that of anyone else, though there be fingerprint traces all over each page, nonetheless it is safe to say that a career shifts shape. So blind Justice with the scales is an apt metaphor—as long as we remember that we're on the threshing floor itself, that time may tilt the balance, pressing heavy-thumbed and at near-random on a side.

This is a function of variety. It is comparatively easy to judge a tennis match or a diving competition; it is simple to determine which piece of pottery is defective, where the violin's varnish has bubbled or the joining cracked. The coincidence of estimates in a gymnast's scorecard sometimes makes one feel as if the judges are in league. It's a little less clear in a piano competition, perhaps, or in the submission of blueprints for an architectural project—but here too the parameters have been defined, the standards made available. To the degree that a form has amplitude, however, it grows harder to assess.

I have carried with me for some time—and it is all the more attractive because unclear—the notion of writers as artisans, of artists engaged in a guild. The model is that of the medieval guild, with its compelling triad of apprentice, then journeyman laborer, then master craftsman—this last attained after a lifetime's study and practice of the craft. That writing is a craft as well as art, that one must learn to dado the paragraph's joints, so to speak, to prime the scene's canvas—this is something we take, I think, increasingly for granted. But the stages of apprenticeship to master craftsman seem at the least confusing; it is not a mere matter of time. Who provides the walking papers; who does the training, the teaching; who ratifies our membership and says, "Welcome to the guild . . ."?

There are several plausible candidates. There are agents, editors, publishers; there are critics and prize-giving committees; there are writing programs, hydra-headed lately, and writing conferences and festivals and magazines and an audience of strangers growing intimate as we whisper secrets—with the high hope that thousands will read them—we might hesitate to tell to a close friend. There is inward certainty, discovery: the knowledge that we now can manage what we once could not. There are strange and compelling contests to enter: the lottery called influence, the lottery called fame. But surely one of the ways we know we are writers is when writers tell us so, pointing out a way through the dark wood.

Yeats called it "singing school"—then hastened to insist that none such obtained in Ireland. Not long ago we writers were strangers to academe's grove; now we fit to those grooves like a needle, wearing blunt with usage. And the assumption here, of course, is that practitioners may represent the art with greater precision than critics, that those who teach had better also be those who do. It is a nice distinction, however; we do not assume that a voice teacher need be a better singer than the students he or she may coach; not all managers of baseball teams were baseball heroes earlier; excellence as writer is not the single measure of those who profess it, who teach.

Writing cannot, we are told, be taught; it must nonetheless be learned. How does one make sense of such a seeming-paradox, and one with which an increasing number of us live?

Antonello da Massina was working as apprentice in his master's studio. The commission was nearly complete, the master engaged on his self-portrait in the lower right-hand corner, behind the donor's image— a kind of signature. He was bitten by a disease-bearing mosquito and was ill for months. From his sickbed he issued the order that the project be completed; from what looked as if it might prove his deathbed, he rose to examine the work. He pronounced himself well pleased. Looking more closely, however, at what was no longer a self-portrait he leaned forward to notice a black speck on the neck. "What's this?" he inquired of Antonello, "what is this?" "Master," said his student, deferential, "that's the mosquito that so nearly killed you." The painter doffed his cap. "Antonello," he announced. "You're the master now."

The whole impulse toward "self-expression" is a recent and possibly aberrant one in art. Legions of accomplished writers found nothing shameful in prescribed or proscribed subjects or in eschewing the first-person pronoun. The apprentice in that artist's shop might mix paint for years or learn to dado joints for what must have felt like forever; only slowly and under supervision might he approach the artifact as such.

Nor is "signature" important. The bulk of our literature's triumphs have been collective or anonymous; who can identify the authors of the Bible, the *Ramayana, Beowulf*? More important, who cares? The *Iliad* and *Odyssey* are by an unknown bard as are, for all practical purposes, the plays of William Shakespeare. This is not to say that these works don't display personality—the reverse is more nearly true—but rather that the cult of personality should fade. It too is recent and, I think, aberrant; it has nothing to do with the labor of writing as such.

All this conjoins with the nature of language and our presumed literacy—a natal familiarity with English that, more often than not in the contemporary author, breeds contempt. No one presumes to give a dance recital without having first mastered the rudiments of dance, to perform Mozart before they've learned scales, or to enter a weight-lifting contest if they've never hoisted weights. Yet because we've been reading since five, we blithely assume we can read; because we scrawled our signature when six, we glibly aspire to write.

And here, I think, is where the issues of apprenticeship and judgment intersect. Imitation is flattery's form. No first sentence is impossible. The writer is the literal lord of his created domain. (Some first sentences are, admittedly, more possible than others; the reader may stop reading after the opening phrase.) We can point to any world we wish; we make up the rules of our game. By the second sentence, however, we have fewer possibilities; we begin to follow our own lead. A story that starts from a first-person present-tense vantage would dizzy the reader if it shifted to third-person and the past tense instantly; one that starts in Zambia had better not move to Rhode Island in the second phrase. And if the writer chooses such disjunction, then the third sentence somehow ought to indicate he knows what he is doing—that the story deals with shifting vantage points. This is a contract we make with the stranger's attention—or, perhaps, that of the judge. The game we invite a reader to join has a coherent system, and we should not cheat nor alter the rules halfway through.

I do not mean that every story must be linear or that the reader fathoms it by the first paragraph's end. Any situation worth exploring is progressively revealed. But if we understand a woman to be forty we should not learn ten pages later that she's twenty-two; if we're told—authoritatively—that X has been a murderer we should not find at story's end that it was really Y. So the process of delimiting continues through the piece; the third sentence follows the second as the second did the first. The thirtieth follows the twenty-ninth, excluding what once might have been. There should be, ideally, only one last line. Of the infinite range of possibility with which the writer began he is left with a single legitimate closure—all other possibilities having been foreclosed. This holds true for dialogue as well as for descriptive prose. If a character's last line must be, "I ain't sure I love you now," he can't use the alternative, "Cyril's in dubiety with reference to hate."

So the teacher-judge must first attempt to parse the petitioner's system—to measure, as it were, the distance between intention and execution. Justice is, more often than we care to acknowledge, a matter of interpretation, a "reading" of the law. If you're looking for an adventure story, you won't likely be compelled by *A la Recherche du temps perdu*; if you want to read about the contemporary South, you'll be disappointed by *Oliver Twist*. This is self-evident but nonetheless something we tend to forget; each work of original fiction creates and must be measured by its own—often unstated—terms. And what we ought to judge therefore is consonance with such engendered expectation: the degree to which the game's rules have been played.

Ford Madox Ford provided, in the case of D. H. Lawrence, an exemplary instance of judgment. What follows is, I think, a paradigmatic example of the teacher's role. Its strategy insists on imitation, its purpose the reverse. The speaker is Bernard Greenhouse, one of the founding members of the chamber ensemble, the Beaux Arts Trio. In the period of which he speaks, Greenhouse had already achieved an important concert career. Yet he felt the need to continue his studies—to complete, as it were, apprenticeship. (In my book, *The Beaux Arts Trio: A Portrait*, this story emerges in fragments; I have excised myself as interviewer for the sake of continuity.)

"Casals was, as you know, very much occupied with the Spanish Republican cause in 1946. We had a lengthy correspondence, and he refused to teach me. But I did not accept the negative reply. So I took a troop transport right after the war—after I'd come out of the navy. I enrolled in the American School at Fontainebleau as a means to get a visa. And I took, in addition to my cello, several cases with all sorts of food which I knew would be in short supply—baking chocolate, tinned butter, that sort of thing. After I arrived in Paris, I wrote another, final postcard asking whether he wouldn't hear me play just once. And I received a card in Paris, saying if I came on such and such a date, he would be pleased to hear me play—providing I would give a check to the Spanish Republican charities. When I received the card I was, of course, overjoyed. I made arrangements to take the train to Perpignan and then the mountain railway up to Prades. And I arrived at the railway station speaking barely a word of French. There was someone with a handdrawn cart who took my valise; I carried the cello. We went down the main street into Prades and to the Grand Hotel. But the owner shook his finger at me and said— the porter translating—'No more cellists can come to my hotel. I already had one. Casals. He disturbed all the guests.'

"So I had to wend my way over to the midwife's. She happened to have a room free at the time, a room just barely wide enough for the bed— with no possibility of practicing. The same day I went to the Villa Colette and knocked on Casals's door. I was let in. Within minutes Casals came down from his studio, still in his pajamas; he had been writing letters. And he said, 'You have come a long way and been very persistent. Why have you come here to study with me?' We sat down, had a long discussion. I gave him my background and told him some of the works which I had performed; I said he had been my idol ever since I was ten. He said, 'You go back to your room and come back in two days in the morning, and I will hear you play.'

"Well, the next days were anxious ones for me. I went back on the appointed morning, entered the room, and Casals still hadn't dressed. He was still in his pajamas. He said, 'Well, now, you warm up a bit, play a bit so that you get your hands in good condition and I will be back as soon as I have dressed and shaved.' I took the cello out of the case and worked for twenty minutes or so, and there was no Casals. I had had my back turned to the door, and when finally I turned I could see his bald head in the doorway—he had been listening at the keyhole. When he saw that I had turned my head, he came into the room, still in his pajamas, still unshaven, and he said, 'I really didn't want to dress. I wanted to hear you without having you nervous.'

"Then he started asking for the repertoire, and he requested many pieces. After an hour or more of my playing—during which he indicated nothing more than the piece and the passage he wanted me to play—he said, 'All right. Put down your cello, put it away, and we'll talk.' And I thought, now here comes the worthwhile contribution to a Republican charity. But he said to me, 'Well, what you need is an apprenticeship to a great artist. I believe in the apprentice system. Stradivarius, Guarnerius, Amati . . . they turned out so many wonderful violin makers. And I believe the same thing can hold true in making musicians. If I knew of a great artist I could send you to, I would do so,' he said, 'because my mind is occupied with the Spanish Republican cause. But since I don't know whom to send you to—and if you agree to stay in the village and take a lesson at least once every two days—I will teach you.'

"So I went back to Paris for my trunks, came back and settled in. At this point the gentleman who owned the Grand Hotel—when he found out that I had chocolate and good American dollars—changed his mind about having a cellist in residence. So I moved into the Grand Hotel, had a palatial room with a view, and from that point on I started to work very hard. I had three or four lessons a week.

"When I asked Casals how much he would charge a lesson, he said twenty dollars. In those days such a sum was considerable. But one day I arrived in great spirits and I played a beautiful performance—forgive me, I think it *was* beautiful—of the Brahms F Major Sonata. And when I finished he said, 'You know, you played so well today I won't accept the twenty dollars.' And I was deliriously happy. But the next lesson, unfortunately, I didn't play so well, and he accepted the twenty dollars. This went on until finally he said to me, 'You know, I can't accept this money from you; I know it's going to be difficult. But someday when you're able to, I would like you to write a check for the Spanish Republican charities and make a considerable contribution.' And this is a promise I've kept.

"We spent at least three hours a lesson. The first hour was performance; the next hour entailed discussion of musical techniques; and the third hour he reminisced about his own career. During the first hour, he sat about a yard away. He would play a phrase and have me repeat it. And if the bowing and the fingering weren't exactly the same as his, and the emphasis on the top of the phrase was not the same, he would stop me and say, 'No, no. Do it this way.' And this went on for quite a few lessons. I was studying the Bach D Minor Suite and he demanded that I become an absolute copy. At one point I did very gingerly suggest that I would only turn out to be a poor copy of Pablo Casals, and he said to me, 'Don't worry about that. Because I'm seventy years old, and I will be gone soon, and people won't remember my playing but they will hear yours.' It turned out of course that he lived till the ripe old age of ninety-seven.

"But that was his way of teaching. He was very insistent about it—extremely meticulous about my following all the details of his performance. And after several weeks of working on that one suite of Bach's, finally, the two of us could sit down and perform and play all the same fingerings and bowings and all of the phrasings alike. And I really had become a copy of the Master. It was as if the room had stereophonic sound—two cellos producing at once. And at that point, when I had been able to accomplish this, he said to me, 'Fine. Now just sit. Put your cello down and listen to the D Minor Suite.' And he played through the piece and changed *every* bowing and *every* fingering and *every* phrasing and all the emphasis within the phrase. I sat there, absolutely with my mouth open, listening to a performance, which was heavenly—absolutely beautiful. And when he finished he turned to me with a broad grin on his face, and he said, 'Now you've learned how to improvise in Bach. From now on you study Bach this way.'"

Let me finish, therefore, with a set of seeming-paradoxes. The only way to learn one's art is through back-breaking labor that must not seem like work. After the seeming-impossible has become difficult, the difficult habitual, and the habitual easy, true mastery begins. We must listen with absolute deference to the verdict of the judge—whether it be praise, dispraise, or the most likely, a suspended sentence—then appeal. We must work through derivation toward the original voice—remembering that "originality" is likely to be a compound of influence so multiform and various it cannot be assessed. We need to know an oxymoron from chiasmus to know freedom within limits as the root and force of syntax. Our certainties will turn to doubt, our rote learning grow improvisational.

Remember that the poet, lost in the dark wood, had the great good luck—in the middle of his journey, in the middle of the road of his life—to find another poet pointing out the way. But remember also that the story of instruction, of Virgil's guiding hand, comes to us from Dante's point of view. Look for the fly, if not in the ointment, on the teacher's neck.

What's in a Name?

My name is Stanley. Could you be mugged by a Stanley? Could a Stanley rape you? Tops, I might molest your kid, but *you'd* never know it, and neither would she. What, a little suntan lotion rubbed along the bottom of her swimsuit like a piping of frosting around a birthday cake? What, a spot of spilled tea on the sunsuit, my finger in the bespittled handkerchief moist from what it wouldn't even occur to you was drool before it was saliva, and vigorously brushing across what won't be breasts for another half dozen years yet, my grunt the two or three tone gutteral hum of deflection, nervous and oddly dapper as the tugs, pats, and twitches of a stand-up comic, distracting as the shot cuffs of magicians and card-sharps, all random melody's tangential rove? Because how could you ever even guess at my intentions and interiors, my inner landscapes and incisor lusts, the thickening at my throat like hidden shim, the ponderous stirrings of my ice-floe blood, deep as resource, buried as oil in my gnarled and knotty groin, my clotted sexual circuits? Could put it past you plenty, believe me, holding the kid's shoulder, the little girl's, for the leverage, drawing her within the fork of my white old thighs, a pervert like a master artisan, fixing her there like a piece of carpentry. Or violating her in absentia, my eyes on her kindergarten picture, my snoot in her laundry, in her eight-year-old grimes. All contacts troubled, gone off, amok but deceptive, accidental, clever as a pickpocket's.

Protected by reputation, see, my triumph of the human spirit, that heart of gold which I don't possess but people attribute to me anyway, mistaking cholesterol for karats, hypertension for love, innocence by association, by stereotype, dismissing me finally, all the world waving me through Customs like that guy in the audience at the night club whose lap the chanteuse sits in, kissing his bald spot, pinching his cheek, and telling folks what a good sport he is, leading the applause.

Protected finally by all my grotesque cuddlies—the limp, the cane, my toothless, grampsy ways, my fatty's belly and threatless aura, my ducky's waddle and feeble's klutz, my *Stanleyness* on me like a wimp heraldrics. Hey, I'm kidding. Only offering credential here, only flashing badge, showing my hand, franked under the ultraviolet like a kid's at the dance.

Stanley is as Stanley does and you are what you're called.

Stanley is your brother-in-law, your C.P.A., your cousin in Drapes. He collects stamps, washes his car, belongs to Triple A, and keeps a weather eye on the gas mileage. He is, that is, as all of us are, the fiction of his sound, all his recombinant glottals, labials, fricatives, and plosives. He's his flaps and trills. He's his spirants, I mean. He is, I mean, the vibrations of his name.

For great characters demand great names. (Of writers I admire, only Henry James—itself a fine name—lumbers his characters with bad ones. I'm thinking of Henrietta Stackpole, I'm thinking of Ralph Touchett, of Fleda Vetch and Milly Theale. I'm thinking of Madam Merle, of Casper Goodwood, Pansy Osmond, and Hyacinth Robinson. I'm thinking of Margaret Thatcher.) Here's a roll call for you. Beowulf and the Wife of Bath. King Lear but not Titus Andronicus. Hamlet but not Garp. Snow White, Pinocchio and Mary Poppins but not Cinderella. Peter Pan but not Captain Hook. R2D2, Hans Solo, C3PO and Obie wan Kenobie but not Princess Leia. Leopold Bloom but not Stephen Daedalus. (Who can explain it, who can tell you why? Fools give you reasons, wise men never try. Rodgers and Hammerstein but not Weber and Rice.) Harry Morgan, Harry Bailey, Harry Angstrom, Harry Lime. J. R. Phil Esterhaus. Babbitt. Mr. Toots. John Jarndyce. Mr. Tulkinghorn. Flem Snopes. Will Varner. V. K. Ratcliff. Dick Diver, Jay Gatsby. My Uncle Toby. Dorothea Brooke and Mr. Casaubon. Jiminy Cricket. Tom Jones, Humphrey Clinker. Hazel Motes. Becky Sharp. Captain Dobbin like a reliable horse. Emma Bovary, Emma Woodhouse, Julian Sorel. Swann and the Guermantes. Vautrin. Hans Castorp. Levin. Father Zossima. Bartleby. Hester Prynn and Arthur Dimmesdale. Angel Clare, Old Goriot, Elizabeth Bennett and her four sisters. All the not-to-be-pronounced names of God.

I want to tell you about Louis Paul Pelgas, the first Director of Admissions at any school in the Thirteen Colonies Conference, but before I begin it will be necessary to provide you with some sometimes dense, and often apparently trivial, historical background.

Clifton College is a small liberal arts college in what are, quite liter-

ally, the outer edges of Pennsylvania. It is out of the way even for Norbiton, Pennsylvania, even for Chapel County. Look at a map. Surrounded
on two sides by West Virginia in the extreme southwestern corner of
what—it's that close to the West Virginia line, that close to the Ohio
one—is referred to by its inhabitants as the "state" rather than the "commonwealth" of Pennsylvania (possibly to lend a little aura of the average
to what is uncompromisingly an atypical part of the nation), Norbiton,
like a heel in an old shoe, exactly snugs the perfect right angle in the
tight corner where its western and southern borderlines meet.

This tiny portion of Pennsylvania had been unofficially a "state" since
antebellum days when, feeling itself both physically and spiritually
closer to the gravitational pull—Chapel County was the only county in
Pennsylvania where it was legal to keep slaves although, due to the impossibility of cultivating crops in its harshly alkaline soil, except for the
handful of "house niggers," exchanged as a sort of gag gift between one
local merchant and another, there was never any appreciable slave population there—of its Virginian and West Virginian antiabolitionist
neighbors than it was to Harrisburg, three hundred fifty-seven miles distant, or Philadelphia three hundred sixty-nine miles off, or even to Pittsburgh, which, though less than one hundred miles away, was, for eighty
of those hundred, accessible only through what John James Audubon
himself has described in his notes as ". . . wilderness so cluttered and
remote that its very sky is uninhabitable by the birds of the air, wilderness so cluttered and remote that that sky is itself wilderness." "A dry
hole," he remarks in an 1847 journal entry, "which for all its varied veg-
etation, succulent berries, meaty nuts and abundant fruit, is as zoolog-
ically lifeless as the moon. I cannot sketch there. My inks, oils and water
colors go off like stale milk and lose their ability to congeal or adhere to
paper. My pencil leads liquefy and my lines melt and run. There is a
liquorish rifeness in the air so profound it lasts the autumn and can burn
holes in the snow, or make—so viable is the half-life of the fermented
spirits of all its fierce flora, its growth and undergrowth, its leaves and
barks—an illusion of its 'frozen' streams and lakes, of ice apparently two
and even three inches thick which is not only impossible to stand upon
but worth your hat to set down on its obdurate-seeming surface. It is a
wilderness so impregnable that no jack rabbit, dog, possum, coon, turkey
or even insect, let alone any animal as fragile and exotic as a bird, could
possibly get close enough to it to thrive."

Nor is any of this typical John Audubon hyperbole. After a failed late-
nineteenth-century attempt to survey the thousand or so square miles
of this "queer, thick country"—Audubon's phrase—Phil and Pembler

Roberts released foxes, dogs, and other small mammals at the margins of The Thicket. (Called "The Thicket" at the Chapel County end and "The Woody" at the Pittsburgh one, one recalls Pembler Roberts's famous comment: "Viewing the unspoiled, unnibbled trees, leaves and grasses in 'The Thicket' is as different from viewing them in 'ordinary' nature, a sylvan woodland or forest, say, as gazing at the defined, beautifully articulated stars in the country is from looking up at them in town.") Seeing them founder and return to their release points, they seemed, in Phil Roberts's analogy, "like confused, guilty hunting dogs who have lost the scent." (The experiment has been successfully repeated for seventeen years in Professor Roger Barr's Psychology 101 classes. Julia Rayburton, while still a junior at Clifton College, devised a variant of the Pembler and Barr experiments. Wishing to test the very letter of Captain Audubon's 1847 journal entry, Ms. Rayburton stood at the edge of The Thicket—now, with the advent of bulldozers, trenchers, and the introduction of other heavy earth-moving equipment, reduced to a plot no larger than a decent-sized park in a medium-sized city—and scattered kernels of white corn, the favored food of all agrarian birds, into it in full view of three hungry bluejays who'd been kept in cages and deprived of food for more than eight hours. The jays, who had carefully and even rather slavishly followed the short trajectory of the corn— Rayburton is left-handed but tosses corn with her right hand—were unable to retrieve any of the kernels. They flew up and around but never entered the air space above The Thicket, thus offering proof of Professor Barr's speculations regarding "density theory," the psychological-cum-sociological postulate that "all bodies repudiate areas smaller than the space required to provide their egress!" The implications this has for America's crowded prison system are, of course, immense. Professor Barr's and Julia Rayburton's findings have already been cited in four court rulings and must be *sub judice* in who knows how many more.)

If this isolated and somewhat remarkable edge of the commonwealth had unofficially chosen to think of itself as a state since, you'll recall, the mid-nineteenth century, it ought to be said that no one really knows why the citizens of Chapel County preferred one designation over another. (What's in a name, eh?) Even as late as 1837, when Chapel and Green counties split off from each other (for reasons, incidentally, which had more to do with the close identification of The Thicket with the town of Norbiton than they did with slaver or antislaver sentiments), the term "commonwealth," not "state," was the legal nomenclature in each of the seventeen articles of incorporation. In fact, Chapel County has only *officially* been designated part of the "state of Pennsylvania" since Maurdon Legurney, both Mayor of Norbiton and County Supervisor, was chosen to represent Chapel County at the Pennsylvania Constitutional Convention of 1878, about a year after the Congress of the recently reunited States of America had put an end to the period of reconstruction. The Convention, referred to in the newspapers of the day—even Horace Greeley sent a correspondent to cover it for the old *New York World-Examiner*—as "The New Reconstruction," was convened at the instigation of the people of Chapel County but was equally the brainchild of Legurney's political protégé, Governor Lamar White, a native of Norbiton who, when Legurney put his name into nomination at the Democratic Convention in St. Louis in 1882, was the first politician ever referred to as a "favorite son," though his family had removed from Norbiton when White was only two years old.

Reconstruction had been, of course, a time of *ad hoc* law, a period of makeshift legislation when some of the most bizarre laws in the history of this or any other nation were passed, almost, it seemed, as a kind of willed whim. It's largely forgotten now, but from 1865 to 1877, when this odd chapter in our history closed, Congress forbade the raising of orchids and carnations. It prohibited the sale of calves' liver in quantities under three pounds and made it a federal offense, punishable by a mandatory seven years in prison, for women to fish from a pier. The statute was vaguely worded, perhaps deliberately, and in the five years it was on the books, no one was actually sent to prison. Ironically, it was the vagueness and unenforcibility of the law that gave rise, during the period, to its public flouting and introduced the term "fishwife" into the American vocabulary. (Less whimsical, but far more dangerous, was a peculiar law of evidence introduced just after the Civil War. This, of course, was the infamous "Mixed Race Witness Rule" which, when crimes were alleged against persons of one race by persons of another, made it obligatory for prosecutor and defense alike to produce witnesses of *both races* to the crime. The rule was obviously directed against the defeated South—it did not apply in non-slave states on the dubious grounds that Negroes were less populous in the North—by a piqued, if victorious, Union. What is perhaps more astonishing than the rule itself is the fact that during the dozen years before its repeal it was five times sent up to the Supreme Court for "challenging," and five times adjudged constitutional!)

As indicated earlier, the Pennsylvania Constitutional Convention was convened in 1878 by a governor who, though he had been a mere toddler when he left and had never been back, was born in Norbiton. As also indicated, this was barely a year after the nation had junked the notion of Reconstruction, the queer period of back-scratch law when all that was necessary to get a law passed was a quorum of cronies who would do unto each other what they would have each other do unto them. As in all periods to which there is an inevitable reaction, that reaction, when it finally came, was a lulu. What were demanded now were unarbitrary and entirely righteous rules of order, logic and sequentiality— a return, if you will, to 1837, when Chapel County quietly signed seventeen articles of incorporation, each of which designated the new county as continuing to belong to the "Commonwealth" rather than to the "*State* of Pennsylvania." (That people in Chapel County held slaves was merely a fact of home rule, of little more significance at the time, really, than the local option that governs the sale of alcohol or is responsible for the blue laws.)

Now, however, there was—at least on the parts of the people of Chapel County, Governor White, and Maurdon Legurney, White's political guru and hand-picked emissary from Chapel County to the Pennsylvania Constitutional Convention—a reaction to the reaction to the reaction. If America wanted sequentiality again, some apostolic succession of convention and right reason, Chapel County, on the very verge of The Thicket, that then still one thousand square miles of all waivered, rebuffed, exempt and repudiate Nature's lush and pointless, extended bramble, wanted, yearned for, and actually *demanded* the return of the random, even if they had to invent a legitimate, legal, due-processed pandect of *de jure* and prescribed code under the fiction of a rigged Constitutional Convention.

Here's what happened:

The people of Chapel County got to Maurdon Legurney, Maurdon Legurney got to Lamar White, and Governor White got a Constitutional Convention for his commonwealth which was in all respects (save for that first cause like a wicked itch that convened it in the first place), splendid, making Pennsylvania a paradigm of justice and good sense which became a model of high democracy. With this exception—the little legalistic eye teaser buried in the middle of chapter VII, article 42, section 12, subsection 9, paragraph 19, line 5: "All territory south of 79°, 30' longitude, 39°, 45' latitude, and north of 80°, 30' longitude, 40°, 45' latitude, and all peoples residing within said territory, shall henceforth, to the contrary notwithstanding, upon receipt of a vote of the majority in any constitutionally convened poll or public plebiscite as defined in chapter III, article 18, section 34, paragraph 1, line 1, not to be interpreted as incorporating the provisions of chapter IV, article 9, paragraph 1, line 16, in accordance with the doctrine, '*inclusio uniuis est exclusio alter-*

ius,' have the right to designate itself, and themselves citizens *of,* in perpetuity, subject to no contingent remainders or to conditional limitations or any other encumbrances, the State of Pennsylvania."

What, quite simply, this did was permit Norbiton, Pennsylvania, and all of Chapel County, and *only* Norbiton and *only* Chapel County, since only Norbiton and Chapel County were to the south and north of all those degrees like a temperate zone, and all those minutes like so many conveniently bunched quarters of an hour, all that mathematical, seaborne geography of that inland commonwealth, to (once the plebiscite passed) unsubjugate itself to all the laws then on the books, and all the laws which might henceforth be written to join them, of that only *Commonwealth* of Pennsylvania!

I've already told you. The soil was alkaline. They were only local merchants, only small businessmen. But what Maurdon Legurney, Governor White, and the people of Chapel County had given themselves up to was the return of the random, permission to wallow in, muddle, and romp in their carefully legislated labyrinthine, skimble-skamble, higgledy-piggledy, helter-skelter, harum-scarum anarchy.

They opened whorehouses, and nobody came.

They beat their horse stables into gaming casinos and their horses stood in the rain while the local merchants stood high and dry inside, forlorn at the crap tables, which, despite all the spit, polish, elbow grease, and good honest effort that the remaining house niggers now emancipate-proclamated into ordinary domestics at the stroke of the presidential pen could put into them, still smelled faintly of crap. And nobody came.

"I tell you, boys," Legurney, back from all he'd accomplished for them at the Constitutional Convention at the capitol in Harrisburg, told them, "the world's our oyster. Norbiton, Pennsylvania, could be a regular Sin City, U.S.A. It's just too bad we're so far off the beaten track."

"Think of it, boys," said Oldham Broom, a pretty fair country tailor in his time, but now the kingpin numbers runner for all Chapel County, or, more precisely, numbers walker, or, yet more precisely still, not numbers runner, or walker, or any kind of numbers mover at all, or even just any common, ordinary, garden variety arithmetician, but full-fledged Theoretical Mathematician, each day drawing the lottery and picking what would have been the winning combinations if only somebody had put down the two, four, six bits or buck other side of the ante, and solemnly contemplating the mysterious and elegant laws of chance, "double sixes three days running. What do you suppose the odds against something like *that* are?"

"It's just too bad we're so far off the beaten track," Maurdon Legurney said.

And at first moved their stills out from their old hole-and-corner hiding places into direct sunlight, and then—advertising was coming into its own about then—out onto the public sidewalks, and then, if they were tipsy enough from sampling their own brew, or maybe even just still sober enough to manage it, might carry a few bottles over to the empty Norbiton jail and offer to put them up against the sheriff's own, going from tipsy to cockeyed, cockeyed to maudlin, and maudlin to philosophical over the course of another slow, businessless, lazy afternoon.

"Folks in this part of the state couldn't get themselves arrested if they tried," Ed Flail, former operator of Norbiton's leading drygoods store and now one of the town's most prominent dealers in stolen goods, remarked to Sheriff Leon Edgers.

"That's a fact," agreed Billy Slipper, poacher, sports fisherman and hunter out-of-season of other people's trout and game.

And got an Amen from the county's rustlers, pimps, pickpockets, and other scoundrels.

Because it was true. Crime *didn't* pay. Not in Norbiton, not in Chapel County.

They were sitting on the porch of the Norbiton Inn. Maurdon Legurney, now a broken and melancholy man, nominal lame duck Mayor and County Supervisor with just a scant five-and-a-half years left to run on one or the other of his overlapping terms, started to say, "I tell you, boys, it's just too bad we're so . . ." But they didn't want to hear it.

"Again with the beaten track," Ed Flail said.

"Yeah, shut up about that damn beaten track, already," Sheriff Edgers told His Honor.

But it was true. They were. And who knew this better than Legurney himself who had not only been to the capitol in Harrisburg within the year but had come back from it as well, making not the giant but expeditious swing from Norbiton at the bottom, western limits of Pennsylvania the one hundred miles up to Pittsburgh and then, by rail, from Pittsburgh on a more or less straight easterly shot to Harrisburg two thirds across the commonwealth, but the long, piecemeal, switchbacked, drawn out, up-hill-and-down-dale, down-hill-and-up-dale, zigzag journey through woodland and across farms where there were no roads, an honest-to-God, on-foot trespasser slash poacher far from the beaten and unbeaten track either when he wasn't an out-and-out, horse-

backride hitchhiking beggar? Practically slaloming himself the length
and breadth of the all-but-Commonwealth-of-Pennsylvania. A Pennsylvania which near where he was was still only this fits-and-starts civilization, borrowing even its place-names from all the tamed cities and
myths of place, towns, and villages tinier than towns, tinier than villages, calling themselves Paris, Rome, London, Vienna, calling themselves Athens, Cairo, Istanbul, even Chicago. The better part of two
entire weeks until he even got to the part where the spur started where
you waited for the freight train that brought you to the whistle stop that
took you to the place where if you managed to get there by a Tuesday
you had only to wait till Thursday or Friday till you could catch the train
to Harrisburg.

So it was true. Off the beaten track. Off the beaten path. Off, for all
practical purposes, the goddamn compass itself. So they knew that, who
were only these local farmers. Whose feathered, attenuate world had
been shaped, though they'd forgotten this, were too close to it, who
couldn't see the forest for the trees or any of those one thousand or so
thorny square miles of difficult bramble that somebody on the Norbiton
side had once thought to call The Thicket. (Which hadn't been surveyed,
hadn't been mapped, and which, for all any of them knew, might contain
somewhere within its tough terrains lost, fabled cities of the Indians,
tall mountains, vast deserts, gritty sand dunes, deep inland seas.) Suddenly reminded only then, by Legurney's lugubrious account of his long
and epic but boring odyssey, despondent, failed and failing criminals
manqué on the porch of the Norbiton Inn. And who (the fellow who
suddenly reminded them lost too) mentioned that he'd heard tell that,
speaking of Pittsburgh, it was an oddity of geographical history that
though they was off the beaten track now, in the old days a right smart
of folks had come down all the way from Philadelphia and Harrisburg
and the Poconos and just all over, even from out of state, to see it.

"Speaking of Pittsburgh?"

"Well from all over except Pittsburgh."

"*Except* Pittsburgh."

"Well they had their *own* half. Where'd they get any call to go traipsing
all over hell and gone if all they wanted to look at The Woody was
to—"

"The Woody?"

"Well ain't that what they call it up there? I thought they called it by
a different name. I thought they called it The Woody."

"Yeah? Well?"

"Well, all I was going to say was that if they wanted to see it all they ever had to do was just turn their heads back over their shoulders and there she'd be."

And someone else remembered that Norbiton had been practically a boom town in those days, and that wasn't it funny the way things changed, that why even this porch we're standing on wasn't always the porch of just any old country inn but was part of a regular hotel.

"The Hotel Norbiton?"

"Thicket House," said Oldham Broom who till now hadn't opened his mouth.

"Oh yeah, Thicket House. I recollect hearing talk of that now."

And then all of them began to pitch in with their memories. And collectively remembered that The Thicket had been a sight, even a tourist attraction, years before there was a railroad in Pennsylvania, let alone national or state parks.

"Commonwealth parks," Billy Slipper said.

"Yeah," said Ed Flail, "commonwealth parks."

Somebody remembered reading somewhere that the first picture postcard was of The Thicket, and someone else that the first hotel in America, named for its view or proximity to a point-of-interest was in 1792 when Thicket House was built. They recalled all manner of things.

It was Maurdon Legurney himself who recalled all the old talk about slaves in The Thicket.

"Maurdon!" Sheriff Edgers said.

"Gettysburg's only the largest and most famous of Pennsylvania's battlefields," Legurney said.

"Maurdon!" the sheriff said.

"Shit," Legurney said, "if the citizens of a community ain't entitled to the use of their own legatee'd and birthrighted natural resources I'd like to know who is then?"

"Maurdon, damn it to hell, shut up."

"Well who? Who is?"

"I'm warning you, Maurdon," the sheriff told his mayor. "Maurdon, I'm warning you."

"Why'd God put it here then? Can somebody tell me that? Why'd the good Lord give us a sense of humor to appreciate it in the first place? Why'd—"

"Maurdon, I'm not telling you again!"

"—He teach folks to plant and farm or dig up all the precious metals deep down in the mines? Why'd He stock the rivers and seas with fish and give us our rifles and our shells and our abiding, manly instinct to hunt?"

"Maurdon—"

"He makes some good points there, Leon," Ed Flail said.

"It's briars, goddamn it!" Legurney went on. "It's all pins-and-needled, barbed-wired, saw-toothed, razor's edgery. It's all spiked, prickly and pointy, stinging bristliosity. And what don't bite, nail, and sharp you to death would rash your skin clear off your bones. Because what ain't briars is all itchweed, poison oak and poison ivy, poison sumac allergens!

"*Why'd He inspire us to come up with chapter VII, article 42, section 12, sub-section 9, paragraph 19, line 5, and all the godgiven, goddamn, chickenshit, loophole rest of it?*"

"What?" the sheriff asked. "What's that?"

"What if it *is* tacky? What if it *is*? Because if we ain't subject to the strict letters of the laws of the Commonwealth we ain't liable to being sued neither, Leon."

"Aw, Maurdon," the sheriff said. "Maurdon, aww."

So the whorehouses came down, and the stills were silenced, and all the energies of the people of Chapel County were redirected into beating the old Norbiton Inn back into its original avatar. It became Thicket House again.

The Thicket opened for business in the spring of 1881. It had taken two-and-a-half years to build the thirty-seven miles of great wooden wall, the wide, tall planked platform, accessible by ladder, that rose around the perimeter of The Thicket and sent off cantilevered shoots deep into that queer and lifeless jungle.

They came from all over the Commonwealth, from Ohio and West Virginia and Maryland and up and down the entire eastern seaboard, from Kentucky and the border states and the states of the Confederacy that was, and from the west and even from foreign lands and it became, you might say, America's first theme park.

The people of Chapel County were famous for their sense of humor, those gag-gift slaves they had once exchanged with each other, the "house niggers" whose trust they'd patiently cultivated in the years immediately preceding the Civil War, the abolitionist sympathies they faked, the underground railroad mythology they perpetuated.

"Follow," they'd said, drawing a slave aside and whispering to him, pointing to The Thicket and seducing him with the dream of freedom, "the drinking gourd!" And steer or lead him in the direction of the infrequent, illusory clearing or occasional false trail.

Or *I* say they'd say. As I've attributed to Legurney and Slipper and Oldham Broom and Sheriff Leon Edgers and the others *most* of the dialogue I've put down here. Because, except for Audubon's journal entries and Phil and Pembler Roberts's remarks, which are documented, we'll never really know who actually said what. The beginnings of a conspiracy are often smoky and seldom known, and all this was over one hundred years ago. But we know who was there and, because of the attendant publicity, have a pretty good idea of their personalities. The New York, Wheeling, Philadelphia, Harrisburg and even Pittsburgh papers tell us what happened. So it had to be *something* like the way I've put it down. It had to be.

The rest is quickly told.

After the sawmill went up and the logging teams arrived, after the estimated million trees had been cut down, and the two-and-a-half years of construction was completed, and The Thicket officially opened, and the public came to climb the ladders that led to the exalted overview atop the high planks set on a wooden scaffolding like the jerry-built crisscrosses of condemnation, the thirty-seven miles of braided grid like a rough cat's cradle of loosely crocheted timber, after the first tentative, trepidatious, dread weight they put on the reinforced railing, after their first rubberneck gawk, *after the first remains of the runaways had been spotted*—remember: there were no signposts to lead them to them, no plaques; the carpenters who were the first to walk these planks, or get any sort of view at all from them, never told what they'd seen, and anyway it was advertised in the newspapers as a sort of "treasure hunt" even though there was no treasure, no prize, and all it really ever was was only this crazy sort of bird watching—not clumps of the skeletal dead— or at least not ordinarily—although there is the odd photograph of dead slaves huddled together for warmth or comfort or solace, embracing each other in loving, awful, open death, their twining elbows and ulnas, their backbones and collarbones, their flanges and humeruses, their scapulas, their sternums, their rib cages, their carpals and frontals, their cheek bones just touching—home at last the house niggers—*after* all this, they waited for more than two years—this would have been the summer of 1883—letting word of mouth do its job, the reports in the press, suckering them in, building the tip, specific about the summer—timing was everything—because they had to choose a season not just when the peak was sure to be crowded—the idea of the two-week paid vacation had begun to catch on at about the same time that work was begun on the great wooden wall—but a time when the weather was dependable, when they could rely upon the long spells of hot, dry weather, when the rain, if it came, was likely to be the sort of fierce, brief deluge of which all traces are gone one or two hours after it has ceased.

They kept their counsel and agreed on July 18, 1883, which fell on a Saturday that year, not just a time when a lot of folks—there was a railroad in Norbiton now—would be enjoying their summer vacations but was part of a weekend, too—timing was *everything*—so that even those folks *not* on vacation would be in town to take advantage of the generous weekend discounts offered by Thicket House. They were quite lucky. The weather had been splendid for upwards of three weeks, no rain—they weren't farmers in Chapel County; the soil was too alkaline; no corn was ruined, no soybeans or tomatoes or greens—the temperatures hot but bearable, and the wall filled with holiday makers all along its great, winding wooden length. Pelgas and the others were ready. The wall was a tinder box. When Louis Paul and the other domestics, after first preparing the most strategic struts, pilings, and braces with oil, finally ignited it, it went off like a firework. Two hundred and fourteen tourists and holiday makers either burned or fell to their deaths on the thorns and briars, the burning brambles and bushes, incinerated and drowned in the lake of blazing liquors of the primed, fermenting fruits forty feet below them.

By law, there were no laws in this corner of the state. There was no conspiracy. There was no arson. There was no murder. There were not even any courts, and the jail, unused for years, was only another curiosity on the tour. As honorary as Maurdon Legurney's titles, as emptily symbolic as the badge the sheriff still wore. So they *had* to lynch them.

Who knew if, in defense of what they'd done—the domestics were all dead; they had no defense—the claim of the citizens of Norbiton and Chapel County, that The Thicket had merely been "salted," was true? That they'd dug up the graves of white men and Negroes already legitimately dead and slowly, careful as puppeteers, lowered their bones into The Thicket? There could be no lawsuits so nothing was ever proven. And, at the time, the records were simply unavailable to the hordes of yellow journalists who descended on Norbiton to investigate what had happened. Indeed, they didn't even know if there *were* records.

For the record, there were records.

Here is a partial list of slaves encouraged to believe they could escape into The Thicket.

The Emmas Woodhouse and Bovary. The Harrys Morgan, Bailey, Angstrom, and Lime. Tom Jones. John Jarndyce. Phil Esterhaus. Dick Diver. V. K. Ratliff. Dorothea Brooke. Flem Snopes. Becky Sharp. A Titus and a Hamlet. A Cricket and a White. C3PO. A Dobbin. Someone else, whether male or female has never been ascertained, known as J. R. A. Tulkinghorn. A person named Gatsby, initial J. Henrietta Stackpole. Elizabeth Bennett, Hester Prynne, Arthur Dimmesdale. A Babbitt, a Toots, a slave girl named Leia. A group of blacks probably from the Caribbean: Julien Sorel, Swann, Casaubon, Vautrin, an old man known only as Goriot, and all the members of the Guermantes family. Hazel Motes, Angel Clare, Hyacinth Robinson. Uncle Toby.

I've not told you yet about the Director of Admissions named Louis Paul Pelgas. You will be thinking, of course, that he is descended from the Louis Paul Pelgas who led his fellow domestics to torch the wall. And probably have surmised that because he studied American history at the University of Minnesota and did his doctoral dissertation on the terrible incidents of the commonwealth turned state, that he accepted the directorship of Admissions in order to exclude whites and turn Clifton College into what, under his tenure, would probably have become an all-black school. But you would be wrong. This particular Louis Paul Pelgas is white and no relation. Coincidence. Nothing but coincidence. Because of his name and the associations it has for the people of Norbiton, you might suppose he takes a lot of ribbing. He doesn't. The fact of the matter is, he's not all that interested in administration. He's looking for another post, has sent out several dozen letters, half a hundred *curricula vitae*. No takers so far, though he's promised his wife he'll keep trying. Well it's the job market. The job market stinks. It's a lousy time for historians. And he hasn't published.

Gee, I haven't told you that much about names at all, have I? Unless detail functions, as perhaps it does, as a kind of noun, and a menu of proper names as a sort of register of fact. What I suppose I've been talking about is connection. Connection, invention, and all the enumerate, lovely links, synapses, and nexuses of fiction.

Oom boom!

Esmiss Esmoor!

Only connect!

RICHARD FORD

Reading

For H. S. B.

I learned to read—I mean learned to read carefully—in 1969, when I was twenty-five years old. I was in graduate school then and trying to figure out if I should begin to write short stories. I was married and living in a small apartment. I'd quit law school the year before. I had gone a long way from home—to California—and I did not know very much. I didn't even think I did.

Nineteen sixty-nine was an awful year in the Vietnam War and a bad year in the country. The Tet offensive had been the year before, and everyone saw the whole war as a loss. Among us graduate students there was a related and distinct unease, almost a squeamishness, about what *we* were doing—writing; an unease that manifested itself as a hot and unforgiving demand for relevancy in everything we said and intended and studied and, most important, asked of others. And, especially, we measured our courses that way. They needed, we felt, to be very, *very* relevant; to our lives, but to our dreads also, to our predicaments, our genders, our marriages, our futures, to the war and to the sixties themselves—an era we knew we were living through even as we did it.

And, naturally, nothing quite measured up. I had a course in the *bildungsroman*, read Lessing, Rousseau, Mann, Henry Adams. And it all seemed just too bookish by half; too much to do with history and Freud, both of whose lessons we distrusted and made fun of as reductive. I read all of Hardy's poems after that, all seven hundred or so pages in the big green Macmillan edition, and couldn't bear them either. They seemed oldish, pale and insulated from my interests. What we did like, of course, we didn't need or mean to study: *Man's Fate,* a clear book of truth; both the wonderful Kesey books; *The Crying of Lot 49, At Play in the Field of the Lord, The Ginger Man*—books premised in ironies, a mood more and more attractive when the sincere and practical connections between us and the world could not be convincingly drawn.

Contemporary writing itself had not been in much of a signifying mood. Donald Barthelme's stories were in our minds. Ron Sukenick's. Barry Hannah. William Kotzwinkle. They were all writing wonderfully. And the disjointures and absurdities, the hilarity, the word-virtuosity of those writers—all of whom I still admire—seemed right for our time and us. The world was a whacking wreck, California its damned epicenter. And we were stranded there, absurdly. And absurdity is never completely irrelevant to the facts of any life.

Exactly what we wanted is not clear to me. Though likely it was not one thing, alone. We were young. We were not particularly educated. And, like many beginning writers, for a time we were addicted to the new in everything. We were makers and less so takers-in, and we thought *ourselves* in the relevance business. Barthelme and those other guys were our colleagues, whether they knew it or not. And to be vulnerable to teaching suggested about us and these classics we resisted— tameness. Encapsulability. There wasn't time for Mann. *Irrelevant*, I have come to believe, is a word one often uses to put oneself forward. And what I truly think is we wouldn't have recognized relevance if it had come up and kissed us on the lips.

Part of my school training as a writer, however, provided that I could learn how to teach. It was felt by my teachers—writers themselves— that if we students ever became the real things, we would probably never be able to support ourselves that way and so could teach as a fallback while we busied ourselves toward agents, book contracts, editors, movie and paperback deals, big bucks—whatever else is at the end of that line of hopes. And strange to say, if my classes did not seem spot-on relevant to me, this prospect of teaching somehow did. Teaching *was* a kind of practical preparation for life, after all, and it did not seem hard to do. It had pleasures. It involved the admiration of others—something I wanted. And teaching literature seemed allied to writing it in some way abject studenthood did not. And so I said I would do it, and in fact was very glad to do it.

What exactly this teacher training entailed was going before a class of undergraduates, asking them to read several short stories and novels chosen and discussed among us assistants by an overseeing professor, and then, for three days a week, teaching. Teaching fiction. And what I found my problem to be was that I couldn't imagine the first thing to do, because I didn't, in any way I could convey to another human, know how to read.

Oh, I'd read plenty. I felt I was a *reader*, and I expected to be a writer. I'd been an English major at a big midwestern university and escaped with good grades. I had actually "taught" high school English a year and worked as an assistant editor for a Hearst Corporation magazine, and had, it seemed, experience to make me worth the risk of being put in a classroom full of eighteen-year-olds. Only as I began to prepare I was drawing a blank.

I can still say the things I knew about fiction then—most of it brought along from college. I knew several terms: Characters were the people in fiction. Symbols were the objects in stories to which extra meaning adhered (the raft in Huck Finn, for example, was a symbol). Point of view, I understood, referred not to a character's opinion about something, or the author's, but to what means the story was told by. First, third, omniscient. I knew that beginnings were important parts of stories and, as in "The Lady with the Pet Dog," sometimes they contained the seeds of the entire story (I did not know why that mattered, though). I knew primitive myths sometimes underlay fairly simple-seeming stories. I knew irony was important. I knew, nervously, that the language of a story or novel often meant more or less or even something entirely different from what it seemed to, and that understanding it—the story—meant understanding all the meanings at once. Meaning itself was a term, though I'd never been altogether sure what it meant.

And I knew other things. I knew how to "read like a writer." We talked about such things in our workshops. Certain books had practical lessons to teach. Nuts and bolts: how to get characters efficiently in and out of fictional rooms (Chekhov was good here); how to describe efficiently that it was dark (Chekhov again); how to weed out useless dialogue ("Hi, how are you?" "I'm fine, how are you?" "I'm okay. Thanks." "Good to hear it." "Good-bye." "Good-bye." That sort of stuff). I learned that a good opening ploy in a novel was to have Indians—if there were any—ride over a hill screaming bloody murder. I learned that when in doubt about what to do next, have a man walk through the door holding a gun. I learned that you couldn't get away with killing off your main character in a short story—though I was never told why, and neither, I guess, was Hemingway.

All these hands-on lessons were things I was mulling. Yet they didn't really seem worth teaching to young readers, people for whom making literature was not yet a career selection, nor was reading it even a given in their lives—in fact was possibly as disagreeable as a dentist's visit. Going about teaching literature in this way seemed like teaching someone to build a sleek and fast car without first treating them to how it felt to split the breeze in one. They'd never know exactly what it was all good for.

What seemed worthwhile to teach was what I *felt* about literature when I read it—those matters of relevance set slightly aside. That was why I wanted to write stories, after all. Literature was pretty and good. It had mystery, denseness, authority, connectedness, closure, resolution, perception, variety, magnitude—*value*, in other words, in the way Sartre meant when he wrote, "The work of art is a value because it is an appeal." Literature appealed to me.

But I had no idea how to teach its appealing qualities, how to find and impart the origins of what I felt. I didn't even know when to bring in my terms, or if they were right. I quickly came to feel that being an intermediary between an expectant mind and an excellent book is a conspicuous and chancy role to play. And I imagined myself sitting behind a metal desk staring at them, *Madame Bovary* open before me, passages underlined, silence commanding every molecule of the still air, and having nothing whatsoever to say, while being certain something should be said. Or worse—having only this to say: "What's the point of this book?" And *then* having nothing to say when the right answer came and as a voice inside me screamed, *mystery, connectedness, authority, closure, magnitude, value.*

These first preparations for teaching occurred over the Christmas holidays, in 1968. I went to my tiny graduate-student office and pored over my stories, over and over and over, without advance. "A Guest of the Nation"; "Death in the Woods"; "The Battler"; "Disorder and Early Sorrow"; "The Wind Blows." I could practically recite them. But I had no idea what to say *about* them. I still can feel the panic of pure inessentialness cold on my neck as literature rose against me like a high wall behind which was a deep jungle. I was to take people through there not just safely but gainfully, only I had no business even setting out.

In an office down the hall from where I was panicking that winter was a man named Howard Babb. I knew him because he was to be the chairman of our English department the next fall, and he was director of the course I was readying to teach. Mr. Babb liked us writers—even more, we felt, than he liked the Ph.D. types whose literary training he saw over. We seemed like true amateurs to him, not even serious enough to be gloomy, and it was in his good character to think of himself, or at least to portray himself, in precisely that way. Later, when I knew him better in the few years before he died, and I was his young colleague, I would overhear him say again and again to some student, about some piece of literature he was instructing, "Now, of course, I don't pretend to know a goddamned thing about any of this business, mind you. I would only in a simpleminded way venture to say this . . ." And then he would go on to say what was truest and best and smartest about a story or a novel. He merely did not claim to be an expert, and possibly he wasn't, though he knew a great deal. Simplest just to say that his mind stayed remarkably open to literature, whereas an expert's sometimes does not.

I will say a word or two about Howard Babb here because he was a singular man—human and inspiring—and because his influence over my life as a writer and as a reader was direct and unqualifiedly good. A day, indeed, doesn't go by now that I do not think of him.

At that time, I knew about him only a very few things, as was once the case between students and their professors—no first names, no dinner invitations or ball games attended together. He was a big Yankee man—in his late forties—with a Maine accent, a bluff, good temper and a deep, murmurous voice with which he would occasionally talk loudly for effect. He had left college to be a sailor, and cursed like a sailor, though he was not undignified. He had tattoos on his arms that you could see when he rolled up his white sleeves. He smoked Tareytons in secret when he was at school, and sometimes drank at faculty parties and talked even louder. He'd been a student of Walter Jackson Bate at Harvard, and later a colleague of John Crowe Ransom and Peter Taylor at Kenyon. He was married and had a son. He walked with a heavy, hodcarrier's purposive gait—bow-legged, arms a little out from his shoulders, as if he was always stalking something. He seemed like a tough guy to me, and I liked him the first moment I saw him.

Toughness aside, though, he loved Jane Austen and George Eliot. He loved Conrad and Richardson and the eighteenth century. He knew a world about narrative and wrote and talked about it smartly, though he never became famous for it. He was, I thought even then, as out of place in southern California as a man with his history and affections for lasting virtues could ever be. And possibly to accommodate those divisive forces—though maybe the line of cause runs exactly opposite—he immersed himself with a fury in literature: reading it, teaching it, and talking about it. And for our purposes—his students—his fierceness, his zeal for teaching, his fervor for literature and its importance to us, comprised his entire attitude toward life, his whole self. No discrepancies. No ironies. No two-mindedness about how he felt, say, when the Irish soldiers kill their poor prisoner in "A Guest of the Nation," and how he might feel were such an awful dilemma ever to be his own. Or our own. Literature had direct access to everyday life. The day, in fact, that he read aloud to me those fearsome final words of O'Connor's, sitting alone in his shadowy office on a winter afternoon almost twenty years ago, I listened without moving. And when he was finished he just stared at the floor, leaning on his knees, the book opened in his big hands, and maybe for five minutes we did not speak a word—not one word—so large were both our feelings for what we'd heard. And what I knew was that anything that happened to *me* afterward, after that seized moment, I would never feel the same about again. Here, I think, was relevance, first encountered, and here was pleasure of a quite rare kind.

But before then, back on that cheerless snowless Christmas, I had yet to encounter it. And what I did, at my wits' very end, was pick up my book of stories and walk down the empty corridor to Mr. Babb's office at the end of the hall. He was there through those holidays, reading alone without overhead light, making his minute margin notes, preparing for his courses while his colleagues were elsewhere—on their sailboats or skiing or attending conventions. I stood in his open doorway until he looked up and saw me. He stared a moment. "Well," he said softly, "what in the hell do you want? Shouldn't you be off farting around back in Mississippi, or wherever it is you're from?" This was friendly.

"No," I said. "I have a problem here."

"Well okay, then." He sighed and closed his book. "Come on in and sit down." And that is what I did.

Not surprisingly, if I could not teach those stories, neither could I say to Mr. Babb how or why I couldn't. This seems axiomatic now—proof of ignorance. But even more awful was that I didn't want to admit I didn't know. Silence has always been the accomplice to my ignorance; and ignorance, unsuitedness, unpreparedness always my coldest, most familiar fears. I have never approached anything difficult and truly new without expecting to fail at it, and quickly; or without generalizing how little I knew and dreading being told.

What I said was this: "I am having trouble knowing *exactly* how to go about teaching this Anderson story."

The Anderson story, as I've said, was "Death in the Woods," one of his great, signature stories, written in the thirties and separate in style and sympathy from the famous "Winesburg" tales from fifteen years earlier and the aftermath of the war. In "Death in the Woods," as in those few other Anderson masterpieces, "I Want to Know Why," "The Egg," "The Man Who Became a Woman," an adult narrator tells a series of events recalled from his childhood, a seemingly simpler time, when the speaker was but a receptor—though a keen one—for whom life's memorable moments became the stuff of later inquiry and recognition. It is a classic story structure, one I have come to know well.

In Anderson, a man remembers a woman he saw once years earlier, in the small town where he was a boy. The woman was poor and poorly treated by her brute husband and her brute son. Yet she fed and provided for them on their poverty farm while the two men went off drunk and carousing. On a certain trip back from town, where she had traded eggs for meat and flour, the woman—named, sadly, Mrs. Grimes—pauses to rest at the foot of a tree, and surprisingly though painlessly freezes to death as snow and then clear night set on. In a spectral and unforgettable scene (one the narrator imagines, since he could not have witnessed it) Mrs. Grimes' dogs begin to run wild circles around her body and eventually drag her out into the night radiance and feed themselves on the provisions she was bringing home—though not, it should be said, on Mrs. Grimes, whose palely beautiful body goes untouched—". . . so white and lovely," the speaker imagines it, ". . . so like marble."

Much is plain in this wonderful story, even to the least lettered reader. When I first read it, in 1969, it seemed longer and complexer than when I read it today. But its large concerns seem the same ones I must've known then, if intuitively: the cruelty inherent in us all; our edgy similarity to the spirit of wild beasts; the uncertain good of advancing civilization; the mystery and allure of sex; adulthood as a poor, compromised state of being; the ways by which we each nurture others; the good to be got from telling. Mystery, closure, connectedness, magnitude—value. Anderson wrote inspired by all these grand disturbances and their literary conceits. I think of him still as one of our great, great writers.

And I meant to teach him. He was on the syllabus, though I could not then have found the words I've just said.

"Tell me, Mr. Ford," Mr. Babb said, still softly, when he'd sat in silence for a while, flipping pages through the story in my anthology, glancing at my underlinings, raising his eyebrows at my notes, sniffing now and then, humming at a line of Anderson's he admired. He knew the story by heart and loved Anderson. I knew that in the way a graduate student must know the tastes of his professors and assume them shamelessly. "Tell me just this," he said again, and looked up at me quizzically, then at the ceiling, as if he'd begun rehearsing some life of his own from years ago, which the story had pleasantly revived. "What, um, what do you think is the most interesting formal feature of this story? I'm, of course, not talking about anything particularly complicated. Just what *you* think about it." He blinked at me as though in the mists of this marvelous story and of his own memory, he couldn't quite make me out now.

And at the instant I write this, I know what was in his mind—though I have never known it before, and would've guessed it was something else; that I would give him the wrong answer, or an incomplete one, and that our talk would commence there. But I understand now that he was certain I had no idea in the world what he could be talking about, and that our tasks would begin from that point—the perfect point of origin. Zero. The place where all learning begins.

"I don't know what you mean by 'formal feature,'" I answered in a good, clear voice. And with that I gave up some large part of my ignorance. I must've sensed I'd learn something valuable if I could only do that. And I was right.

"Well," he said, bemused. "All right." He nodded and sighed, then turned in his swivel chair to a green chalkboard on the wall, stood, and with a chalk wrote this list.

Character
Point of View
Narrative Structure
Imagistic Pattern
Symbol
Diction
Theme

These, of course, were words I'd seen. Most of them had been swirling around my thinking for days without order or directive. Now, here they were again, and I felt relieved.

These expressions, Mr. Babb said, sitting back in his chair but still looking at the list, described the formal features of a piece of fiction. If we could define them, locate them in a particular piece of fiction, and then talk about any one of them in a careful and orderly way, reliant on the words of the story and common sense, asking perfectly simple questions, proceeding to deductions one by one, perhaps talking about other features as they came to mind—eventually we would involve ourselves in a discussion of the most important issues in a story, or in a novel.

In every story he himself read, he said, some one formal feature seemed to stand out as a conspicuous source of interest, and he could investigate the story that way. *The Great Gatsby*, for instance, was *narrated* in a way he thought especially interesting. Point of view was then the issue: Who was Nick Carraway? Why was he telling the story? What peculiar advantage or disadvantage did he have as its teller? Was our understanding of the story affected by the fact that he told it? If so, how? Did he—Nick—judge other characters? How? Was he always telling the truth? What if he wasn't? Why did I think so?

In "Silent Snow, Secret Snow," the lustrous, enigmatic master-story by Conrad Aiken (also on the syllabus), how could one make sense of this unusual snow that seems increasingly to buffer the child whose life is at the story's center? Is it actual snow? Why do we think it is or isn't? Could we reasonably imagine it to represent anything besides itself? Only one thing? What did this have to do with other features of the story? The child's character? The setting? His parents? Here we were investigating an image.

Story to story, each had a path-in signaled by a prominent formal feature, with one feature's effects and our observations about it implicating another—point of view leading naturally to an interest in character, leading onward to some wider sense of how, as the story progressed through its own structural parts (scenes, settings, flashbacks), character and image and narrative strategy intertwined and formed the whole, until by our directed questioning we could say what seemed most complexly at issue in the story. Theme, this was—though no one should hope to identify that matter succinctly or to say it in a phrase. It was last but not foremost. Foremost was one's intimacy with the story.

In the Anderson, Mr. Babb said, one might start with a simple-minded set of questions and observations about who it was who told that story to us. Was it just a straightforward matter of an anonymous voice telling a story in the most unembellished way? *No.* Wasn't the teller a character? *Yes.* Did he tell it as it happened? *No.* Could one, on close examination of the very words chosen in the story, distinguish different concerns—even preoccupations—of the speaker besides just the facts of the old woman's death? *Yes, yes, yes.* And with each answer elicited couldn't we reasonably say, "And how does this materially contribute to my understanding of the story?" Or, in plainer words: "So what if this is true?" "So what if this is not?"

What opened for me in the course of this single conversation was a larger number of small lights, partial recognitions I could only partially appreciate, but that over the years have developed and seemed among the most important I've ever made and, toward reading literature, the most important of all. Mr. Babb, naturally, never told me exactly what to do, and our talk never left the plane of the hypothetical/conditional ("one *might* ask this; isn't it possible to wonder that? surely this is not completely irrelevant . . ."). But he taught. He taught me not only an orderly means to gain entry to and intimacy with a complex piece of narrative, but also that literature could be approached as empirically as life, to which after all it was connected. As in life, our literary understandings, even our failures at understanding, were founded on a series of commonsense responses—not necessarily answers—that were true to the small facts, the big movements, and the awes and dreads and pleasures we all felt as we made our way along. Literature was not only accessible, but relevant to life, inasmuch as the same matters were of issue in both: How do I love whom I love? How can I go on each day with or without those persons? How will this day end? Will I live or will I die?

It will be understood that when I left Mr. Babb's office that late December afternoon, I did so with a much less clear view of reading literature than I have today, even though my view now is still clouded by the ignorance of all I've yet to read and will never read, and by the "complicating" experience of having spent the next eighteen or so years trying to make stories as good as those Anderson ones I loved and that affect me to this moment. Still, I went away feeling confident—pleasurably confident—that the method I'd just seen practiced bore an utterly natural relationship to any piece of fiction I would ever read, examine, or teach. I believed that the stories which had pleased me, awed me, frightened me with their interconnected largeness were actually *constructions of* those formal features Mr. Babb had described. Good stories— whether or not they were made so intentionally by authors—were basically arrangements of knowable images, word patterns, of dramatic structure and symbols. They were *made of* characters and points of view and possessed themes. Moreover, reading any story with this knowledge amounted to the truest experience of knowing it. I'm certain I taught my first students that, and taught others, too; made discovering forms and verifying them an end, not just a pedagogy, a device. It is almost inevitable I would, given my novice's need to order a universe and since fiction can be fitted in so nicely to this symmetry. My mind rested there, I suppose I can say. And many people, I suspect, students and their teachers, too, never get beyond that static, intermediate stage of reading— knowing which point of view is which, sensing what an old symbolizing animal man is, comparing and contrasting poor Jake Barnes and lucky Bill Gorton *as characters*; never get around to asking what all this has to do with life—asking the final question of relevancy: So what?

Thinking back to then, I'm sure Mr. Babb didn't believe in such a pat, synthetic view of literature, but instead that we synthesize these forms in an effort to organize our progress through difficult writing, tracing their shapes like constellations in a wild heaven. The proof was the awe he preserved, the affection, the eagerness with which he returned to the same passages and stories over and over, still curious, pleasantly baffled, willing to be amazed, reverent of all that the books continued to give him. It was I—not smart enough and just beginning—who championed a method before the method's full use and limits could be understood.

And it is—I suppose appropriately—only because of writing stories rather than being an excellent reader that I figured out that this formalism was a faulty account of how stories of any length got made and are best known.

Stories, and novels, too—I came to see from the experience of writing them—are makeshift things. They originate in strong, disorderly impulses; are supplied by random accumulations of life-in-words; and proceed in their creation by mischance, faulty memory, distorted understanding, weariness, deceit of almost every imaginable kind, by luck and by the stresses of increasingly inadequate vocabulary and wanting imagination—with the result often being a straining, barely containable object held in fierce and sometimes insufficient control. And there is nothing wrong with that. It doesn't hurt me to know it. Indeed, my admiration for the books I love is greater for knowing the chaos they overcame. But there is very little I can say, then, about the experience of writing stories that will make the experience of parsing them formally seem a completely apt way to know them. Even the word—formal—seems wrong-spirited to such an amateurish and un-formal business. *Characters*, those "rounded" people in good books whom we say we recognize and know like our cousins, are at heart just assemblages of sentences, ongoing, shifting arrangements of descriptions and purported human impulse and action hooked to a name—all of it changeable by adding and subtracting or forgetting words—yet hardly ever sharply convincing to me as "selves." Point of view, that precise caliper for measuring meaning in Mr. Babb's scheme, is chiefly an invented mind's voice which I can hear and "write through," and whose access to language and idiom seems, at least to start, adequate for some not quite certain telling. Imagery—at best—is a recurrence of sentence patterns and emotional tics and habits I would often rather trade in for more diverse and imaginative resources in language. And symbol. Well, symbol is anything the reader says it is.

And for every writer it's different; different means and expectations, different protocols under which a story accumulates, different temperaments and lingo about how to do it—different work in every way—as should be.

A formal template for studying narrative can guide us orderly into such creations as these, permit a desired intimacy with sentences, aid our confidence and encourage our thinking by abstracting us from parts of the story we can't grasp yet, then in due time leading us to the other parts, so that eventually we see and can try connecting all that's written. But an organizing or explaining system which doesn't illuminate the haphazard in any story's existence can't be a real comprehension. Such schemes are always arbitrary and unstable—wrong (if still useful) in that at their worst they reduce a complex story to some matter of categories, and pose as cure-alls to our natural wonder and awe before great litera-ture—reactions that originate less in ignorance than in the magnitude of the story itself; reactions we shouldn't relinquish but hold on to for dear life—as pleasure.

But pleasure can arise even from this very friction between the story read and the story written. And not a single, simple pleasure, but several, with shadings and history. Even as unsevere and practical-minded as the formal procedure taught me when I learned to read closely is in some sense an imitation of its subject—one with a consoling use, in this case. And imitation has always appealed to us: "The pleasure . . . received is undoubtedly the surprise or feeling of admiration occasioned by the un-expected coincidence between the imitation and its object." That was Hazlitt's idea. And Addison takes it straight to the point: ". . . Our imag-ination loves to be filled with an object or to grasp at anything that is too big for its capacity"—which is what happens when a method of knowing cannot altogether account for its natural subject in all its com-plexity.

This friction between my school method and my experience might just as well be renamed pleasure. Each is valuable to me, each quickens interest in the whole truth, and each can accommodate the other. Plea-sure, in this scheme, arises when what was unknown, or unknown as pleasure, can be perceived that way; when, in a sense, pleasure is rein-vented.

I still feel dread and wonder in the face of literature from time to time—usually in a novel, often so much that I can't parse it with sat-isfaction. Maybe my spirit for parsing has been worn down. Joyce makes me feel that way. Ford Madox Ford, sometimes. Céline. Gide. Pynchon: awestruck—although I think these writers' aim is to make me feel that. And I simply experience chaos—literary chaos, the story's apparent nearness to its own disorderly beginnings—more agreeably than I once did. I try to accommodate the story read to the one written, which is what Mr. Babb did and would've had me do from the beginning. He probably knew, however, that there's pleasure in first learning and then unlearning, that it is one of literature's other great relevant lessons for life. And I am satisfied that his pleasures have finally become mine, and that I was at least a willing student. For that I could not be more grateful.

A Diarist on Diarists

*This inescapable duty to observe oneself: if someone
else is observing me, naturally I have to observe
myself too; if none observe me, I have to observe myself all the closer.*   —Kafka, November 7, 1921

*I fall back on this journal just as some other poor
devil takes to drink.*   —Barbellion

I am enamoured of my journal.   —Sir Walter Scott

Diarists: that shrewdly innocent breed, those secret exhibitionists and incomparable purveyors of sequential, self-conscious life: how they fascinate me and endear themselves to me by what they say and do not say. If my friends kept diaries, and if I read them, would I know them as well as I know Kafka, standing in front of his mirror, playing with his hair? And Virginia Woolf, languishing because of a snide remark made about her novels by an undergraduate. And poor Dorothy Wordsworth, trying valiantly to stick to descriptions of sunsets while losing all her teeth. And Pepys, giving a colorful account of his latest fight with his wife. And Camus, coolly observing, "Whatever does not kill me strengthens me." Or plantation owner William Byrd, "dancing his dances" and "rogering his wife" (code words for bowel movements and sexual intercourse). Or the anonymous Irish scribe driven to confide into the margin of a medieval text: "I am very cold without fire or covering . . . the robin is singing gloriously, but though its red breast is beautiful I am all alone. Oh God be gracious to my soul and grant me a better handwriting."

In the old days everybody kept diaries. That's how we know that "Carlyle wandered down to tea looking dusky and aggrieved at having to live in such a generation": from Caroline Fox's diary; and that Henry James "kept up a perpetual vocal search for words even when he wasn't saying anything": from his nineteen-year-old nephew's diary; and that when Liszt played, he compressed his lips, dilated his nostrils and, when the music expressed quiet rapture, "a sweet smile flitted over his features": from George Eliot's diary. People came home from their dinners and visits and wrote down what others said and how the great men looked and who wore what and who made an ass or a pig of himself ("A little swinish at dinner," the diligent Dr. Rutty wrote of himself in his eighteenth-century diary).

Those who stayed home alone also documented their evenings. ("I dined by myself and read an execrably stupid novel called 'Tylney Hall.' Why do I read such stuff?" wrote Macaulay.) Even a literate body-snatcher gave an account of himself before he turned in at night: "March 16, 1812, Went to Harps got 3 Large and 1 Large Small, 1 Small & 1 Foetus, took 2 Large to St. Thomas's, 1 Large to Guy's."

Are there fewer diarists now? It seems so, to me, but perhaps I'm unusual in that I have not one friend who keeps a diary—or at least who admits to it. Sometimes I'll happen upon a diarist and we greet each other like lonely explorers. Last spring I discovered a fellow diarist over lunch, and what a time we had discussing the intricacies of our venture-in-common, our avocation . . . specialty . . . compulsion? We confessed eccentricities (he has a pseudonym for the self that gambles; I often reread old journals and make notes to my former selves in the margin). We examined our motives: why keep these records, year after year? What would happen if we stopped? *Could* we stop? We indulged in shop-talk; hardbound or softcover? lined or unlined? about how many pages a night? proportion of external events to internal? Did one write more on bad days than on good? More or less on quiet days? (More, we both decided.) Did we feel honor-bound to report in at night, even when exhausted—or intoxicated? Ah, it was a good lunch we had.

"I should live no more than I can record, as one should not have more corn growing than one can get at. There is a waste of good if it be not preserved." This, from Boswell, expresses the aspect of duty that many diarists typically feel. Queen Victoria continued her diary strictly as a duty from the age of thirteen to eighty-two. Unfortunately, much of it reads like it. Many diaries, left by long-forgotten owners in attic trunks, describe neither affairs of state nor the table talk of great geniuses nor the growing pains of profound souls. But a sense of *accountability* emanates from these old books. ("Went with Maud to Chok's for a soda. J. L. lost two heifers from shipping disease . . . nothing of interest to record today.") Man and woman was beholden to the *recording* of God's hours, be they interesting or not.

> No mighty deeds, just common things,
> The tasks and pleasures each day brings.
> And yet I hope that when I look
> Over the pages of this book,
> Twill be (and, if so, I'm content)
> The record of five years well spent.

This, from the title page of my mother's college diary, offers captured memory as incentive to daily diligence. *Nulla dies sine linea*, it orders, and my mother obeyed, detailing in tiny handwriting, in a variety of inks, the social and mental highlights of 1932–36. People seemed to go to the movies every day, sometimes twice in one day. They ate a lot of spaghetti—but, of course, there was a Depression. No longer a diarist, my mother offered the little blue and gold book to me (we had to pick the lock—she had no idea it was even hers until we opened it). Her parents had given her the five-year diary as a going-away present for college, and she felt she owed it to them to write in it. I'm glad she did. How many daughters can read—in purple ink—about the night they were conceived?

Now I'm the only practicing diarist in my family. Not one of my friends keeps a diary, as I've mentioned. "To tell the truth, I've never thought I was that interesting," says one. "I'm not a *writer*," says another. A third writes letters, sometimes three or four every evening, and says this serves the purpose of a diary. Another person who is a very prolific writer has advised me to "put all that material into stories rather than hide it in your journals. When you feel haunted or sad, write a story about a person, not necessarily yourself, who feels haunted or sad. Because, you see, it's the feelings that are universal, not the person."

Art, fiction, if it is to be public, must tap the universal. A diary by its very nature is the unfolding of the private, personal story—whether that story be told from a distance (the "I" in a political diary, observing affairs of state; the "I" in the captain's log, marking latitude, longitude, and the moods of the sea) or with the subjectivity of a person whose politics and moods and sea-changes exist inside his own head. I need to write a diary, just as I need to write fiction, but the two needs come from very different sources. I write fiction because I need to organize the clutter of too many details into some meaning, because I enjoy turning something promising into something marvelous; I keep a diary because it keeps my mind fresh and open. Once the details of being me are safely stored away every night, I can get on with what isn't just me. So, as I explained to my friend, the fictional and the diary-making processes are not interchangeable. I had to keep a diary for many years before I could begin writing fiction.

Like Victoria, I, too, began keeping track of my days at the age of thirteen. But it was not because I felt the young queen, whose comings and goings would one day be read by the world. Nor did anyone make me a present of a sumptuous diary with a lock and key that cried out to be made the repository of secrets. I made my first diary, with half-sheets of notebook paper, cardboard, and yarn, and I wrote in it passionately, because I felt there was nobody else like me and I had to know why—or why not. "I don't believe people exist whose inner plight resembles mine; still, it is possible for me to imagine such people—but that the secret raven forever flaps about their head as it does about mine, even to imagine that is impossible." That is Kafka at thirty-eight, speaking for me at thirteen—and for diarists not yet born.

There are many books about diarists, and some of them make fascinating reading. What is odd, however, is that many of the authors do not seem to be diarists themselves: they write with the air of scientists, observing this peculiar organism called a "diarist" from the other side of a polished lens. F. A. Spalding states in *Self-Harvest, a Study of Diaries and Diarists* that we seldom if ever find development within the individual diary, either in what is recorded or in the manner of recording it. Also that "diarists who hope to aid memory continue to the end to complain of the lack of it." Also that diaries do not seem to teach diarists "how the better to spend my time for the future," even if they read over their diaries, "and few do so." Spalding also says that, except for Scott and Byron, "there is hardly an example of a diary written out of a first class creative mind." "We cannot imagine a Shakespeare keeping a diary," he says. In fairness to Mr. Spalding, he wrote his book before access to the Kafka diaries was possible—or Virginia Woolf's; though maybe he wouldn't have considered these writers first class creative minds. As for Shakespeare, that enigma, who can say with certainty whether he did not jot down his moods and plots for plays into a little book that lies crumbling in the earth or awaiting its finder in some forgotten cranny?

Every true diarist knows that having a relationship with a diary is like having a relationship with anyone or anything else: the longer it lasts, the more it is bound to change. When I began my diary, at age thirteen, I traversed that naked space between my mind and my little book's pages as hesitantly as a virgin approaching a man who may or may not prove trustworthy. Now, two-and-a-half decades later, my diary and I have an old marriage. The space between us is gone. I hardly *see* my diary anymore. And yet, there is a confident sense that we are working together. We have been down many roads together, my diary and I (I use the singular, but what I call "my diary" resides in many separate books—some of them lost, others maimed or destroyed [more on this later]), and I have been neglectful and insincere and offhand and have not always shown respect in regard to this fellow-traveler of mine. In adolescence, I weighed him down with feelings of gloom and doom; in late teens, I wasted his pages cataloguing the boys who fell into, or eluded, my snare; in my twenties, I drove him to near death-from-boredom with my lists of resolutions, budgets, and abortive plans for "the future." Sometimes I shunned the sight of him, and I wrote my secrets on sheets of loose paper—not wanting to be bound by him— and, of course, those pages are now lost. In my thirties, as my craft of fiction was consolidated and I felt I had "something of my own," I returned to him with new respect. I told him when good things happened, and shared ideas for future work. As I became less trapped in my universe of moods and recognized my likeness to other people and other things in the universe-at-large, my entries began to include more space. Now there are animals and flowers and sunsets in my diary, as well as other people's problems. As a rule, I complain less and describe more; even my complaints I try to lace with memorable description, because . . . yes, Mr. Spalding, diarists do reread their diaries, and how many times I have exclaimed aloud with rage when I looked up a year or a day, hoping to catch the fever or the flavor of the past, and found only a meager, grudging, "I feel awful today." So now I write for my future self, as well as my present mood. And sometimes, to set the record straight, I jot down a word or two in old diaries to my former self—to encourage, to scold, to correct, or to set things in perspective.

As for memory, I don't complain of the lack of it or use my diary to improve it, as Mr. S. would have me do. It is rather that I know one of us has it—my diary or me—and so, if I can't remember something, I look it up. (Though, as I've said, sometimes nothing's there except a mood nobody wants anymore.) Yet, though I frequently look things up, or sometimes browse through a year, I have never read my diaries straight through, and possibly never will. I have tried, a couple of times, but there are simply too many of them, and, after a while, I get the peculiar dizziness that comes from watching a moving train while on another moving train. One cannot live two lives at once, for long periods of time.

Early or late, there comes a time in every diarist's life when he asks himself: "What if someone should read this?" If he truly recoils at the thought, he might take measures to prevent it, writing in cipher like Pepys, or in mirror-writing (da Vinci's notebooks) or in a mixture of foreign languages. One seventeenth-century schoolmaster wrote his diary in a notebook so small as to be illegible without a magnifying glass, the whole in abbreviated Latin. (The diary was four inches by two and a half inches; and there were seventy lines to the page!)

But far, far more prevalent, I think, is the breed of diarist who writes for *some* form of audience. This audience may be God, it may be a friendly (or unfriendly) spirit (witness the way some diarists must justify their self-contradictions and shortcomings); or it may be one's future self (at thirty-eight, Virginia Woolf wrote in her journal that she was hoping to entertain herself at fifty) or . . . in many cases, more often than we may care to admit . . . we write for some form of posterity. How many diarists can honestly say they have never once imagined their diaries being "discovered," either before or after their deaths? Many of us hope we will make good reading. (I occasionally catch myself "explaining," in my diary: putting in that extra bit of information that I know quite well but cannot expect a stranger to know.)

In *The Golden Notebook* Doris Lessing writes about a pair of lovers, each of whom keeps two diaries. It is understood tacitly between them that one diary may be "secretly read" but the second diary, the really private one, may not. Of course, one of the partners cheats and the couple is sundered forever because of this unpardonable breach. I know perfectly well that if I had a partner who kept a diary (or two diaries) I would probably cheat. Several times over my diary-keeping years, people have read my journals. Some sneaked and were caught (perhaps others sneaked and were not); a few let me know about it, in a variety of ways. One left a cheerful note: "Enjoy the halcyon days!" Another tore out a handful of pages. Another tossed the whole book into the Atlantic Ocean. On several occasions I have actually read parts of my diary aloud to someone. But too much "publicity" is destructive to a diary, because the diarist begins, unconsciously perhaps, to leave out, to tone down, to pep up, to falsify experience, and the *raison d'être* of the undertaking becomes buried beneath posings.

The prospect of people reading my diaries after I am dead does not disturb me in the least. I like to think of pooling myself with other introspective hearts: madmen (and women), prudes, profligates, celebrities, outcasts, heroes, artists, saints, the lovelorn and the lucky, the foolish and the proud. I have found so many sides of myself in the diaries of others. I would like it if I someday reflect future readers to themselves, provide them with examples, warnings, courage, amusement even. In these unedited glimpses of the self in others, of others in the self, is another proof of our ongoing survival, another of the covenants eternity makes with the day-to-day.

DAVID HUDDLE

Taking What You Need, Giving What You Can: The Writer as Student and Teacher

The kind of writer and the kind of teacher of writing I am these days is powerfully informed by my experience as a student of writing. As an undergraduate I had four semesters of creative writing, and I completed the work for two different graduate writing programs. Altogether I studied under eleven different writing teachers. If ever there was a product of the American creative writing industry, I am it. And yet in the composition of this essay, I have come to realize that I was equipped with an essential quality, without which I never would have become any kind of writer at all: I was able to take what I needed from every teacher and every class, and I was able to disregard what I didn't need or what might have harmed me. I'm not sure what to name this quality—survival aptitude, perhaps—but it seems to me necessary for anyone who aspires to make a writing life for him- or herself. It seems to me the one quality that perhaps you are born with or born without. If you have it—if you can take what you need from your experience to nourish your writing—then you can learn to write, and the classroom will be of enormous benefit to you. If you don't have it, then no amount of writing-education will make you a writer.

So I know that writing can be taught, but I also know that only a small number of people can learn to be writers. In my writing classes, I encounter many students who have more talent, more writerly resources (i.e., intelligence, language aptitude, literary instinct) than I have ever had, but who do not become writers. I also encounter a few students whose talents and resources are modest but who nevertheless become writers. In the past, I have been frustrated by such unlikely results of my classes. Nowadays I am comforted by that unpredictable element of teaching writing.

In composing this essay and discussing it with my writer friends, I've come to see that just as a real writer takes what he or she needs from a teacher, so, too, a writing teacher gives what he or she can. It is not my duty to tailor my teaching to each individual student; it is not my duty to attempt to make writers of my students. It is my duty to be a certain kind of a teacher, to try to be consistent in the values that I try to convey to my students, and to let them use me as they will—as I used my teachers.

My relationship with writing and with literature is a practical one. I was years coming to understand this relationship, and in the process, I flunked out of the University of Virginia as an English major. In 1962 and 1963, I knew that I was powerfully affected by many of the novels, stories, and poems I was reading for my classes, but I couldn't get the hang of writing papers, saying the right things in class, or *thinking about literature* in the way that apparently my professors thought about it. Not only that, some of the lectures and discussions from those classes seemed to me deeply wrong but in a way that I couldn't even approach articulating.

I remember three different occasions of English major stall-out— trying to write papers on Salinger's *Nine Stories*, Conrad's *Nostromo*, and Melville's *Moby Dick*. These were books that I deeply loved. I wasn't able to make myself write those papers because (I later understood) I couldn't connect what I felt about the books with the way—the conventional way—I thought the papers had to be written. This wasn't really the fault of my literature professors; if I had been able to think of an alternative and personally meaningful way for me to write the papers, my instructors most likely would have accommodated me, perhaps even rewarded me for being innovative. But at the age of twenty, I didn't have enough gumption to invent my own alternative methods.

What's the difference between academic and practical approaches to narrative literature? Thematic concerns, symbolism, literary history, and matters of influence were, in those days, the stuff of the academic approach to literature. A practical-minded reader would be drawn to such elements as characterization, situation, point of view, structure, setting, pacing, symmetry, diction, syntax, and sentence length. An academic teacher is—or was in those days—interested in the ultimate value of a literary work and its connection to other literary works; a writing teacher is interested in how a work works and does not work.

I'm still reacting to those academically inclined professors. Workshop is the word that I put forth in opposition to whatever I see as academic. I'm a committed workshop teacher. I see my job as one of constantly trying to demonstrate to my students the value of a practical approach, not only to manuscripts that pass through our classrooms, but also to works of literature. I want the writing workshop to be a place where it is all right to love *The Sound and the Fury* for entirely different reasons than those that make it attractive to professors and A-plus students of Modern American Literature.

As part of the practical approach to literature, I want my students to see that most aspects of a literary work are down-to-earth matters that are perfectly understandable to a moderately intelligent reader using common sense. Throughout my high school and undergraduate education I encountered teachers who tried to elevate literature to a level apprehensible only by an elite few. This literature-as-a-high-mystery approach serves a couple of functions; it elevates the teacher who espouses it at the same time it excuses that teacher from having to be rigorous-minded in actually thinking about the work itself. Teachers who have practiced this method have done so in large part simply because it is a centuries-old literary-pedagogical tradition, but I tend to be personally irked by it. The message of that kind of teaching is that there is such an immense distance between literature and the student that the idea of any but the most gifted student having literary aspirations is absurd. Which is to say that I now feel that such teaching conspired to deny me and others like me our rightful literary heritage. So one of my most basic aims in the classroom is to try to return that heritage to practical-minded students.

The practical approach to reading literature has direct implications for trying to write good stories and poems. Here are some of the practical aspects of writing I wish to reflect in my teaching.

—Writing is a natural act. You don't have to be somebody else to write well. As much as it's possible to be so, you do have to be yourself—or try to be yourself—to write good poems and stories. But because they've been taught that literature is so far "above them" many of my students feel that they must spout philosophical profundities, espouse noble sentiments, and compose archaically poetical phrases. In short, many of my students see the act of trying to make literature as one that by definition requires them to be other than themselves. And they aren't easily dis-illusionable in this regard. My project for a semester of beginning poetry and fiction writing may be generally described as trying to coax a room full of 20-year-olds to try to be—or to discover—themselves in their writing.

—Reading is also a natural act for a writer. Reading is writing's nour-ishment. Like anyone else, a writer reads for pleasure and instruction, but there is another level at which writers read: ruthlessly and automatically, they consume the writing technology of what they read. Writers learn the craft of writing by reading the work of other writers. I don't think writers of integrity steal from other writers in any direct way, but I do think they incorporate other writers' technology into their own systems. No writer of integrity would say to himself, "Ah, yes, Salinger switches from the first-person to the third-person point of view here in the middle of "For Esme with Love and Squalor," and I am going to write a story utilizing this very successful device." At the same time, I think that any serious writer would not read "For Esme with Love and Squalor" without remarking that change in point of view, without thinking about it, and without incorporating observations and conclusions about that device into his or her own writing technology. Imitating the device itself would be the crudest articulation of how one writer learns from another. More likely, the reading writer's point-of-view decisions will be informed by the Salinger story in only subtle ways.

Within their individual sensibilities—the true source of originality—writers carry around what they've learned from other writers. Within that part of me that is peculiar to David Huddle also reside William Faulkner, Ernest Hemingway, Peter Taylor, Eudora Welty, Flannery O'Connor, Raymond Carver, John Cheever, J. D. Salinger, Richard Yates, George P. Elliott, Hannah Green, and two or three hundred other writers. I am honored to have them as my guests.

I wish all of my discussions of writing to be informed by my reading, and I wish to demonstrate to students that I see my writing life as being carried out in the company of other writers carrying out their writing lives. I wish to demonstrate to students that I am a writer primarily because I love other writers' stories, novels, poems, and essays. Occasionally I'll put it bluntly to a student: If you don't love reading short stories, then you have no business trying to write them.

—Criticism—or responding verbally to manuscripts—is a natural act. In this case, I have a two-front war to wage with my students: there are those who wish to make pronouncements about the worksheets that we discuss (e.g., "This story fails because its author stereotypes the main characters"), and there are those who feel that they are not trained critics and therefore they have no business criticizing anyone's work and furthermore an author's story is the way it is because that's how the author wanted it to be and who are they to take issue with the author's intentions?

One tactic I exercise here is that of ascribing aesthetic will to literary works; I suggest that stories yearn toward a state of perfection, that it is up to an author to give a story what *it* wants or needs, and that it is up to a critic to help the author discern a story's desires. This is not nearly as much of a fairy tale as it sounds in this fast version; my own experience of writing has been one of developing sensitivity to the signals my work is giving me as I compose it. I tell my students that when I first began writing, I always had a plan and I stuck to it as strictly as possible, trying to ignore the distracting ideas that came to me in the composing process; I tell them that I still begin with a plan, but that nowadays I try to accept most of the ideas that come to me in the composing process. I tell them that such ideas are, in my opinion, true inspiration, and that I have found the inspiration that comes this way, from within the work, to be much more reliable and useful than the other kind, the kind that comes when you're taking a walk in the woods, watching a sunset, or listening to your favorite music.

—Receiving criticism may not be a natural act, but it is a valuable skill, very much worth developing. A crucial introduction to this development can be the standard workshop practice of requiring an author to be silent during the discussion of his or her work. A workshop where an author can't keep quiet but feels compelled to defend and explain the work under discussion is a counterproductive experience for both the author and the people who are trying to offer helpful criticism. I remind authors that they are not required to accept any of the criticism they are offered, and I suggest that they not be hasty in deciding whether or not to use a piece of criticism or a suggestion. A suggestion that seems insulting during and immediately after workshop discussion may next week be the key to a brilliant revision. Ideally, over the course of days and weeks, authors will consider the discussion of their work and will make changes at their leisure.

Every semester, in my beginning poetry- and fiction-writing classes, I read one of my own stories and some of my own poems to my students. This is not a pedagogical activity for the thin-skinned. In a workshop of fifteen or sixteen people, there will always be at least one who can ask a devastating question. ("Why did that girl walk out of that bar that way?") Nowadays I pride myself on not being defensive in class, on listening carefully to whatever is said about my work, and on making it clear that I will consider anything and everything that is said to me about my work. This is not just acting on my part; I have benefited a great deal from criticism I have received from my writing classes. But that doesn't mean that I don't often walk out of such classes with my soul bleeding.

("Didn't they understand that she walked out of the bar because of the song playing on the jukebox?")

But I'm a better writer for having submitted my writing to the workshop for scrutiny, and I hope my workshops are more nourishing communities as a result of my having brought my work into them. An important lesson I took from George Garrett, my mentor at Hollins College in 1968–69, was the value of a writer-teacher's companionship. That Garrett treated me like a writer helped me begin thinking of myself as a writer. At the time he was treating me so generously, I questioned his judgment and diminished the amount of esteem I accorded to him. We're all familiar with that dynamic: "If he thinks I'm a writer, then he can't be all that great a writer himself." Nowadays I understand what a noble thing it is that George has done over the years for his many hundreds of writing students: he has extended himself toward us in such an absolutely democratic way as to prevent the kind of idolization that many other writing teachers encourage. By treating us as writers, he helped us become writers. Garrett's manner toward his students requires them to see him as a regular guy trying as best he can to get some good writing done, and there could certainly be no more useful an example for an apprentice writer.

I've been lucky to have had a number of writing teachers whose treatment of me as a fellow-artist has helped me carry out my work. The first story-writing class I took was at the University of Virginia in 1963 from a formidable nonwriter, Professor John Coleman, a brittle-witted, quick-tongued guy whose practice it was to read the students' stories aloud in class and to correct and ridicule them as he read them. In some cases, he had the student read his own story aloud—by coming to the front and standing before the class—but he continued to interrupt with corrections and comments in the course of the reading.

There were two or three of us that he favored, and I was lucky to have received Coleman's mercy, but his general technique for that class was to set us students against each other in seeking his approval. The University of Virginia was an all-male school then, and the atmosphere of that classroom had a kind of locker-room ruthlessness about it. We laughed at our classmates as they were subjected to Coleman's humiliations; his teaching conspired to make us admire him and to despise each other.

My next writing teacher was James Kraft, a young man who had just received his doctorate from Virginia, a very energetic and hospitable teacher. Kraft wasn't a published writer, but he had been working on a novel for a while, and he wasn't a cruel teacher. I came to his class, in the summer of 1967, straight out of the army's 25th Military Intelligence Detachment stationed in Cu Chi, Vietnam, and of course what I was writing then were stories about military experience. Between being discharged from the Army in Oakland, California, and coming to Charlottesville, I'd spent a week with my parents in Louisville, Kentucky, sunbathing by their apartment complex swimming pool and trying to impress the lifeguard, a pretty high school girl named Nancy. In my heroic efforts, I'd dived into water that was too shallow and had skinned my nose rather dramatically. As a result of my week of civilian life, I showed up in Jim Kraft's class as this Vietnam vet looking dark-skinned and recently wounded, as if I'd just stepped out of the jungle with a string of Vietcong ears attached to my belt. Kraft and the other students treated me with a rather horrified respect, and whatever I might have written, they were not likely to criticize it harshly. I wasn't writing stories with much authenticity, but Kraft addressed my work with a seriousness that always surprised me. I remember that the one nonmilitary story I wrote had a character in it named Leviticus—simply because I liked the sound of that name—and preparing for class the night before that story came up for discussion, Kraft read the entire book of Leviticus, trying to understand my biblical allusion. If he was irked when I told him that I had no reason other than the sound of it for using that name, he didn't let on. From him I learned as a writer not to be careless in my choices and as a would-be teacher that taking a student's writing seriously encourages the student to take it seriously, too.

Peter Taylor was my next writing teacher, for his first and my last two semesters at the University of Virginia. Though I later came to revere him, in 1967 Taylor was no one I'd ever heard of before he came to Charlottesville. He had a kind of humble, shambling air about him that did not encourage veneration. In class his manner was without authority. He brought in books and read aloud from them, mostly Chekhov, though I also heard him read Faulkner's "That Evening Sun," and Caroline Gordon's "Old Red," and a fair portion of Katherine Ann Porter's "Old Mortality." He spoke about characters and scenes the way you'd talk about things that happened in your family or among your friends. This was in a graduate-level class—he had been kind enough to let me enroll in it—and for about the first month and a half, he read to us in class and talked with us in this unsettlingly ordinary way about what he'd read. I had handed in a couple of stories, and I was impatient to have them discussed in class, and I knew that several other students were even more disturbed than I was at Taylor's unproductive use of our class time.

Taylor held conferences with some of us about stories. He had an office in a little dimly lit, musty-smelling house on the other side of Jefferson Park Avenue from Cabell Hall, and over there, too, he seemed to me to lack the exotic aura I expected a real writer to have. It was sort of like going into your uncle's law office and talking about your plans for perhaps attending law school. Taylor did not go over your manuscript sentence by sentence. Rather, he spoke generally about disappointingly nonliterary issues of the story and about fiction writing in general. A couple of things I remember his telling me were that it was awfully hard finding what you wanted to write about and that he had been grateful to see that his subject matter was family. He also told me once of his father's being mad at him about a story he wrote that had a character in it very much like a family aunt; meeting him at the airport shortly after the story's publication, his father told him that if Taylor had been around when he had read the story, he would have hit him. He told me that he sometimes left blanks in his stories when he couldn't think of the right word or the right sentence; he said that he liked going over and over his stories because it gave them a kind of "gnarled" quality.

Mr. Taylor requested a conference with me to talk about one of my stories that I'd been especially eager to have discussed in class. Its denouement came in a scene where a man and a woman are engaged in sex in the female-superior position on a kitchen table when the woman's husband comes in and murders her with a shotgun. Now that I remember it, it seems to me that Mr. Taylor took me into a small room behind his office for our conference, and it became evident to me that talking about this story embarrassed him a great deal, but he gave me to understand it was a lesser embarrassment than trying to lead a discussion of it in class would have been. One of the things he said then was that he personally had nothing against a dirty story—he claimed to have written a few of them himself—but that he didn't think a person who might not wish to read such a story ought to have one inflicted on him- or herself in a workshop. If that session sticks in my mind, it also sticks in Peter's. From then on, over the years, whenever anyone reported back to me that they'd seen Peter Taylor and mentioned my name to him, they'd say he shook his head over the kind of stories I was writing in those days. So far as I know, Peter still thinks of me as a quasi-pornographer.

When Peter finally did get around to discussing our stories in class, he took it upon himself to read them aloud to us. He said that he thought it would be useful for us to hear our stories read in another voice and to hear all of them read in the same voice. Well, he was right about that, you could hear things about your story when he read it that wouldn't have been evident otherwise. If he had trouble with a sentence, you knew it needed some reworking; if he read a passage as if he savored it, you knew you'd done something right. Again, his actual talk about our stories was so ordinary and commonsensical that it frustrated me and frustrated most of us. We'd jump in with negative observations whenever possible, and Peter let us have our say, but most often he was in the position of defending a story against the criticism of the majority of the class. At the time, this way of running a class seemed to me all wrong and further evidence that Peter Taylor wasn't much of a writer and wasn't really suited to be a writing teacher.

In spite of his reservations over my subject matter, most unobtrusively Peter Taylor brought about a personal relationship with me that I think in some part was calculated to enable me to know him, to know something about his life as a writer.

My regard for Peter Taylor's work and his teaching has increased over the years, so that I now see that even at the time I was in his classes, I was learning more than I thought I was. For one thing, it was the first genuine workshop I'd attended, the difference being that we students were encouraged to form bonds with each other, even if some of the bonding came out of our impatience with Peter. John Coleman and Jim Kraft had been good writing teachers for me, but theirs had been writing *classes*—in that the channels of energy went from student to professor and back from professor to student—not *workshops*—in which the class is a community of writers working with each other under the leadership of a senior writer.

After Peter Taylor at Virginia and George Garrett at Hollins, I entered Columbia University's MFA program, where my first teacher was Richard Elman, a quintessential New York City writer. I'd done a good deal of writing the summer before I moved to New York, and so I brought in about 125 pages of new work to show my new writing teacher. A few days later, Elman held a conference with me in which he told me very bluntly that if I was going to write like that, he would have no interest in me throughout my time at Columbia. This was pretty devastating for me because, at considerable sacrifice and expense, my wife and I had moved to the city so that I could attend Columbia; now Columbia, in the voice of Richard Elman, was telling me before I even got started that I was a failure. My opinion is that that was a pretty reckless thing for a teacher to do to a student. Elman's point, as I now understand it, was that I was trying to rely more on craft than on heart, and somewhere along the line I did need to have that news delivered to me. I spent a month or so feeling pretty lousy about it, but then I started writing my way out of my doldrums. I felt like I had survived an assault on my writing life, and I felt stronger for having done so. So even though I would probably not be so blunt as Elman was to me, I give him credit for having done something for me that a writing teacher can sometimes do for a student, get him back on the right track.

Hannah Green was my second writing teacher at Columbia. Compared with Richard Elman, Hannah was an angel of positive reinforcement and a very low-profiled presence in the workshop. Among her rare qualities was her capacity to be affected by what she heard or read in class. She responded very emotionally to workshop work, and she was unembarrassed about her responses, valuable behavior for me to witness, since I had schooled myself in the Faulkner-Hemingway ethic of holding back emotion as both a personal and a literary code. One particular memory of Hannah that I hold very close is of sitting beside her during Tillie Olsen's visit to our class and Tillie's reading of "Hey Sailor, What Ship." The story is about the pain of an alcoholic's destruction witnessed by people who have loved and respected him, and while I sat listening to it, I found my eyes focused on Hannah's wrist, which at some time in her life had been broken and had healed at a slightly crooked angle. I was also aware of some small sounds Hannah made as we listened to the story together, quiet ohs and ums that registered the story's hurt. I of course didn't weep because of the story, but Hannah did, openly and unashamedly. In some part I feel that Hannah Green legitimized my emotional involvement in my reading and in my teaching, and she reinforced the value I'd already taken from Taylor and Garrett that a writer's company was at least as valuable as his or her classroom teaching.

The one truly bad writing teacher I have ever had was Anthony Burgess, who was working for both Columbia and Princeton in the same term and was living in New Jersey. Burgess would take no student manuscript home with him to read and would hold no office hours with any student. A few aggressive ones gave him rides to and from the airport in order to have some personal contact with him. He was always late for his classes, and he seemed to blame us for it; once he came in almost an hour late and shouted at us who had sat around the seminar table waiting for him, "I don't know what you people want from me!" He left early whenever he could get by with it. During class time, he went around the seminar table, holding mini-conferences with students, looking at a page of their work, skimming down that page until he found a word choice that he wished to discuss with that student. He would hold forth for a while on a particular word, and then he would go on to the next student. After three weeks of Burgess, I managed to transfer out of his class and back to Richard Elman's; Elman might have been reckless, but at least he took his teaching duties seriously. Nevertheless, I learned about teaching from Burgess the way you can learn about writing by reading a really lousy book.

Lore Segal was my writing teacher for my final semester at Columbia. Lore wasn't sleeping very well that spring, and she spent her hours of insomnia annotating the thesis manuscripts of those of her students who were graduating. Lore made it clear that she liked my stories, but my God, did she give them a going-over with her editing pencil. From her, I learned a view of teaching writing that connects liking somebody's work with giving it the most painstaking scrutiny. For me, this continues to be a necessary principle since my natural lazy inclination is to think that if I like something, it probably doesn't need much editorial attention from me. I'm still a pretty lousy manuscript annotator, but I do have Lore's good example firmly planted in my brain.

This has been a roundabout way of demonstrating that my own teachers' primary gifts to me were not the exotic secrets of writing but were in fact the ordinary methods of living a writing life and making human connections with other writers. A writing workshop is, in its ideal sense, a community of writers trying to help each other accomplish their best writing. Its first level of value is in its being a community, a gathering of people whose company nourishes each person's writing life.

What a workshop is not is a committee that repairs faulty manuscripts. Most of the time manuscripts can be improved through sensitive revision in response to workshop discussion. But the process is not a mechanical one in which critics tell the author what is wrong with a story and how to fix it, and the author goes home and does what the workshop told him to do. The dynamic of a workshop is oblique, indirect, subtle, and occasionally perverse. Listening to workshop discussion of one story may lead an author to a realization of how to write another much more urgently felt story. Listening to workshop discussion of a story's ending may bring the author to a solution of a problem with a story's beginning, of which only the author is aware. I believe that workshops can be immensely useful but that they are only rarely useful in obvious and logical ways. I also believe that their usefulness is strongly determined by the level of community commitment of their members. Writers caring enough about the work of other writers to give it their time and attention has a generally nourishing effect on the work of both writers.

Some of the most valuable things I have been taught as a writer are intangibles that have come out of my having carried on my work in the company of other writers carrying on their work. These are values that

I hope to pass on to my students, both in and out of workshops, through example, through mental telepathy, through having these values inform everything that I say about writing. These are elements of a writers' code, and though I can't articulate them all, I can nevertheless convey an idea of what I'm talking about:

—The one relationship that counts is that between you and your writing. If you feel good about what you're working on, then you're in good shape, and if you don't feel good about it, then you need to figure out what to change so that you do feel good about it. What you're working on right now is what matters, not what you have written and not what you're going to write.

—Writing is writing's reward. The best part of story writing is to be working on a story in which you are wholeheartedly and wholemindedly engaged. The support and encouragement of friends, family, and even strangers can help, but finally you have to find your reasons for doing it *in doing it.*

—Write for the good of the work—as opposed to writing for others or writing for yourself.

—Serve your stories relentlessly by doing everything you can to make them as good as you can make them (i.e., letting others read them, trying to revise them to perfection, carrying out appropriate research instead of trying to fake it).

—Write stories you *want* to live with. This isn't always possible—or it's hard to know if a story you're working on will become one you want to live with. You have to write a number of stories that you need to cast off from yourself and not live with. But it's useful to remind yourself that your reason for writing these things is because you want certain stories of your own to live in the world with you.

—Write often enough that you miss it if you don't do it. To have a real writing life, you must be writing at least this often. Going to your writing should seem a pleasure rather than a burden to you; if it isn't a pleasure, then you need to shape up your writing life.

—Demand of yourself that you grow in your ability, your ambition, your achievement. If you don't feel you're getting somewhere in your writing, then you need to make some changes. Grow or rot, those are your choices. It is one of the happy functions of the writing workshop—the community of your writer-friends—to keep you growing.

Against Metaphor

Any opposition to metaphor, any expression of distrust for metaphor, is I suppose heresy for a poet—particularly when a poet proposes to address the issue not simply as a point of technique but as a matter of aesthetic and indeed of political conviction. To me, however, these two things are in many ways one. My thinking on the subject of metaphor commences with politics, with the realization that my writing began when I was in late adolescence, in Mississippi in the late 1960s, in the midst of a series of impulses from what I now choose to think of in Frederick Jameson's terminology as the political unconscious, and in response to a long process of coming to terms, from the inside, with the peculiarly southern American version of apartheid.

Ralph Ellison has taught us—absolutely aptly—to understand that in places where there is institutional racism (as I suppose also in the mind of any individual who is a racist, but I'm thinking collectively now), members of the oppressed race are "invisible" to their oppressors: *The Invisible Man*. However, it ought to be understood that Ellison's formulation is a metaphor, a beautifully and devastatingly accurate one— so successful a metaphor, in fact, that it encourages us to forget that it *is* a metaphor. If we come to think of it too simply (as we tend to do with metaphors that are truly effective), we forget the obvious fact that black people in the South were never actually invisible; they simply were not seen by whites—seen as equals, seen as "real" human beings, seen as *actually there*, in the same way whites were actually there. Obviously, what we are talking about is nonliteral, metaphorical vision, since to the flesh-and-blood eye, any flesh-and-blood body is as visible as any other. I can propose an equal but opposite metaphor that lets us understand things from another point of view: black people in the South in which I grew up were not invisible, we might say—white people were blind. They suffered from institutionalized—and metaphorical—blindness.

A few years ago I began thinking about this fact in the course of a meditation on my own upbringing, and I was forcibly struck by the deep complexity of an appalling but obvious fact: institutionalized blindness perpetuates itself through education. White parents in the South spent generations plucking out their children's eyes.

I remember the logic behind the desire to carry out this program, a false logic proceeding from an assumption which appeared (to racists) as fact, but was actually veiled or unacknowledged metaphor. The chain of "logic" ran this way: (a) I begin with the assumption—and this is the crucial point at which fact is blurred by figure: that that person over there is less real than I am because of her blackness: that person is an animal (or *like* an animal), an object, a piece of property, a "spook," a nonentity; (b) I base a whole subsociety on this metaphorical assumption, which I allow to masquerade as fact, exploiting that nonentity, who is after all now reduced by my mental operation to only that; (c) if I ever admit to myself that my motivating assumption is false, my whole world view falls apart, as a consequence of which (d) anyone who questions the initial metaphor is the enemy; and therefore (e) I must educate my child to think as I do (pluck out my child's eyes) because what right-thinking parent can stand idly by and allow his or her child to become the enemy?

So stated, this chain of "reason" is patently absurd; it yields at once to a rational attack. However, metaphor has a way of defeating or defusing rational argument.

There is, I think, a tendency in language toward compression over time, toward the leaving out of connectives that become burdensome with long repetition. The language wants to become increasingly dense and efficient. Emerson's observation in "The Poet" that "language is fossil poetry" is itself a metaphor for this precipitative behavior of language. A sentence has a way of becoming a phrase; a phrase has a way of becoming a single word; by this process we communicate more quickly, with greater connotative density. This process operates by and large in the realm of the social unconscious, where the evolution of language and the evolution of mores are more or less inseparable. Thus, without anyone's noticing it, the proposition "I shall behave, for my own gain, toward that person over there *as if* she were less human, less real, than I am" is rapidly shortened to "That person *is like* an object," and again to "That person *is* an object." A proposition that was in the beginning obviously—rhetorically—a hypothetical *as if* has taken on the form of a statement of fact. And then the entire proposition may find a home in a single word that is powerfully charged with unconscious assumptions: the word *nigger*, for instance, which, no matter what else you may say about it, is obviously a word full of force, else it would not be as objectionable as it is. It is a metaphor disguised as a concrete noun. Its force comes from the history of which it is a concretion, the assumptions, the unacknowledged *as if* that it contains and conceals.

One of the dangers of metaphor is that it has precisely the grammatical structure of a statement of fact—or of a lie, for that matter. It requires a vigilant mind, sometimes, to be aware of the differences among metaphors, lies, and statements of fact.

Another danger of metaphor is that it may allow or even encourage us to forget literal truths.

Here's a centrally operative piece of text from Freud's *Civilization and Its Discontents.*

Have we a right to assume the survival of something that was originally there, alongside of what was later derived from it? Undoubtedly . . . In the realm of the mind . . . what is primitive is so commonly preserved alongside of the transformed version which has arisen from it that it is unnecessary to give instances as evidence. . . . In mental life, nothing which has once been formed can perish. . . . Everything is somehow preserved and . . . in suitable circumstances (when, for instance, regression goes back far enough) it can once more be brought to light. Let us try to grasp what this assumption involves by taking an analogy from another field. We will choose as an example the history of the Eternal City. Historians tell us that the oldest Rome was the *Roma Quadrata*, a fenced settlement on the Palatine. Then followed the phase of the *Septimonium*, a federation of the settlements on the different hills; after that came the city bounded by the Servian wall; and later still . . . the city which the Emperor Aurelian surrounded with his walls. We will not follow the changes . . . any further, but we will ask ourselves how much a visitor, whom we will suppose to be equipped with the most complete historical and topographical knowledge, may still find left of these early stages in the Rome of today. . . . The best information about Rome in the republican period would only enable him at most to point out the sites where the temples and public buildings stood. Their place is now taken by ruins, but not by ruins of themselves but of later restorations made after fires or destruction. It is hardly necessary to remark that all these remains of ancient Rome are found dovetailed into the jumble of a great metropolis. . . .

Now let us, by a flight of imagination, suppose that Rome is not a human habitation but a psychical entity with a similarly long and copious past—an entity, that is to say, in which nothing that has once come into existence will have passed away and all the earlier phases of development will exist alongside the latest one. This would mean that in Rome the palaces of the Caesars and the Septimonium of Septimius Severus would still be rising to their old heights on the Palatine and that the castle of S. Angelo would still be carrying on its battlements the beautiful statues which graced it until the siege by the Goths, and so on. But more than this. In the place occupied by the Palazzo Caffarelli would once more stand—without the Palazzo having to be removed—the temple of Jupiter Capitolinus; and this not only in its latest shape, as the Romans of the Empire saw it, but also in its earliest one, when it still showed Etruscan forms and was ornamented with terra-cotta antefixes. . . . And the observer would perhaps only have to change the direction of his glance or his position in order to call up the one view or the other.

There is clearly no point in spinning our phantasy any further, for it leads to things that are unimaginable and even absurd. If we want to represent historical sequence in spatial terms we can only do it by juxtaposition in space: the same space cannot have two different contents. Our attempt seems to be an idle game. It has only one justification. It shows us how far we are from mastering the characteristics of mental life by representing them in pictorial terms.   (pp. 16–19)

In this passage, Freud must, for the sake of his argument—for the sake of metaphor—categorically separate *city* from *mind* in their *literalness* in order to be able to recombine them metaphorically and thus make his point. This is one of the untrustworthy facts about metaphor. Its rhetorical function is to connect and equate things; it is over this characteristic of metaphor that teachers of literature (myself included) often find themselves waxing sentimental in the safety of the classroom. But in order to make overt the likeness of its terms—their *likendness*—it must first *covertly assert or assume* their unlikeness. It must divide the two terms into vehicle and tenor.

If I come to work and say, for instance, "The boss is a bear this morning," I'm saying something partly descriptive, of course; and the first person who ever compared grouchiness to bearlikeness was also saying implicitly, "Look, isn't this a clever way of describing the boss's mood." When it is fresh, a metaphor calls attention to its own figurativeness. All that goes more or less without saying. But something else is also implicit: "Actually," we're saying, "the boss *isn't* a bear. Actually the boss is only vaguely *like* a bear. How could the boss *actually* be a bear?" Once the metaphor is uttered (and especially once it becomes a cliché— as it likely will if it is sufficiently witty and fitting) then it becomes far less possible to entertain the possibility that the boss *might in actual fact be* a goddamned bear.

That's comforting, of course. Maybe one reason a vaguely ironic metaphor like "the boss is a bear" becomes a cliché at all is that it functions as a little talisman of social protection. As long as I can say "The boss is a bear this morning," then it seems less likely that he or she might actually be one.

But—and this is the terrifying thought—what if it turns out that the boss *actually and literally is* a bear: a bear wearing a boss suit, a bear waiting, as soon as we turn our backs, to rip us to shreds and gobble us up raw?

If that's the literal truth, wouldn't it be useful to know it?

Metaphor functions as a wonderful and powerful mental mechanism, which like most such things is double in its effects—it gives and it takes away. I'll admit I'm not much worried about the connection between bosses and bears. If you think this example ridiculous, that's fair enough—I've chosen it partly for its striking ridiculousness. That way leads to things, as Freud says, that are absurd (if not in this case entirely unimaginable).

But there may be other examples that are less trivial. If we transpose this idea into the realm of racism, accepting the notion that both the "invisibility" of blacks and the "blindness" of whites are *metaphors* like unto "the boss is a bear," then we see that the fate of the racist is precisely that of the office worker whose boss *really is* a bear, but who has been encouraged by a clever metaphor to forget that dangerous fact.

Suppose, for instance, Freud's metaphor of *city* and *mind*, useful as it is, becomes one of those preventive mental forms—standing like a metaphorical angel with a sword of flame at the gate to some precinct of thought, or of concrete reality—that refuses to let us consider certain things? Metaphors *appear* to be synthetic, but have an analytic backwash that may be insidious by virtue of being implicit. Useful as Freud's metaphor is, and original as it was when he thought of it, is it possible that by its very being it prevents us from thinking about the city-mind connection as *utterly literal, utterly concrete*?

We consider the connection between city and mind, Freud says, "by a flight of imagination." To consider so he calls "spinning a phantasy," "an idle game." The unreality of the connection, the unconcreteness of it, he thus makes overt. But for the purposes of the point I'm trying to make, I need to get back on the Eden side of Freud's metaphor, to the more primitive and pristine and, I think for present purposes, more effective notion that (like boss and bear) city and mind may in fact be concretely and literally one and the same.

Part of the beauty of Freud's writing generally is the greatness, the precision, of his irony. As has often been pointed out, he is the very flower of Romanticism; but since he's a late Romantic, he has a strong streak of Mercutio in him. In *Civilization and Its Discontents*, he makes bad jokes in the face of his own death, sharing with Mercutio a great tragic sense of humor. Conversely, part of the greatness of Carl Jung—

who otherwise is so cockeyed on so many subjects—is his realization of the potential for corrosiveness in Freud's irony, and his insistence on a certain "primitive" or atavistic point of view, a sort of negative capability in the face of metaphor, or in the face of what may at any moment turn into metaphor and thus threaten its own concreteness in the mind.

Two anklets were found in the stomach of a crocodile shot by a European. The natives recognized the anklets as the property of two women who, some time before, had been devoured by a crocodile. At once the charge of witchcraft was raised; for this quite natural occurrence, which would never have aroused the suspicion of a European, was given an unexpected interpretation in the light of one of those presuppositions which Lévy-Bruhl calls "collective representations." The natives said that an unknown sorcerer had summoned the crocodile and had bidden it to bring him the two women. The crocodile had carried out the command. But what about the anklets in the beast's stomach? The natives maintained that crocodiles never ate people unless bidden to do so. The crocodile had received the anklets as a gift.

This story is a perfect example of that capricious way of accounting for things which is a feature of the "pre-logical" state of mind. We call it pre-logical because to us such an explanation seems entirely illogical. But it only strikes us in this way because we start from assumptions wholly different from those of primitive man. . . . If three women go to the river to draw water, and a crocodile seizes the one in the center and pulls her under, our view of things leads us to the verdict that it was pure chance that that particular woman was seized. The fact that the crocodile seized her seems to us natural enough, for these beasts do occasionally eat human beings. For primitive man such an explanation completely obliterates the facts and accounts for no aspect of the whole exciting story. Archaic man is right in holding our view of the matter to be superficial and even absurd, for the accident might not have happened and still the same interpretation would fit the case. . . . What we call chance is to him arbitrary power. It was therefore the intention of the crocodile—as everyone could observe—to seize the woman who stood between the other two. If it had not had this intention it would have taken one of the others. But why did the crocodile have this intention? These animals do not ordinarily eat human beings. This assertion is correct—quite as correct as the statement that there is no rainfall in the Sahara. Crocodiles are really timid animals, and are easily frightened. Considering their numbers, they kill astonishingly few people, and it is an unexpected and unnatural event when they devour a man. Such an event calls for explanation. Of his own accord the crocodile would not take a human life. By whom, then, was he ordered to do so? (*Modern Man in Search of a Soul*, pp. 127, 132)

So, what's the truth? A crocodile is mindless. A crocodile is all intention. The temperature is 75 degrees. The boss is a bear. What does it mean that the basic syntactical structure of a metaphor is *exactly* that of a simple declarative sentence, a simple direct statement of a fact?

> To my right,
> In a field of sunlight between two pines,

The droppings of last year's horses
Blaze up into golden stones.
(James Wright, "Lying in a Hammock at William
Duffy's Farm in Pine Island, Minnesota")

Really? Surely not. But maybe . . .

How *do* we tell the difference, in speech and in writing, between facts and metaphors? What tips us off? *The temperature is 75 degrees* may be true or false, but it is no metaphor, despite its form—we know this by our sense of the relative concreteness of the subject, verb, and adjective, which are all on one rhetorical plane, and by the mundane subordination of the adjective to the noun it modifies. *The boss is a bear* is almost certainly untrue, we think—but is it a metaphor or is it a bald-faced lie? Do we determine this by tone? Doesn't our understanding of the rhetoric of this statement depend on how we perceive an intention of the phrase (which must finally be an ironic intention)? What does the metaphorical crocodile who says this to us want—to grin at us with big mossy teeth, or to eat us up?

Her heart was pure as the driven snow may be absolutely true, but it is certainly a simile; the case of simile is somewhat different from that of a "straight" metaphor because it is overtly rhetorical and thus allows its mechanism to show. Make a simple metaphor of it: *her heart was driven snow*. That's more interesting, but a hell of a lot more uncertain: is the emphasis now on the heart's purity, or its driven coldness? Furthermore, the statement is most certainly false, or at least as false as our friend the bear.

Can it be that, as Francis says to Rudy in William Kennedy's *Iron-weed*, "Every stinkin' damn thing you can think of is true"?

We do of course usually know the metaphorical from the non-metaphorical, and one of the ways we tell them apart has to do with our terror of the power of the lie. *The temperature is 75 degrees* may or may not be a lie. We don't fear such a statement usually, because it's easy to verify. Stick your head outside—yup, around 75; or nope, it's snowing.

How about *the earth is round*? Strange territory, that one. Most of us accept it on faith most of the time as having been proved by people we trust. Could such a statement be metaphorical, under any circumstances whatever?

Her heart was driven snow. Well, the only direct means of verification would be to lay her on the operating table and cut her chest open. Nobody would ever do such a thing driven only by a figure of speech—or would they? I maintain that it happens all the time: people undertake *to do* because of figures of speech. Someone somewhere might cut her chest open to verify or disprove a phrase. It's a dangerous idea and therefore perversely appealing: to cut her open might be rewarding, or it might be deadly. How can you know until you try it?

What if a disembodied voice tells you *your dog is God?* Fact, lie, or metaphor? The answer you choose to this multiple-choice question will determine everything. And what if your dog then tells you to shoot people? *People are targets,* says the poodle. ("So," Faust exclaims when his dog turns out to be Mephistopheles, "this was at the poodle's core!") Farfetched as it sounds, this sort of thing seems to happen with disturbing regularity to schizophrenic serial murderers like Son of Sam.

The boss is a bear. This one causes us the least trouble of all because we *know* what it means, or think we do. Because it announces its nonliteralness so thoroughly, we don't think we have to verify it. We feel safe at once. We can smile, even. We can feel superior; we can be ironic, we can feel wise. (Though what do we believe if this sentence is uttered in the dead of night, in a voice of godlike authority, by the poodle?)

It is certainly true that being made a fool of, under certain conditions, can be a dangerous thing.

Metaphor, viewed singlemindedly, turns easily and readily into a sort of talisman against uncertainty. Metaphor can fill us with a feeling of superiority to simple brute facts (the untrustworthiness of them, their dangerousness, or their perceived powerlessness in the face of the pure protean forms the mind can turn them to within its own domain) and superiority to statements about concrete realities (which might turn out vitally, even fatally, to be falsehoods). Metaphors may make us feel safe from being made fools of by words or by the world not because metaphors are relentlessly ambiguous, as we sometimes suppose, but precisely because they are *not.* Any statement that may be understood both as patently nonliteral and as patently false *is not a threat,* to this way of looking at it.

Which would be worse—to be made a fool of by a crocodile, or to be eaten by one? It depends, I guess, whether the crocodile is real or metaphorical. (I suppose you could be made a fool of and *then* eaten—the worst of both worlds, but a commonplace in folktales.) And isn't this really why we want to explain the crocodile—so we can feel superior to it, and hence safe from it?

And that is precisely when things get really dangerous. What if there really is a conscious intention inhabiting the *medulla oblongata* of the crocodile? What if the boss really is a bear? And if there's even the ghost of a chance that the boss might be a bear, we'd be better off remaining totally literal-minded, like Othello before he falls under the spell of Iago the liar, the metaphor spinner. Shakespeare is a master of metaphor's hideous slipperiness; his work is constantly teaching us to see double in very precise ways. Othello at his most straightforward—as a pure one-dimensional literalist—can fight bears without flinching. But what if matters are more complicated than they appear at face value? Then Othello is a fool again.

Sometimes hardheaded literal-mindedness is the best defense against misleading figures of speech and forms of thought; but sometimes such an approach is as fatal as gullibility. At least half the time, the only cure for a bad metaphor is a better one. Either, or—either, or: there's no end to the cycle. Even poor pure-as-the-driven-snow Desdemona doesn't offer a decent solution. True or false: *it's 75 degrees outside*. Stick your head out the door and verify. True or false: *your husband is sufficiently crazed with jealousy to kill you*. Stick your head in the noose, as it were, to find the answer.

Oops—it was concrete truth again.

It is well known that great minds have wrestled with the question whether it is the glorious sun that illuminates the worlds, or whether it is the human eye by virtue of its relation to the sun. Archaic man believes it to be the sun, and civilized man believes it is the eye—so far, at any rate, as he reflects at all and does not suffer from the disease of poets. He must strip nature of psychic attributes in order to dominate it; to see his world objectively he must take back all his archaic projections.   (Jung, *Modern Man in Search of a Soul*, p. 145)

Yes. But *always*? Especially if there's any truth to this:

... have we a right to assume the survival of something that was originally there, alongside of what was later derived from it? Undoubtedly ... in mental life, nothing which has once been formed can perish. ...   (Freud, *Civilization and its Discontents*, p. 15)

So the answer is simple, finally: the mind can do more things than one at the same moment.

Sun *and* eye. Boss *and* bear.

But that's not really simple at all, is it? The proposition is as simple as Shylock, who is thoroughly—and precisely—double in Shakespeare's text, if not in any particular production of the play: victim *and* villain.

City *and* mind.

This "illogical" insistence is, I suppose, the "disease of poets."

Freud's point—the central truth of his metaphor—is that the mind not only *can* have things both ways at once, it can't *help* it. The mind not only *can* have its cake and eat it, it can't *help* doing so. Once the cake is in the mind, it is there until the mind dies and is burnt to a fine white dust and scattered into the air, over the earth. No matter how much the idea of *eating the cake* is in the mind, the original idea of the cake is in there too.

And that, one is tempted to say, is the difference between mind and world. But wait: we have to be consistent. If it's sun *and* eye, if it's city *and* mind, then it must also be mind *and* world. And that means, for me, that Freud is wrong to stop short in his Roman metaphor. Unlike Shakespeare, Freud appears to fail to notice, in this one instance, that his doubleness must be precise and unrelenting in order to be complete, and in order to be complete in that way, it must be grotesque (like Shylock, like Iago, like Lear).

Perhaps the proposition *mind and world are separate* is not a statement of fact but a metaphor.

Obviously, I have a certain axe to grind with Freud about his metaphor of the city. In fact, my grievance is not primarily with the metaphor itself, but with Freud's own disowning of it, his deflation of it—though I insist that the deflation could not have taken place without the metaphor's being there to begin with. The pattern, I repeat, is this: first implicit separation of vehicle and tenor, then explicit but rhetorical reconnection of the two (in the course of which one term retains its literalness and the other is apotheosized, deliteralized, in the imagination), and finally (usually implicitly, but in this passage from Freud the last move is made explicit) utter and complete separation of the two, denial of their equality in literalness.

The boss, we are reassured by our metaphor, *is really not a bear.* Freud is convinced, in the end, that "the same space cannot have two different contents (p. 19)"; he says this as if it hardly needed saying at all. But I grew up in a place in Mississippi where two worlds, two towns, actually coexisted in one space. There was a white Macon, Mississippi, built on top of, or inside of, or surrounding, a black Macon, Mississippi. There were white institutions and monuments occupying the same dimensions as black ones. And in order to see through the situation—which was a political enormity, a terrible evil—one had to develop a precise double vision; otherwise one could see only the white world or only the black world, but never know both. But the only truth, the only reality, was the simple and literal reality of *both*, not as two but as one.

I had to know that the split world of segregation existed; I had to know that the single world of human beings living in one place—in a single interdependent community—existed; I had to know that what was clearly and concretely *there* was not the same thing that existed in the minds of the inhabitants, and that in this separation of mind and world there was a deep and destructive wrongness. Furthermore, I had to know that I was myself one of the inhabitants, participating in this separation (with the assumption that the black side was the subservient vehicle, which does all the carrying, and the white side was the privileged tenor, which is only along for the ride) and what I thought I was seeing was not necessarily what was really there.

Salvation—clarity—depended on two complementary motions of mind: first, seeing through the doubleness of that world; second, learning to see a single world again. I did not have to learn to recreate that world into the oneness I desired; I had to learn how to see the oneness that was *actually there*. Doubleness—metaphor—in that place was a curse. To deny metaphor's bewitchment its reality, to attempt to make of it nothing but a fancy, would have been to render it omnipotent.

What Freud for his own reasons refuses to acknowledge when he insists that his Roman metaphor is a mere "phantasy" is that cities (and even tiny towns in rural Mississippi), societies, politics, are acts of mind, acts of imagination. I want to assert that they are in fact highly concrete works of art. Naturally, some of them are better works of art than others. The one in which I grew up was an especially bad example, not simply badly executed, but, like so many others the world over, executed with bad intent and in bad faith.

What I had to learn was that the only cure—the *only* cure—for bad art is good art.

To say that I came seriously to the writing of poetry at the age of 18 or so in order to complete the task of curing my culturally imposed blindness—to grow new eyes, through poetry, in place of the ones which had been plucked out of my head—would be to risk both sentimentality and falsehood. At the time, I consciously turned to poetry not as therapy but as an escape from politics, from a political situation that seemed to me utterly horrible because, as I had come to see, I had spent years on the wrong side of it. I grew up indoctrinated in racism; the politics of the civil rights movement unmasked me to myself (which is a debt I owe forever to the heroes responsible). At that point, knowing that I had indeed turned into the enemy "my people" had prayed I would never become—enemy of the world in which I had grown up, and thus of much of what I inevitably was and am—I needed to turn away from all of it. If I had been stronger, if I had had more personal resources, I might have been able to do more at the time—join the movement, actively press for social change. As it was, the best I could manage was to live my own guilt and turn to disciplines, ideas, and worlds undreamed of by my former selves.

Poetry, I thought, constituted both such a discipline and such a world—not despised in the rural South from which I came, but rather ignored, unknown. As it turned out, however, poetry was also precisely the discipline I needed in order to learn to see again. My eyes were not gone, in fact—that "plucking out" to which I have referred is itself a metaphor. I had simply learned not to use my eyes. The discipline of poetry, to which I came by an extraordinary stroke of luck, schooled me *not* in the value of the beautifully figurative, which I already knew: it taught me to see *through* the figurative (*through* in a double sense, as through a smoke screen and as through a lens) to the value of the literal.

Treated in the right way—when understood fully, pushed to its absolute uttermost limits and seen through—metaphor has the capacity to teach this lesson and return us from its ghostly metadimension to ourselves and to each other. Metaphor plays with vital protean forms of language—that is, those forms that transform and condense into what we accept as "statements of fact"—out of which human beings build their fictions about the nature of the world. It is deeply important to play with these linguistic forms; only thus do we learn what is and what is not trustworthy in the forms of thought that depend on them. And as every artist knows, it is important that this play go on in an unconstrained way. But because metaphor is one of the great powers of language, and is therefore both rewarding and dangerous, this play must also be careful and responsible, the way we require science to be as careful and responsible as possible. The failures of science in this regard are often physically tangible; those of art, perhaps, are less so. But the fact remains that doubleness (as opposed to duplicity) is an enormously demanding, imperative, hazardous, and by definition ambiguous pursuit, which must be got just right in order to be anything other than confusing and destructive. The possibility that it may be got exactly right, though, is the salvation of metaphor, of double vision, the "disease of poets": if we come to see everything double, in a precise and disciplined way, then we may hope to hold the terrible paradoxes of our situation before ourselves, and truly know them.

Getting Started

It is useful when you begin a novel to evoke certain guidelines if not actual rules that have given you aid and comfort during the periods of tribulation that marked the beginnings of your Novels Past. You are never, of course, so given to imperatives as when you don't know what you're doing and, therefore, haven't begun. This helps to explain an obvious contradiction in most book reviews: a notable absence of any understanding of the examined work in tandem with a flood of imperatives regarding what the work ought to have been. First novelists, especially, are afflicted with the need to give advice—witness Tom Wolfe's advice to us all, regarding our proper subject matter (lest we end up bantering among ourselves, like so many poets). But I digress, a common weakness with all beginnings.

Beginnings are important. Here is a useful rule for beginning: Know the story—as much of the story as you can possibly know, if not the whole story—before you commit yourself to the first paragraph. Know the story—the whole story, if possible—before you fall in love with your first *sentence*, not to mention your first chapter. If you don't know the story before you begin the story, what kind of a storyteller are you? Just an ordinary kind, just a mediocre kind—making it up as you go along, like a common liar. Or else, to begin a novel without an ending fixed in your mind's eye, you must be very clever, and so full of confidence in the voice that tells the story that the story itself hardly matters. In my own case, I am much more plodding; confidence comes from knowing the story that lies ahead, not in the limited powers of the voice that tells it. This calls for patience, and for plotting.

And most of all, when beginning, be humble. Remember that your first, blank page has this in common with all other blank pages: it has not read your previous works. Don't be enthralled by the sound of your own voice; write with a purpose; have a plan. Know the story, *then* begin the story. Here endeth the lesson.

The authority in the storyteller's voice derives from foreknowledge. In my opinion, a novel is written with predestination—a novel being defined as a *narrative*. A *good* narrative has a *plot*. If you're not interested in plot, why write a novel? Because plot provides momentum, plot is what makes a novel better on page three hundred than it was on page thirty—*if* it's a good novel. A good novel, by definition, keeps getting better. Plot is what draws the reader in—plot *and* the development of characters who are worthy of the reader's emotional interest. Here endeth another lesson.

Is this advice for everyone? Of course not! "Plot" isn't what compels many novelists to write, or some readers to read. But if you choose to write a novel without a plot, I would hope three things for you: that your prose is gorgeous, that your insights into the human condition are inspirational, and that your book is short. I am directing my remarks, of course, to those writers (and readers) of *long* novels.

Would a film director begin to shoot a picture without a screenplay? I would never begin a novel without knowing the whole story; but even then, the choices for how to begin are not simple. *You* may know exactly where the story begins, but choosing where you want the *reader* to begin the story is another matter. And here cometh another lesson for the writer of long novels: Think of the reader. Who is this reader? I think of the reader as far more intelligent than I am, but a child—a kind of hyperactive prodigy, a reading wizard. Interest this child and he will put up with anything—he will understand everything, too. But fail to seize and hold this child's attention, *at the beginning*, and he will never come back to you. This is your reader: paradoxically, a genius with the attention span of a rabbit.

I am amazed that mere consideration of the reader, nowadays, often marks a writer as "commercial"—as opposed to "literary." To the snotty charge that Dickens wrote what the public wanted, Chesterton replied, "Dickens *wanted* what the public wanted!" Let us quickly clear up this name-calling regarding "commercial" and "literary": it is for artistic reasons, in addition to financial wisdom, that *any* author would prefer keeping a reader's attention to losing it.

Three obvious but painstaking components either succeed in making a novel "literary," or they fail and make it a mess: namely, the craftsmanlike quality of the storytelling (of course, in my opinion, a novel should be a story worth telling); the true-to-life quality of the characters

(I also expect the characters to be skillfully developed); and the meticulous exactitude of the language (discernible in every sentence and seeming to be spoken by an unmistakable voice).

What makes a novel "commercial" is that a lot of people buy it and finish it and tell other people to read it; both "literary" novels and failed, messy novels can be commercially successful or unsuccessful. The part about the reader *finishing* a novel is important for the book's commercial success; both good reviews and the author's preexistent popularity can put a book on the best-seller lists, but what keeps a book on the list for a long time is that a lot of those first readers actually finish the book and tell their friends that they simply must read it. We don't tell our friends that they simply must read a book we're unable to finish.

In my own judgment, as a reader, the faults of most novels are the sentences—either they're ambitious or they're so unclear that they need to be rewritten. And what's wrong with the rest of the novels I don't finish is that the stories aren't good enough to merit writing a novel in the first place.

One of the pleasures of reading a novel is anticipation. Would a playwright *not* bother to anticipate what the audience is anticipating? The reader of a novel also enjoys the feeling that he can anticipate where the story is going; however, if the reader actually does anticipate the story, he is bored. The reader must be able to anticipate, but the reader must also guess wrong. How can an author make a reader anticipate—not to mention make a reader guess wrong—if the author himself doesn't *know* where the story is going? A good beginning will suggest knowledge of the whole story; it will give a strong hint regarding where the whole story is headed; yet a good beginning must be misleading, too.

Therefore, where to begin? Begin where the reader will be invited to do the most anticipating of the story, but where the reader will be the most compelled to guess wrong. If anticipation is a pleasure, so is surprise.

My last rule is informed by a remark of the late John Cheever—in his journals—that he was "forced to consider [his] prose by the ignobility of some of [his] material." My advice is to consider—from the beginning—that *all* of your material suffers from ignobility. Therefore, *always* consider your prose!

In the past, I have deliberately loaded my first sentences with all these admonitions in mind. The first sentence of *The World According to Garp*: "Garp's mother, Jenny Fields, was arrested in Boston in 1942 for wounding a man in a movie theater." (The sentence is a shameless tease; "wounded" is deliberately unclear—we want to know *how* the man was "wounded"—and that the person "arrested" was somebody's *mother* surely suggests a lurid tale.) The first sentence of *The Hotel New Hampshire*: "The summer my father bought the bear, none of us was born— we weren't even conceived: not Frank, the oldest; not Franny, the loudest; not me, the next; and not the youngest of us, Lilly and Egg." (Well, what is shameless about this is that *anybody* bought a bear. The rest of the sentence is simply an economical means of introducing the members of a large family. In fact, this family is so large, it is cumbersome; therefore, a few of them will die deaths of convenience rather early in the novel.) The first sentence of *The Cider House Rules*: "In the hospital of the orphanage—the boy's division at St. Cloud's, Maine—two nurses were in charge of naming the new babies and checking that their little penises were healing from the obligatory circumcision." (This beginning operates on the assumption that orphanages are emotionally engaging to everyone; also, how people are named is always interesting, and the matter of "obligatory circumcision" suggests either religion or eccentricity—or both. Besides, I always wanted to put "penises" in an opening sentence; the word, I suppose, sends a signal that this novel is *not* for everyone.) And the first sentence of *A Prayer for Owen Meany*: "I am doomed to remember a boy with a wrecked voice—not because of his voice, or because he was the smallest person I ever knew, or even because he was the instrument of my mother's death, but because he is the reason I believe in God; I am a Christian because of Owen Meany." (When in doubt, or wherever possible, tell the whole story of the novel in the first sentence.)

All of those first sentences were not simply the first sentences I ended up with; they were, with one exception, the first sentence of those books that I wrote. (In the case of *Garp*, the *first* first sentence was the sentence that is now the last sentence of the book: "But in the world according to Garp, we are all terminal cases.")

In the case of the novel I am now writing, I have narrowed the possible beginning to three choices; I haven't made up my mind among these choices—so it is still possible that a fourth alternative will present itself, and be chosen, but I doubt it. I think I shall proceed with something very close to one of these.

1. "A widow for one year, Ruth Cole was forty-six; a novelist for twenty years (counting from 1970, when her first book was published), she'd been famous only a little longer than she'd been a widow—in fact, in Mrs. Cole's mind, her husband's death and her literary success were so closely associated that her grief overshadowed any enjoyment she could take from the world's newfound appreciation of her work."

This is a plain, old-fashioned beginning: it holds back more than it tells, and I like that. The character is a woman of some achievement; we may therefore expect her to be a character of some complexity, and—as a recent widow—we can be assured that we enter her life at a vulnerable moment. This beginning continues to build on our impression of Mrs. Cole *at this moment.*

"Furthermore, she'd always perceived any recognition of her writing—both when the praise had been spotty and now that it was profuse—as nothing more than a seductive invasion of her privacy; that such sudden and so much attention should come to her at a time when she most sought to be alone (and most needed to grow accustomed to being alone) was simply annoying. Fame, to Mrs. Cole, was merely a trivial vexation among the more painful torments of her loneliness. She wanted her husband alive again, she wanted him back; for it was only in her life with him that she'd been afforded the greatest privacy, not to mention an intimacy she'd never taken for granted."

We stand on solid ground with this beginning; we already know a lot about Mrs. Cole and her situation. We may be interested in such a woman, at such a time in her life, but there is no hook; the beginning is *too* plain—it lacks even a hint of anything sensational.

Try again.

2. "Dr. Daruwalla had upsetting news for the famous actor, Inspector Dutt; not sure of the degree to which Inspector Dutt would be distressed, Dr. Daruwalla was impelled by cowardice to give the movie star the bad news in a public place—young Dutt's extraordinary poise in public was renowned; the doctor felt he could rely on the actor to keep his composure."

This, of course, is the beginning of a novel by Ruth Cole; it is one of *her* beginnings. Mrs. Cole continues in a tone of voice that promises us she will, occasionally, be funny. "Not everyone in Bombay would have thought of a private club as a 'public place,' but Dr. Daruwalla believed that the choice was both private and public enough for the particular crisis at hand." And the second paragraph provides the "hook" I feel is missing from my first beginning.

"That morning when Dr. Daruwalla arrived at the Duckworth Sports and Eating Club, he thought it was unremarkable to see a vulture high in the sky above the golf course; he did not consider the bird of death as an omen attached to the unwelcome burden of the news he carried. The club was in Mahalaxmi, not far from Malabar Hill; everyone in Bombay knew why the vultures were attracted to Malabar Hill. When a corpse was placed in the Towers of Silence, the vultures—from thirty miles outside Bombay—could scent the ripening remains."

This is certainly a more mysterious beginning than my first—not to mention more foreign. The language (that is, Mrs. Cole's) is more lush and dense than my own—this beginning is altogether more exotic. But pity the poor reader when he discovers that this is *not* the novel he is reading; rather, it is a novel *within* the novel he is reading. Won't the poor reader feel misled too much? (To mislead is divine, to *trick* is another matter!) However, I am aware that I will never get the reader to read Mrs. Cole's Indian novel as closely as I want him to *if* the reader knows it is merely a novel within a novel; by beginning with Mrs. Cole's novel, I make the reader read it closely. What a choice! And so I come, cautiously in the middle, to the third possibility.

3. "*Son of the Circus,* the seventh novel by the American novelist Ruth Cole, was first published in the United States in September 1989; the excitement was mitigated for the author by the unexpected death of her husband—he died in his sleep beside his wife, in a hotel in New York City; they had just begun the promotion tour."

This is not yet quite the blend I want—between what is plain and old-fashioned, and what is exotic—but it comes close to satisfying me, *provided that* I begin the so-called Indian novel quickly, before the reader becomes *too* involved in poor Mrs. Cole's widowhood (not to mention the bad timing of her husband's demise). And that last line—"they had just begun the promotion tour"—hints at a tone of voice that will prevail both in Ruth Cole's fiction and in my telling of her actual story; any consideration of one's prose must include a consideration of the tone of voice.

But what I miss (from Mrs. Cole's beginning) is greater than the kind of purity gained by the third possibility. Both the first and third beginnings tell the reader what *has* happened to Ruth Cole; Mrs. Cole, on the other hand, tells us what Dr. Daruwalla is *going to* do—he's going to give an actor named Inspector Dutt some bad news. What *is* this news? I want to know. And Dr. Daruwalla may be so used to vultures that *he* does "not consider the bird of death as an omen," but we readers know better: of *course* the vulture is an omen! *Anyone* knows that! Therefore, at this writing, I am inclined to begin my novel with Mrs. Cole's first chapter, or part of it. If Mrs. Cole's story is good enough, the reader will forgive me for my trick.

Even as I write, a fourth opportunity presents itself to me: instead of starting with Mrs. Cole's novel or with Mrs. Cole, it is possible to begin with someone else reading her novel—perhaps her former lover.

"At that moment, the German stopped reading; he was a golfer himself, he did not find dead-golfer jokes amusing, and he was overwhelmed by the density of the description—the pace of this novel was unbearably slow for him, not to mention how little interested he was in India. He was not much of a reader, especially not of novels, and he despaired that he was less than halfway through the first chapter of a very long novel and already he was bored. (The last book he'd read was about golf.) But special interests, none of them literary, would compel him to keep reading the novel he'd momentarily put aside.

"He knew the author; that is, he had briefly been her lover, many years ago, and he was vain enough to imagine that in her novel he would find some trace of himself—that was what he was reading for. Once he penetrated the story—past the dead golfer—he would find much more than he'd bargained for; his imagination simply wasn't up to the task he'd set for himself, but he didn't know that as he sat fingering the German translation and smiling boorishly at the author photograph, which he found faintly arousing."

And by the time you read this, I may be considering a fifth possibility. Anyway, once the beginning is locked in place, it is time to invite similar scrutiny of the next chapter and then the next. With any luck, you will hear from me (and Mrs. Cole) in about four years.

My Grandmother on My Shoulder

So much of childhood lies buried in the mysteries of the synapses. Repressed because unbearable—perhaps because it conflicts with some necessary myth we have constructed to explain our ancestors. Or perhaps simply because it pains us to remember.

So much of self-knowledge is just recovering memory. This is one of the saving graces of aging. Memory sails back through the seas of dying gray matter and we grow sane enough to bear our own consciousness. Short-term memory, the old ones tell us, dies away like melody on a summer night. But ancient buried chords return, as if played on a harpsichord with some strings broken. A recitative with words missing, a partial transcript of an unrecoverable conversation.

I grew up in an old-fashioned European family in New York. Perhaps that is one reason I feel so much at home in Italy. Grandmother, Grandfather, Mother, Father, three sisters, housekeeper—we might as well have been a family of the last century.

My grandparents came from Russia and spoke Russian and Yiddish when they did not want the children to understand. My parents were called by their first names, like children; my grandparents were "Mama" and "Papa."

Papa painted in the tall studio facing north toward the Museum of Natural History (in one of those turrets, I later learned, Margaret Mead, one of my heroines, wrote). As befitting the patriarch, he had the only studio. My mother, also a painter, folded and unfolded her easel as the time to work permitted. And my grandmother? She cooked and baked and worried over us. I never thought of her as having creativity at all—and I never learned her recipe for brisket or apple pie or even roast potatoes.

I painted still lives with my grandfather, but it was my grandmother who taught me, in some mysterious way, to be a woman. It was my grandmother who taught me to be the second sex. It was my grandmother I had to kill before I could become a writer.

Every woman artist has to kill her own grandmother. She perches on our shoulder whispering: "Write nice things. Don't embarrass the family." But "nice things" are rarely true things. The truth about human beings is rarely "nice."

And so we are divided—we creators of the female gender. In some way we identify with the patriarch—or how would we have become creators at all? And in some way we identify with the murderer; the one we murder—"Mama"—is ourselves.

I have asked myself again and again how is it possible that the women's revolution has started and stopped so many times in history—beginning with the suddenness of an earthquake and often dying away just as quickly. Women spill oceans of ink, change some laws, change some expectations—and then subside; and become their grandmothers again. What is this dialectic that drives them? What is their guilt that causes them to sabotage their own gains?

It is not merely biology—the softening effect of estrogen on the human female—and the years of bearing and rearing. For we no longer bear and rear for all our lives, and often we are stronger and more determined for every child we bear. The secret is to be found, rather, in the long dependency of the human creature and the many years it takes to form those curious mosaics we call our memories. In those mosaics there are both "male" and "female" forms. Onto the "female" we project all that we must repress, stifle, kill within ourselves. Onto the "male" we project all that we must assert in ourselves in order to create.

If this were conscious, everything would be easy—including change. But it is far from conscious. We do not *know* that we value the male and devalue the female. We do not *know* that we are divided against ourselves. We do not *know* we have internalized "Papa" as right and "Mama" as wrong.

So we twist in the wind: identify with Mama and we deny our creativity; identify with Papa and we need to kill our grandmothers in order to assert ourselves.

Every book I have written has been written on the bleeding corpse of my grandmother. Every book has been written with guilt, powered by pain. Every book has been a baby I did not bear, 10,000 meals I did not cook, 10,000 beds I did not make. I wish, above all, to be undivided, to be whole (this, in fact, is the theme of all my work), but I remain divided.

Like a person who once committed a terrible crime that went unpunished, I always wait for the ax to fall.

My grandmother died in 1969. Ten years later I wrote this poem, attempting to capture something of the feelings her example raised in me:

Woman Enough

Because my grandmother's hours
were apple cakes baking,
& dust motes gathering,
& linens yellowing
& seams and hems
inevitably unraveling—
I almost never keep house—
though really I *like* houses
& wish I had a clean one.

Because my mother's minutes
were sucked into the roar
of the vacuum cleaner,
because she waltzed with the washer-dryer
& tore her hair waiting for repairmen—
I send out my laundry,
& live in a dusty house,
though really I *like* clean houses
as well as anyone.

I am woman enough
to love the kneading of bread
as much as the feel
of typewriter keys
under my fingers—
springy, springy.
& the smell of clean laundry
& simmering soup
are almost as dear to me
as the smell of paper and ink.

I wish there were not a choice;
I wish I could be two women.
I wish the days could be longer.
But they are short.
So I write while
the dust piles up.

I sit at my typewriter
remembering my grandmother
& all my mothers,
& the minutes they lost
loving houses better than themselves—

& the man I love cleans up the kitchen
grumbling only a little
because he knows
that after all these centuries
it is easier for him
than for me.

Now, a decade later, these feelings are even stronger.

Seeing the hatred and envy that women have of other women, the passionate denunciation of female progress, I have often wondered, where does the intensity of the hatred come from and why are women so bitter toward those among themselves who press for change?

If you have been a good girl all your life and have adhered to good-girl rules, mustn't you attack the bad girl, the one who breaks rules and gets away with it? Cheated by life with grandma on one shoulder, cheated by playing by rules invented by man to keep us meek, we often attack the very ones who seek to free us—a case of wanting to kill the messenger.

Unless this dialectic changes, women will never progress. They will begin their revolution but never complete it. They will win freedoms only to have their daughters give them back.

In the sixties and seventies, we thought it was only a case of having enough women in power. What we had not bargained for is that often women in power do not advance the cause of their own sex.

Identified with the male because the male in our culture means assertion, often women in power behave like men—or worse.

Nancy Reagan, Imelda Marcos, Margaret Thatcher, Leona Helmsley— these are not women who advance the cause of women. These are women who have imitated all the worst aspects of male power and have cut off not one breast (like the Amazons of old), but two.

A truly revolutionary movement of women would be one that asserted and glorified the real strengths of the female—nurturance, the ability to connect with emotion, the ability to make human beings connect with and nurture one another. It is a false feminism that abandons the strengths of womanhood for an unbecoming imitation of the arrogance of the male. It is a false feminism that dictates that women become artificial men in order to assert their power.

Where does this leave the female creator? In a quandary, usually. The quandary I have described above. My grandmother sits on my shoulder and I seek to kill her. Is there an alternative way to be a woman artist? Is there an androgynous freedom beyond female and male?

A memory from childhood drifts back through the synapses. I am lying in the big bed between my parents. Perhaps I am four or five. I have awakened with a nightmare and my sleepy father has carried me into bed and placed me between himself and my mother.

Bliss. A foretaste of heaven. A memory of the amniotic ocean—the warmth of my mother's body on one side and of my father's on the other. (Freudians would say I am happy to separate them—and maybe they are right—but let us shelve that question for now.) Suffice it to say that I am happy to be here in the primeval cave. Suffice it to say that I am bathed in the radiance of paradiso.

Back, back in time. I lie on my back and the ceiling seems a kaleidoscope of diced peas and carrots—nursery food—comforting and warm. My parents' mingled smells and mine. Family pheromones. Familiar smells out of which we are born. For the moment, there is no world but this, no siblings, no teachers, no streets, no cars. Eden is here between my sleeping parents and there is no banishment in sight. I deliberately hold myself awake to savor this heaven as long as I can. I fight off sleep to savor the moment of *paradiso* threading through the *purgatorio* of everyday life, the *inferno* of school and sisters, of competitive sandbox wars, and the cruelty of other children.

This is where we all begin—in the paradiso of childhood. And it is to this place that poetry seeks to return us. Poetry and love. We seek them all our lives. The poles of our being—love and death: the parental bed and the grave. Our passage is from one to the other.

My grandmother on my shoulder is upset. She doesn't want me to write these things. She believes the course of wisdom in a woman's life is to keep silent about all the truth she knows. It is dangerous, she has learned, to parade intimate knowledge. The clever woman smiles and keeps mum. My problem is that books don't get written that way. Especially not books containing truth.

So we come back, inevitably, to the problem of women writing the truth. We must write the truth in order to validate our own feelings, our own lives, and we have only very recently earned those rights. Dictators burn books because they know that books help people claim their feelings and that people who claim their feelings are harder to crush.

Patriarchal society has put a gag on women's public expression of feelings because silence compels obedience. My grandmother thinks she wants to protect me. She doesn't want to see me stoned in the marketplace. She doesn't want me pilloried for my words. She wants me safe so that I can save the next generation. She has a matriarch's interest in keeping our family alive.

Hush, Mama, the world has changed. We are claiming our own voices.

We will speak not only for ourselves but also for you. And our daughters, we hope, will never have to kill *their* grandmothers.

Two more memories drift back through the decades. The first is of you washing my little hands between your own and saying that you were "washing away the Germans"—with its pun on "germs." The second is of the children—me, my older sister Susannah, and the baby, Claudia, hiding in the cave of the linen closet and playing "Running away from the Nazis." The war is already long over. It is 1947—but in our memories, the war is never over. Three little Jewish girls in New York City, in a world where anti-Semitism seems the remotest possibility, are playing as if Anne Frank's fate applied to them. (And, in some way, of course it does.)

I make a foray into the kitchen for bread and butter sandwiches while my older sister holds the fort (and the baby).

"What are you doing?" asks my Grandmother.

"Oh, nothing," I say, running back for cover with the sandwiches.

"Children!" calls my Grandmother. "Children!"

We pretend not to hear her.

"*Children*," she calls, "What are you playing?"

"Oh, nothing," we say, munching our sandwiches in the closet, hiding from imaginary Nazis.

We cannot say that we are playing love and death. We would not even know how to form the words. But we are playing for our lives, playing for time, and playing as a way of learning life.

My older sister who originated this game was born in 1937. The world was on the edge of war when she first emerged into it, and she absorbed the threat of danger with her mother's milk. I followed her lead, as second children do. The details obsessed me: the baby bundled in the doll carriage; my mission to the kitchen to snatch the sandwiches (bread, butter, applesauce, and powdered sugar); my mad dash back down the hall through imaginary woods filled with imaginary Nazis, shouldering imaginary machine guns; my sense of my own importance as a survivor, provider, purveyor of food.

"In dreams begin responsibilities," says the great Irish poet Yeats. In games begin the serious business of our lives. Still the messenger, still the provider, I am still hiding in the scented cave of the linen closet to write, then rushing out to gather sustenance from the world, then running back to feed the baby and myself.

The baby that I feed is sometimes my daughter, sometimes myself, sometimes my books. But the model of frenzied survival is clear. I alternate between periods of calm and periods of maximum stress. The second World War still rages in my head.

I try to imagine my grandmother's life compared to my own. Born in the 1880s in Russia, raised in Odessa, she came to England in her teens, married, and had two daughters before the first World War began. In the twenties, she raising two small children in New York, having survived pogroms, prerevolutionary unrest, the influenza epidemic, the first World War, displacement, emigration, two new languages, two new lands. And I, the second daughter of a second daughter of a second daughter, bear all these burdens and disruptions in my soul.

I seize them all as opportunities. I embrace the courage and tenacity she passed along to me. But I have won the right to speak of it—a right she never dreamed.

Mama—the world will silence us soon enough. Let us not conspire by silencing ourselves. "The snow falls over all the living and all the dead," said James Joyce. Let us unbury ourselves while we still have breath and life to do it. The world is not so dangerous if we surrender our fear. Think of all we have lived through collectively—we second daughters of second daughters . . . and we are still alive! Let us raise our voices in celebration of that amazing fact of survival. Let us never accept silence as our fate again!

The Prose Sublime: Or, the Deep Sense of Things Belonging Together, Inexplicably

There must be in prose many passages capable of producing a particular kind of aesthetic reaction more commonly identified with poetry. Unlike the classical sublime of Longinus, the prose sublime I have in mind would only in the simplest case depend for its effect on images or fine language; and those purple passages which, because they do so, are generally singled out for notice need not much concern us. In any case, the reaction to prose as to poetry proves in experience to be much the same, a sort of transport, a *frisson*, a thrilled recognition, which, "flashing forth at the right moment," as Longinus has it, "scatters everything before it like a thunderbolt."

In respect to poetry more than one effort has been made to pin down the very physiology of this reaction, albeit too personal and eccentric to be taken as universal. The report goes that Dickinson would feel, physically, as if the top of her head were taken off; her whole body grew so cold it seemed no fire could ever warm it. Housman's testimony is more circumstantial still. His skin, as he shaved, might bristle so that the razor ceased to act; a shiver would run down his spine or he would feel "a constriction of the throat and a precipitation of water to the eyes"; or something might go through him like a spear, and the seat of that particular sensation was "the pit of the stomach." We might suppose that physical sensations so violent and, it would seem, verging on the pathological, would be enough to discourage all reading, but it is not so. We ourselves may have been spared the specific symptoms, but the remarkable similarity of such accounts remains impressive. Perhaps this much could be said, that some sense of elevation or elation may be felt which does not, for every reader, register itself in terms so physical. All the same, the illusion of something physical may be left behind, a shadow or tint not unlike the spreading of a blush, a suffusion of something warm and flowing just beneath the surface. Has not everyone felt something of the kind? The cool-minded R. P. Blackmur admits to "moods when the mere movement of words in pattern turns the shudder of recognition into a blush and the blush into vertigo." But however such feelings should be described matters less than the question of what it is that calls them forth.

The obvious place to look is just where everyone has always looked, in a prose which depends for its power primarily on the quality and distinction of its language. For there can be no doubt that fine prose of itself can and does give pleasure, and pleasure of the very kind to which poetry is normally thought to have first claim. The type of prose generally offered by way of example, however, would compromise the purity of the inquiry—prose that aims to be poetical: Pater or Doughty, perhaps, or self-consciously experimental work like *Tender Buttons* or *Finnegans Wake*. What this says of general ideas about poetry is too embarrassing and Victorian to pause over. We must try to find what we are looking for in a prose that does not aspire to the condition of poetry but is content to remain itself. Let us consider a passage not excessively familiar, one to which nothing of story and almost nothing of character can be adduced to explain its success: a specimen of prose pure and simple.

In the spring mornings I would work early while my wife still slept. The windows were open wide and the cobbles of the street were drying after the rain. The sun was drying the wet faces of the houses that faced the window. The shops were still shuttered. The goatherd came up the street blowing his pipes and a woman who lived on the floor above us came out onto the sidewalk with a big pot. The goatherd chose one of the heavy-bagged, black milk-goats and milked her into the pot while his dog pushed the others onto the sidewalk. The goats looked around, turning their necks like sight-seers. The goatherd took the money from the woman and thanked her and went on up the street piping and the dog herded the goats on ahead, their horns bobbing. I went back to writing and the woman came up the stairs with the goat milk. She wore her felt-soled cleaning shoes and I only heard her breathing as she stopped on the stairs outside our door and then the shutting of her door. She was the only customer for goat milk in our building.

Intense clarity; one-dimensional—everything rendered on a single plane. Whatever beauty the passage has—and it has as much as any passage of this scope can probably bear—depends less on the words themselves and the care taken with them than on this very sense that great care is in fact being taken. This leads to a strong sense of the author's presence as manifested in the style, a style that seems to come directly from the character of the author and is, practically speaking, indistinguishable from it. With Hemingway this sense of the author is rarely, if ever, absent, but that is just the point.

The author here would be felt as present even without the personal pronoun. He is present in the weight of the words picked out and the rhythms of the composed and modeled phrases, as much as in the attitudes and affectations of the Hemingwayesque. To pick up *A Moveable Feast* for the first time, as I did not long ago, years after its original publication, was to be astonished all over again, as in adolescence, by the prose. I found myself content to read through it as if it had no subject, as though the malicious gossip and tall tales were nothing more than an excuse for the exercise of the famous muscular style. The old I. A. Richards distinction between tenor and vehicle seemed to reverse itself. The subject had become mere vehicle; the true tenor—that is to say, what was being articulated by means of all the beautiful, fierce detail—turned out to be the style itself.

Of course that is exaggeration. Yet if the prose sublime is here at all it seems lodged first in this way of using language and only then, though inseparably, in the picture this language brings into such clear and changeless focus. Technically speaking, this may in some sense always be true or partly true, but it is rarely so decisively true as here, and this rarity in itself becomes a factor in the reader's admiration.

But beneath the surfaces of language, beyond even style or Blackmur's "mere movement of words in pattern," there must be other deeper and more hidden sources for the mysterious yet familiar feelings we are trying to trace. A certain idealizing tendency in the criticism of the past might lead us to assume that the most fundamental source of all would lie in what James calls a "deep-breathing economy and an organic unity"; but in practice no example can ever be adequate to the task of representing that. I must doubt, in any case, whether an organic unity can be maintained except by an uncritical assertion of faith and, as for economy, what we instead constantly find ourselves overwhelmed by in novels is just the generosity of their wastefulness. Often enough the reasons for what comes through as the richest life and most sounding harmony in novels never do become clear, though with our favorite authors we learn to trust that somehow, anyhow, everything must, in a sense, belong. When the reasons do too obtrusively loom up, it is right to suspect that some scheme of the author's is being imposed upon the reader.

According to Percy Lubbock, James's great interpreter, the reader of a novel finds it impossible to retain what Lubbock calls "the image of a book" entire. It must be nearly as hard for the author to manage this trick himself. Always, says, Lubbock, "the image escapes and evades us like a cloud." Yet it does not entirely escape. In our memory there remains forever some image of the novel called *Madame Bovary*, and it is not at all the same as the remembered image of *War and Peace* or *The Wings of the Dove*. Ours are doubtless only phantasmal images of the whole—we could never, like a Borgesian character, become the true author of any of these novels—but these cloudy images have still enough of the contours of a wholeness about them to enable us to think of each one individually and quite distinctly.

And is wholeness the question anyhow? More vivid and alive, certainly, are those broken-off pieces of the whole which continue to drift across our consciousness more or less permanently, fragments though they are. In novels these pieces had once figured as scenes or the mere details of scenes; or as characters, characters in the end perhaps independent of the acts by which we had come to know them; or sometimes, though rarely, as a mere phrase or formula: "Hurrah for Karamazov!" Aside from whatever cloudy sense of the whole the reader may have held onto, such pieces are pretty much all that is left to prize, and there need be no embarrassment in conceding this simple truth.

I have said enough to indicate my belief that it would be futile to seek out the prose sublime in any large idea of artistic unity. Such ideas come to seem, in the light of experience, artificial, faintly theological. Even with the old Coleridgean formula—*unity in variety*—it might be well to emphasize, for a change, the uncanonized term of the pair, *variety*. For one form of the aesthetic reaction we are trying to understand seems to occur just at that point when we grow aware that an ever-present and powerful sense of variety has begun to yield to what may never become more than a provisional sense of unity. A number of different things being put more or less together, one after the other, circling, recurring, veering off, they are seen to make a fit, perhaps quite unexpectedly, to be parts of some larger but undefinable complex. There comes over us then a deep sense of things belonging together, inexplicably. Joyce's "basic patterns are universal," observes Blackmur, "and are known without their names." Universal patterns concern me less than patterns of the occasion and, indeed, of so many changing occasions if we had the time to look for them that we could never expect to invent names to cover them all. Something of the mystery in the act of recognition, at which Blackmur hints, is probably always present.

There is a pattern familiar in modern poetry that may point to a similar, if less obvious, pattern in prose. It involves the simple juxtaposition of seemingly unrelated things. Take Pound's "In a Station of the Metro."

The apparition of these faces in the crowd;
Petals on a wet, black bough.

A rather high degree of likeness, based here on visual resemblance, is clearly intended, but the connection is never stated as such. It is a disposition of objects or perceptions, or of objects taking the place of perceptions, that is found here and there in Chinese poetry as well, a type of parataxis in which the implication of likeness is carried by the arrangement itself.[1] Nor should the expository importance of Pound's title escape notice; it forms the bottom note of a triad, so to speak, the three notes of which are set vibrating together in a new chord. To register, further, the social and emotional distance between a modern, urban Metro station and the timeless pastoral of petal and bough is to see how the poem offers one more version of what Dr. Johnson long ago described as the "discovery of occult resemblances in things apparently unlike."

If we examine now a passage in prose, a long paragraph which likewise involves "things apparently unlike," we may catch something of the same pattern in action, though here less plainly laid out and therefore more elusive. The paragraph comes from the novel *Poor White*, by Sherwood Anderson, and it is chosen because, being unfamiliar, it has a chance to show freshly whatever force it may have. It is no more than a broken-off piece of a whole, but a whole in this case that really cannot be said to exist, a novel which survives, if it does, only in pieces, perhaps by now only in this very piece. Anderson seems never to have had a thought longer than thirty pages or so, and in the novel this paragraph rises toward whatever life and beauty it possesses out of a context truly flat and torpid. The plot is not important; there is practically no plot anyhow; Anderson did not like plot.

And then in Turner's Pike something happened.[2] A farmer boy, who had been to town and who had the daughter of a neighbor in his buggy, stopped in front of the house. A long freight train, grinding its way slowly past the station, barred the passage along the road. He held the reins in one hand and put the other about

---

1. A line from Li Po, cited in Wai-lim Yip's *Chinese Poetry*: "Floating cloud(s): wanderer's mood." Yip compares this technique to the montage of Eisenstein, but the comparison should not be pushed too far, if for no other reason than the fact that in cinema, after the pioneer days, montage of this type came to seem arty and theoretical in a way that it does not yet seem in poetry or in prose, where it remains a practical resource. Pound calls the arrangement, or something like it, "planes in relation," and the analogy to sculpture and perhaps painting seems more persuasive than the one to cinema.

2. To identify: Hugh is the inarticulate, dreamy hero; Rose McCoy is his landlady's schoolteacher daughter, who boards elsewhere; Mrs. McCoy is the widow of a railwayman named Mike; and Turner's Pike is a road leading out of a small Midwestern town about the turn of the century.

the waist of his companion. The two heads sought each other and lips met. They clung to each other. The same moon that shed its light on Rose McCoy in the distant farmhouse lighted the open place where the lovers sat in the buggy in the road. Hugh had to close his eyes and fight to put down an almost overpowering physical hunger in himself. His mind still protested that women were not for him. When his fancy made for him a picture of the school teacher Rose McCoy sleeping in a bed, he saw her only as a chaste white thing to be worshiped from afar and not to be approached, at least not by himself. Again he opened his eyes and looked at the lovers, whose lips still clung together. His long slouching body stiffened and he sat up very straight in his chair. Then he closed his eyes again. A gruff voice broke the silence. "That's for Mike," it shouted and a great chunk of coal thrown from the train bounded across the potato patch and struck against the back of the house. Downstairs he could hear old Mrs. McCoy getting out of bed to secure the prize. The train passed and the lovers in the buggy sank away from each other. In the silent night Hugh could hear the regular beat of the hoofs of the farmer boy's horse as it carried him and his woman away into the darkness.

Perhaps we must be told that the railwaymen have worked up a custom of tossing out chunks of coal for the widow McCoy as they pass—times are hard; but we should be able to guess that Rose and Hugh, vague longings aside, are fated never to get together. Something of all this is probably implicit in the tone of the passage, in the emotional sense the scene does in its own way make. Yet it would be hard to find in these "things apparently unlike" very much that we could call resemblance, occult or not. Not everything is reducible to metaphor; there is more to our search than the uncovering of hidden likenesses. The mind recognizes readily enough how the parts of a poetic image fit together—often enough just the two halves of it, side by side—but in prose there is ampler room for maneuver. Any mixing of contraries may stop short of parallel or symmetry; it is the mere act of combining that seems to make the figure. Two or more things being put into play together are found, as by a sort of grace, to coexist somewhat harmoniously. In the Anderson passage the testing moment when this must be recognized or missed arrives with the chunk of coal, which has nothing whatever in common with moonlight or lovers in a buggy. The point is not just that the author states no connection; neither is any particular likeness implied, and it is in just this way that its pattern, if it has one, is markedly different from the Metro Station pattern. There is only the sentence in which the discord is resolved: "The train passed and the lovers in the buggy sank away from each other." The experience has the character of a ceremonial, small mystery; and I would add that what we experience seems to involve a perception of time. It is a classic instance of things coming together even as they pass, of a moment when things may be said to associate without relating. The feeling raised by this perception is one of poignancy; perhaps that is the specific feeling this type of the prose sublime can be expected to give rise to. Made up of unspoken connections, it seems also to be about them. Probably it is not peculiarly American, but I can recall nothing in European novels, not even in the Russians, which evokes and gives body to this particular mood. (A more complicated and sustained example, again from forgotten Anderson, is Chapter XII of his *Dark Laughter*, but it is far too long to quote here.)

This may come in the end to nothing but one more attempt to deal with what is after all inexpressible. Yet something remains. Incidentally, no one can have read through many pages of Anderson without having been struck by the frequency in his prose of this word *something*: "And then in Turner's Pike something happened." The quintessential predicament for any character in Anderson is this: he (or she) wanted something and did not know what it was. It may be the universal predicament, for that matter. In any case, it resembles the predicament the reader of Anderson finds himself in, for he sees and seems almost to understand something without knowing what it is. Not that this feeling is brought about only by the sort of pattern we have been considering; it is rather that such a pattern can, like patterns more clearly universal, also be known, though without its name, for indeed it has none.

In a brilliant essay entitled "Techniques of Fiction," Allen Tate refers to what he calls the "actuality" of a scene in *Madame Bovary*. It is the scene in which Emma, having received a letter of farewell from her lover, dashes up to the attic in a panic; there the sound of her neighbor Binet's lathe turning comes to her; the sound seems to draw her down toward the street, toward the death she already halfway desires. It is this purely coincidental detail of the lathe, which in no foreseeable way has anything to do with Emma's fate, that confers the sense of "actuality" on the scene for Tate. What he calls "actuality" is only a more philosophical or theological way of designating the aesthetic moment when things associate powerfully together without apparent reason; others have used the term "dramatic correlative" for such a connecting, an echo no doubt of Eliot's "objective correlative." Presumably the novelist, by identifying the process, might make use of it at will, though it does not show up as a device in the pages of *The Rhetoric of Fiction*. Nor in the Anderson passage is any sense of actuality which it happens to possess so much built up and managed as it is simply taken for granted, either naively or confidently—rather, let us say, with the very confidence which can be one of the great assets of the naive writer.

Such moments are akin to the Joycean epiphany or to the "frozen pictures" of novels, moments at which the action, pausing, gives way to a held picture, something like the cinematic freeze-frame or a fermata in music; the picture in itself seems to represent, almost abstractly, some complex of meaning and feeling.[3] When Prince Andrey, wounded, looks up at the "lofty" and "limitless" sky, the effect is of a kind of summation, the meaning of which can be and, as it happens, is stated: "Yes, all is vanity, all is a cheat, except that infinite sky." The Joycean epiphany seems likewise to be a form of revelation or insight; the meaning in wait around the last turned corner of narrative is suddenly illuminated by a flash of understanding: "Gazing up into the darkness I saw myself as a creature driven and derided by vanity; and my eyes burned with anguish and anger." This is very beautifully said, and we may for a moment wonder, as Longinus might have wondered, if the effect is not grounded in the flash of style as much as in the flash of understanding; yet both are present.

In Anderson there is not the same push toward meaning; the rendering exhausts the interpretation: "The train passed and the lovers in the buggy sank away from each other." This has everything the Joycean epiphany has except for the crucial flash of understanding; and the plain style of it I find quite unofficially beautiful as well. Such a passage seems hardly to bother with understanding at all; it is a passage of unspoken connections, unnameable affinities, a tissue of association without specified relations. As far as I know, this last species of the prose sublime, being so elusive, has not previously been isolated and identified.

In it, connections, if any, remain unstated; likewise meanings. As used to be remarked of poems, such passages resist paraphrase. Their power is hidden in mystery. There is, at most, an illusion of seeing momentarily into the heart of things—and the moment vanishes. It is this, perhaps, which produces the aesthetic blush.

3. Stage tableaux work a little in this way, especially at curtains, though a sense of contrivance can compromise the purity of the effect. Moreover, whatever expressive tableau the director arranges is often accompanied by a speech which seems to "interpret" the meaning of the picture, as in the last moments of *Uncle Vanya*, for instance. One thinks in the worst cases of the titles which in Griffith accompany the screen image.

SYDNEY LEA

Making A Case: Or, "Where Are
You Coming From?"

In the late seventies, I read an essay by Brendan Galvin on poems he called "Mumblings" (in *Ploughshares*, 1978). In such poems, Galvin says, an unidentified first person "tries to tell the reader how he ought to feel about the nonspecific predicament of an often unspecified person." Yes, I thought, or else the poet addresses an unidentified second person about the cloudy difficulties of his or her relationship with that second person, or yet a third (also unidentified). I, too, disliked the verse Galvin attacked, especially for its evident premise: that a Poet, by assuming that title, could automatically lay claim to an interesting inner life. Surely, I believed, an "I" was interesting only if proved to be, which meant among other things that he or she must cogently reveal an identity in the writing itself.

My recourse was rash. Goaded by my friends and collaborators Jay Parini and Robin Barone, I founded a magazine, the *New England Review*. Its poetry, we vowed, would operate from more accessible premises. "Pronouns are not people"—I recall my cautionary dictum on certain early rejections, one that unquestionably smacked of the tyro's glibness, but whose gist I still approve.

Not that all seventies poets "mumbled" in the way Galvin had mocked. Some relied on image, whether deep or shallow, plain or surreal. And yet these writers, too, seemed often to exclude me from their work's deeper resonances—just as I was expecting some authorial commitment, a poet would turn to notice, say, a pigeon carrying a snip of someone's necktie through a raincloud, or whatever. Subject matter, so to speak, never quite came out in public.

Somebody once accused Edmund Wilson of denouncing as vices all things he couldn't do, elevating his aptitudes into virtues. I want not to be guilty of the same. If, for example, in my own poems I've always inclined, almost catastrophically, to narrative, I've never dogmatically urged the same bent—in part because that would deprive me of a Donald Justice, whose approach I'll never emulate, no matter how deeply I admire it. Nor am I willing to forgo a May Swenson, an Auden, or, more contemporarily, a Jorie Graham, Charles Simic, or William Matthews, to cite a few wildly divergent cases.

Twelve years ago, though, nettled by the self-regard in certain seventies verse, I did couch my editorial commentary in narrative terms, initiating, moreover, an annual *NER* narrative poetry competition (still going strong). And by 1982, much time in my own readings was given over to "The Feud," a fifteen-page verse tale from my second collection. The rancor I felt against excessive personalism found a momentary release in story, or perhaps more properly in character, a concern I sensed we might too easily have ceded to prose writers.

My pitch, however fresh in those years, is commonplace now, when many commentators—not all of them clearheaded or well informed—assert that hyper-privacy has lost our poetry a readership. (This despite the fact that verse today is generally less "difficult"—think of Andrew Hudgins or C. K. Williams—than it was a decade ago.) There's also a movement abroad called the New Narrative.

I've recently wondered why—having once stumped so for narrative—I want now, both as writer and critic, to move on. It isn't only that I'd avoid repeating Edmund Wilson's error, as the more doctrinaire exponents of the New Narrative may be doing; more important, my *inclination* to narrative was always of greater moment to me than story line itself. If it served to brake my *own* narcissism (as pronounced as anyone's), it also provided a more positive, and more intriguing impulse: narrative opened my poems up to rhetoric, by which I, like Jonathan Holden in his *Rhetoric of the Contemporary Lyric,* mean the language of persuasion—and hence of argument, of testimony, even of the abstraction that Ezra the Ur-Imagist warned us to go in fear of. (I speak of immediately recognizable stuff, not of the rhetorical *gestures* that I think all good poems contain.)

But why was rhetoric, so understood, a goal at all? Having as editor and writer not only lectured but also visited many a "workshop," I had noticed, in addition to (and continuous with) "mumbling," a kind of anti-rhetorical rhetoric among participants: "Show, Don't Tell." Over and over I heard it; and at length I bridled, thankful that most canonical poets had never heeded such an injunction. Consider

> The ceremony of innocence is drowned;
> The best lack all conviction, while the worst
> Are full of passionate intensity.

Even though Yeats himself polarized rhetoric (made of our quarrels with others) and poetry (made of quarrels with ourselves), he went ahead and composed those great lines in "The Second Coming."
Or, for further example:

> Getting and spending we lay waste our powers.
> Little we see in Nature that is ours . . .

> Time present and time past
> are both perhaps included in time future . . .

> I have wasted my life . . .

> Publication—is the Auction
> Of the mind of Man—
> Poverty—be justifying
> For so foul a Thing . . .

> I saw the best minds of my generation . . .

The list could be endlessly extended, but whatever our tastes, few would think immediately to send Tom, Jim, Emily, and Allen back to workshop for the sin of too much "telling." And would any of us really scold John, on the same grounds, for the following lines?

> "Beauty is truth, truth beauty,"—that is all
> Ye know on earth, and all ye need to know.

I spent much breath on the virtues of narrative in my early years as editor, teacher, and lecturer; but privately I wanted sanction in my own writing for moves like those above. Indeed, I've composed relatively few pure narrative poems in five collections, a fact that surprises me less today than once it might have, since I see that from early on I sought not so much the freedom to make a story as to make a case—perhaps like Frost's in "Birches":

> . . . Earth's the right place for love:
> I don't know where it's likely to go better.

It was not restraint alone, then, that barred me from cajoling fellow poets into narrative-or-nothing, that made me hedge my bets, proposing storyteller's "values" instead. Yes, I believed, if I could establish *characters*, including the character called "I," if I could suggest *setting* (historical, political, geographical), if I could at least imply *plot*—if, in short,

I could call back to our service some basics of conventional fiction—the reader might accept my trucking with big issues like the perils of revenge (in "The Feud").

The real goal, however, was to find modes of argufying in verse. And if I still feel that narrative can help a poet make a case, I'm increasingly interested in how poets may do so otherwise, in how we may gain authority for overt rhetoric, for assertion, information, so on, without recourse to fiction's tools. How can Keats write that "Beauty is truth" and impel us to deep thought, whereas, whimsically to choose a seventies instance, the originator of "Happiness Is a Warm Puppy" impels me to homicidal fantasy—even though that aphorism and Keats's share the exact same rhetorical structure?

I ask you now to remember "Ode on a Grecian Urn."

This poem, of course, will always be inexhaustible to critics, and my quirky responses won't put matters to rest. For one thing, poems can have equal and opposite pulls, as Keats knew better than most. They are not philosophy; nor, although they can and do *contain* them, are they reducible to their "ideas." For another thing, I'm reacting here not as critic but as writer. There's nothing scholarly, then, in the following observations:

—Keats calls the scene on the urn a love scene, but it's actually one of intended *rape*, the maidens being "loath," "struggl[ing] to escape," a fact that undercuts the often alleged "calm" of the work.
—The urn is said "to express a flowery tale more sweetly than our rhyme": if so, to put it crudely, we *poets* must despair.
—All the questions in the opening strophe concern the referentiality of the urn's images (where's the scene? what's the legend? who are the figures? Keats can't even tell if they're human or divine), and thus are questions about plot, setting, and character.
—They're *rhetorical* questions, the answer to each being "I don't know."

Let's start with that last point. Keats asks his questions in response to the urn's images, which "show." The poet will later make clear, prosodically stressing the word itself, that image cannot "tell." I think this has consequences, say, for the famous opening of stanza 2:

> Heard melodies are sweet, but those unheard
> Are sweeter; therefore, ye soft pipes, play on;
> Not to the sensual ear, but, more endeared,
> Pipe to the spirit ditties of no tone . . .

The cheerful reading is that Keats's "negative capability" permits him to write a poem *even as he recognizes its inferiority to a certain silence*: that of pure image, of scenery transcending "All breathing human passion. . . ." Never mind that this desire for a stasis removed from passional life, and from the need to testify till the tongue goes dry, seems simply un-Keatsian. Consider instead where the second stanza's assertions point: to the turn in stanza 4, with its emphasis on "sacrifice." The "melodist" of the prior strophe, "happy" in his *quiet*, and the "more happy love! more happy, happy love!" (does Keats protest too much?) Both have vanished, not to return.

Keats, in brief, now recognizes the poverty of his prior claims, that silence and slow time are superior to human emotion, unheard airs to heard, unknowable characters, settings, and legends to knowable. Such contentions lead to a dead end, at least for a poet. If Keats reverts to his rhetorical questions in this fourth and pivotal stanza, the answer to each is, still, "I don't know." (Which means, among other things, "I can make no case.") No longer affirming such ignorance and powerlessness, nor finding mere image "more endeared" than testimony, here's what he does:

> And, little town, thy streets forevermore
> Will silent be; and not a soul to tell
> Why thou art desolate, can e'er return.

I'd once have claimed that the poet here craves a narrative solution, is "desolate" himself because there's "not a soul to *tell*"—even on the simplest level—what the urn's depictions enact or signify. Be that as it may, Keats has by the end established a dialectic: silence and speech; image and articulation; showing and telling:

> O Attic shape! Fair attitude! with brede
> Of marble men and maidens overwrought,
> With forest branches and the trodden weed;
> Thou, silent form, dost tease us out of thought
> As doth eternity: Cold Pastoral!
> When old age shall this generation waste,
> Thou shalt remain, in midst of other woe
> Than ours, a friend to man, to whom thou say'st
> "Beauty is truth, truth beauty,"—that is all
> Ye know on earth, and all ye need to know.

The final aphorism is often taken as a further sign of Keats's negative capability: he persists in responding to beauty, even though verbal beauty is *ignis fatuus* compared to that of wrought things. Indeed, some claim that the very stateliness of the ode—its grand rhythms and intricate structures—paradoxically proves this "heard melody" to be as dignified and enduring as the urn's "silent form," which has teased the poet out of thought, collapsing the dialectical values I've just mentioned. In short, the abstraction "Beauty" destroys the proclivity Keats ascribed to Coleridge—"an irritable reaching after fact and reason"—in the very letter that coined the term negative capability.

Though I'm only a stepchild and not a child of Harold Bloom, this reading does seem sentimental to me. For if the silent urn teases Keats out of thought, it does so "as doth eternity." This is not, however, to identify poem and urn *sub specie aeternitatis*, but to see eternity as a succubus, reminding Keats (quite understandably) of mortality. To think of the urn is to think of a burial vessel or a grave. Hence, famously, the *cold* pastoralism that the poet evokes:

> When old age shall this generation waste,
> Thou shalt remain, in midst of other woe. . . .

Though the phrase I have emphasized is enjambed, the break hints that the urn is itself a woe as durable as "others," so that the silent image— "marble men and maidens overwrought"—is associated with wasted "generation," and thus, etymologically, both with the ruin of genius and of procreation, including its "breathing human passion." If the urn is man's friend, then man as poet needs no enemies.

James Cox once joked to me that Keats must perform an unspeakable act on the "unravished bride of quietness" in order for her finally to speak. It was, of course, a joke, outrageous—but only because the closing pronouncement is surely the poet's. And is it—so nonspecific, so abstract—other than a tepid self-consolation? Even if I can somehow imagine the final aphorism of the poem as the urn's utterance, I'm reminded of a bad parent's response to the child who thirsts for explanation: "Why can't I go outside?" "Because I said so; that's all you need to know."

" 'Beauty is truth, truth beauty'—that is all . . .": the line is also linked by rhyme to "Cold Pastoral!" Reading on, we find it's "all ye know *on earth*." Is there some different venue, then? Yes, but a lesser ode of May 1819 warns against it: "No, no, go not to Lethe," Keats writes in "Ode on Melancholy," "neither twist / Wolfsbane, tight-rooted, for its poisonous wine. . . ." It is wrong, as Keats puts it in the more famous ode to the nightingale, even to be "half in love with easeful death." True, he says

> Now more than ever seems it rich to die,
> To cease upon the midnight with no pain,

> While thou art pouring forth thy soul abroad
> In such an ecstasy!

But here's the conclusion of that stanza:

> Still wouldst thou sing, and I have ears in vain—
> To thy high requiem become a sod.

Imagination, figured as Psyche in yet another ode, demands votive testimony. Otherwise, she's bereft.

> No voice, no lute, no incense sweet
> From chain-swung censer teeming;
> No shrine, no grove, no oracle, no heat
> of pale-mouthed prophet dreaming. . . .

A central issue in all these spring odes, I believe, is the poet's need, precisely, to tell. In "Ode to a Nightingale," Keats dreams of removing himself somehow from passionate speech. But where does that leave him?

> I cannot see what flowers are at my feet,
> Nor what soft incense hangs upon the boughs,
> But in *embalmèd* darkness, guess each sweet . . .

There is a hint of the grave, once more, in the play on "embalmèd." We see how feckless, perhaps even deadly, is visionary image. Indeed, visionary image (*we* might say "deep image") is oxymoronic for Keats; it is "viewless"—i.e. invisible—and therefore guesswork. It reduces him to passivity, and, worst, it's a fraud:

> Adieu! The fancy cannot cheat so well
> As she is famed to do, deceiving elf.

If "Ode to a Nightingale" poses different rhetorical questions from those of the urn poem, still their answer is, categorically, "I don't know."

My excerpts are selective, but they dramatize a dilemma of poetry now as then: we must attend to what Richard Wilbur has more lately called "the things of this world"; and yet we cannot be content with them, no matter how splendidly (or grimly) graphic they may be. The music flees if we rely on simple image, as Keats first tries to do in contemplating the Grecian urn; but if we *dissociate* ourselves from simple image and seek some visionary realm, such music as we get is ersatz. We need, as always, a poetry incorporating both image and something nonvisionary beyond it—something that may, yes, involve narrative values but may involve rhetorical ones in addition. Or instead.

I'm campaigning for overt rhetoric, which will not be to the taste of all. And yet one way or another, poetry will make a case, or else it will cease to function as verbal art, earning its praise in other terms—making "a good picture," say, or having "good music." In which instances, why substitute verse for an actual picture, or—as Marvin Bell has cogently asked—"if a poem is only music, what chance does it have" against real music?

In what I consider his greatest composition, Keats exemplifies an attitude not yet discovered in the great spring odes. Originally composed in September of the miraculous year, "To Autumn" adopts the familiar ploy of rhetorical questioning: "Where are the songs of Spring? Aye, where are they?"—which must certainly include the odes from the May preceding. The answer, however wistful, goes somewhat beyond the familiar "I don't know":

> Think not of them, thou hast thy music too. . . .

This Septembral music, to be sure, is also prepared to "flee." The choir of gnats, the bleat of lambs no longer lambs, the songs of fall insects and migratory birds—yes, these constitute a *memento mori*. Yet the poem itself is mellow and fruitful. One could read the whole renowned last stanza as a gentle Imagist piece, the more imagistic and gentle as it moves to closure. We may think of Stevens's famous claim that "Death is the mother of beauty." And yet, can we discover a rhetoric similar to Stevens's here?

Let me say for now that there are many ways to skin the rhetorical cat, and let me swerve momentarily from the strategies of "To Autumn" in order to consider one of those ways: in Robert Frost, whose rhetoric is easy to hear, since that's about all there is. "Provide, Provide" is chiefly persuasion, verging even on preachiness. It offers four short lines of showing—

> The witch that came (the withered hag)
> To wash the steps with pail and rag,
> Was once the beauty Abishag,
>
> The picture pride of Hollywood

—and seventeen of telling.

The lines that "show" are narrative, however minimal (and however short, incidentally, on image): Famous beauty becomes crone. On the strength of this short-short story, the author moves straight to rhetoric,

which begins as wry musing (lines 5–15) and, though Frost doesn't purge
the wryness (he rarely does, in any poem), concludes as realist argument:

> No memory of having starred
> Atones for later disregard,
> Or keeps the end from being hard.
>
> Better to go down dignified
> With boughten friendship at your side
> Than none at all. Provide, provide!

If you agree that Frost here "gets away with" flouting the show-don't-
tell mantra, you may say that he does so exactly because, in that opening
mini-narrative, he has shown, and I won't disagree. My point, however,
will be that narrativity is only one of the many ways of skinning that
cat. If character, setting, and plot—narrative components—validate the
author's point of view in "Provide, Provide," I want to consider other
modes of validation. For, however achieved, authorial and *authoritative*
point of view is what is ultimately of moment here: a poet's authority
will be the energy persuading us to hear out whatever case he or she may
make.

Even though, for example, I took the pronouncement ironically, I
heard Keats out when he said that beauty was truth. No, I didn't believe
him, nor believe that he believed *himself*. But the very dialectical structure of the poem, with its attendant tonal changes, told me enough of
the speaker that I could share in his ponderings. I witnessed not only
how the urn's depictions provoked the loaded questions in "Ode on a
Grecian Urn," but also how these mere images could not respond to
those unsettling questions. As Stanley Plumly has said, "the image has
no voice." It was Keats's own voice I heard: confronted with silence, it
articulated an attitude—not "fair" like the urn's but troubled, complex—*within the poem*. In brief, it summoned me to participate in the
author's quarrel with himself, which, for all of Yeats, resulted in rhetoric—and in poetry also. In rhetorical poetry.

We do not participate; we reject or scoff or get angry when we read
"Happiness Is a Warm Puppy," because it *has* no specifiable "attitude,"
is enounced by no identifiable voice, signals no well-grounded point of
view. Where, to use the old sixties phrase that is the subtitle of this
essay, is such a proposition coming from? That's another rhetorical question, the self-evident answer being our old, dismaying "I don't know."
The puppy slogan is argument, yes, but free-floating argument. It rides
off into the distance on an automobile bumper, leaving me, at least, to
thunder: Who says so?

Whatever it may do on a bumper sticker, in any case, argument or rhetoric in poems must not hover in such middle air. Indeed, by my interpretation of the "Grecian Urn," it was just such hovering that Keats found insufficient, even deathly. Knowing the gesture to be somehow both aesthetically and philosophically wrong, he yet wrote, "Beauty is truth, truth beauty," consciously *allowing* the aphorism to waft upward from its own silent, imagistic context and thus to reveal its desperate breathiness, irrelevance. Only a very great poet, of course, would choose so daring a gambit, would trot out the very mistake he implicitly warns against, would permit his rhetoric to "float free" by way of indicating the perils of such a technique.

"To Autumn" moves me particularly in that Keats not only accepts but also affirms the dislocation of his ego, his "I," from the center of his meditation, seeking to fuse it with a greater general process. In the ode on the urn, as I've just suggested, the quest for authority had led to an all but crippling doubt. Indeed, in *all* the songs of spring Keats's would-be prophet's voice clamored for a spirit's ear—and always unsuccessfully. Now he does not even try to invoke the goddess, doesn't have to: she's already there in what Wordsworth had called "the simple produce of the common day." Far from claiming some "Romantic" special province for The Poet, then, some insight that only his point of view can muster, the author figures himself as just another observer.

The poem, is, paradoxically, great in its posture of modesty. Its rhetoric is compelling in its hiddenness. For if "To Autumn" does possess rhetoric, it seems strangely unconnected with argument ("Beauty is truth," or whatever). Poetic argument instead relies for its effect on the institution of perspective . . . which, ironically, the poem then seeks to dismantle. This is the greatest paradox of all here: that by first vigorously establishing it, the author persuades us to surrender personal point of view as a vanity. Indeed, the desirability of such surrender is the object of his rhetoric, but it is achieved by exquisitely subtle devices.

Thus the opening stanza heaps up its imagery, from which the rhetoric—indirect, quiet—takes its resonance. The world is initially shown to be so abundant that the bees "*think* warm days will never cease. . . ." But the irrelevance of even such a comparatively innocent ego is made clear by the lines that open the second section of the ode:

> Who hath not seen thee oft amid thy store?
> Sometimes whoever seeks abroad may find
> Thee sitting careless on a granary floor . . .

That is: I, the poet, have seen the goddess amid all her sweet trappings—but then, who hasn't? Even the birds and beasts are witnesses. The author immediately reverts to images, which now "chime" with the rhetoric just as the rhetoric has chimed with the imagery. But the central point is that neither is sufficient of itself. Let me further attempt to clarify this tricky contention by repeating that "Imagist poem" in stanza 3:

> Where are the songs of Spring? Aye, where are they?
> Think not of them, thou hast thy music too—
> While barred clouds bloom the soft-dying day,
> And touch the stubble-plains with rosy hue
> Then in a wailful choir the small gnats mourn
> Among the river sallows, borne aloft
> Or sinking as the light wind lives or dies;
> And full-grown lambs loud bleat from hilly bourn;
> Hedge crickets sing; and now with treble soft
> The redbreast whistles from a garden-croft;
> And gathering swallows twitter in the skies.

The passage begins in rhetoric, in "loaded" questions, so that the return to imagery—the purest in the poem—remains grounded in the quietly argumentative attitude: the very un-loading of the language as the stanza progresses suggests the case being made. We have *wailful* gnats that *mourn*; we have "full-grown lambs," sheep ready for slaughter, so that there's some poignancy in their *bleat*. But the crickets merely *sing*, the swallows *twitter*. Keats has moved from images of sight to the cruder one of hearing; but more important, his very verbs of sound grow increasingly generic, almost hackneyed, surely vernacular. His choice of words implies, again, that he is no longer *the* testifier but *a* testifier, common as brutes. Indeed he wants to extinguish his Self's view by conjoining it with a kind of general perspective.

However, in lyric (which for this reason distinguishes itself from certain fictional possibilities, by the way), there can be no general perspective. Lyrical point of view is never omniscient, is always limited; what I'm addressing, finally, is how the limits get established within a given poem. When I say rhetoric must have authority; when I say I want to know where such and such a rhetorical gesture is coming from, be it overt (e.g., "The best lack all conviction") or more latent (e.g., the progressive subversion of image's "significance" in "To Autumn"); when I say I want to know on what grounds a poem's case is being made—it's point of view that actually concerns me.

Whenever we lyricists engage in acts of argument—and I hope we will—or even gentle persuasion, it's a good idea to ask those same slightly wisecrack questions of ourselves, or rather of our poems, that we might ask of the bumper-sticker slogan: *Who says so? Where are you coming from?* For if we let our pronouncements float free, they too will be no more than slogans, irksome in their equivocality. Point of view must be earned, as Puritans say. Nor am I saying anything much different: to make our cases in poetic format, we must establish our credentials; that is the crucial end, though the means to it are likely infinite.

In any event, I suspect that every access to authoritative point of view will lead, as each has with Keats, into considerations of *voice.* And yet voice can be established, too, in countless ways: by the things or images a poem talks about ("To Autumn"); by its grammar or syntax; by exploitation of structure ("Ode on a Grecian Urn" could be studied from this angle and all the others), including responses, obedient or rebellious, to received formal structures (like the sonnet, with its promise of high seriousness, the villanelle, which implies obsession, or the couplet, boding a yen for aphorism), and so on. But vocal authority, however accomplished, is essential. Pronouns are not people. If, having composed a draft of a lyric, we ask ourselves "Who says so?" we must have a more compelling answer than naked "I."

PHILIP LEVINE

Part of the Problem

Recently I was invited to participate in a lecture series at the Folger Shakespeare Library in Washington dealing with the topic "Socializing the Private Vision." The title comes from a quotation from the poet Tom McGrath in which he says, "[South American poets] do not live essentially in a private world, but on history's doorstep, in a time of change. And the problem of [our] poetry is how to socialize the private vision . . ." (*American Poetry Review*). The Folger Library is asking each of the participants in the series "to address in his or her own way the tension inherent in practicing an essentially private art within the context of society." There are others who see the problem of American poetry in very different terms, and it is possible that there are those who do not see a problem, but more of that later.

It would appear that the Harvard critic Helen Vendler runs directly counter to McGrath. In a recent *New Yorker* review of *The End of Beauty* by Jorie Graham, Vendler writes:

The fraught moment of youthful struggle is the moment of Graham's book. American poetry has never had an easy conscience about being merely beautiful. . . . The sheer freedom invoked by Graham is liberating. The downtrodden Benthamism of most ethical poetry—wedded either to the pragmatic claims of the oppressed or to the totalitarian claims of some ethical system—has no poetics by which to rise to the full-winged reach of untrammelled meditation.

I take it Vendler is discomfited by poetry that refuses to be untrammelled by a vision of the world as it is, one complete with "the pragmatic claims of the oppressed," which might include, should we translate that into the language of experience and out of Vendler's post-Orwellian Polbabble, the demands of the starving for food, of the sick for care, of the desperate for release, your claims on me and mine on you. So for Vendler the problem is avoiding all temptation to socialize the private vision so that the poet can rise to Keatsian heights by scorning a poetry of social concern and instead dwelling on the timely (because eternal) question of how we perceive that we perceive or fail to perceive beauty. This leads Vendler to a wonderfully revealing moment:

Graham, the daughter of American parents living in Italy, grew up trilingually (through French schooling) and has an unembarrassed range of cultural and linguistic reference, which she does not censor out of her poems. In contrast, for instance, to Adrienne Rich's language (deliberately impoverished in the service of availability to the uneducated), Graham's is *opulent.*

One might also say in contrast to Vendler's language, which is deliberately obfuscated to meet her notions of what is stylish and to hide her essential elitism. I would defend Vendler's right to be a snob; let us by all means have a poetry for the terribly well educated. Has the lack of such an embroidered, referential poetry ever in this century been the problem? But let us in this rich and pluralistic society have a poetry for some of the rest of us.

In search of a loftier inanity I went wisely to another critic, Stanford's own Marjorie Perloff. Discussing in the *Michigan Quarterly Review* the essential paradoxes at the heart of Adrienne Rich's poetics, she writes, "The desire to write a poetry that denies the mediation of language, the power of words to disguise and transform experience, seems to go counter to the very need for poetry in the first place. . . ." For Perloff it would appear that it is not enough to keep our experience out of poetry, the task is to disguise and change it. Rich, she says, no longer calls for a negative capability, a free play of the mind denied to women by their secondary status, "but a straightforward, readily comprehensible call to action." "However," writes Perloff, "that call is undermined . . . by Rich's conservative rhetoric, a rhetoric indistinguishable from that of the Male Oppressor." And the Male Oppressor turns out to be none other than Robert Lowell, whose impact she sees on Rich's poetry as devastating.

It is as if Rich, the radical lesbian poet, cannot shed the habit, learned by the time she was twenty-one, a Radcliffe graduate and the winner of the Yale Younger Poets Award . . . of having to write a poetry that would win the approval of the judges. . . . When we probe the imagery, the syntax, and the verse forms of *A Wild Patience Has Taken Me This Far*, we find the spirit presiding over the collection is less that of Emily Dickinson than of Robert Lowell.

If that weren't bad enough, she finds traces of William Carlos Williams and Matthew Arnold. (It's rather amazing how personal these critics get and how all-knowing they become about the personal: Rich deliberately impoverishing her language on the one hand and straining after male judges on the other.) Lest Rich abandon all hope for her poetry, Perloff offers advice which might allow her to become the very liberated and potent poet thousands of men and women already find her to be. Rich "has something to learn from more experimental poetry—for example, from the poets, male and female, associated with the journals $L=A=N=G=U=A=G=E$ and *New Wilderness Letters.*" An interesting feat, that of writing a poetry of social and personal change in a style that denies the entrance of the public world. It is clear to Perloff that Rich, the fledgling feminist poet, must expunge all traces of Lowell and turn to the $L=A=N=G=U=A=G=E$ poets for new forms, new ways of seeing and recording, which is to say that in order to reach contemporary women and inspire them to lead lives dedicated to feminist principles, Rich has got to adapt her voice to an aesthetic that eliminates the presence of Rich's own experience. But of course it has been Rich's ability to capture her own experience and that of other women that has given her poetry the authority it has. How can you tell me what it is like to be a woman of imagination, brilliance, and power unless you tell me what it is like to be a woman of imagination, brilliance, and power, which is of course what Adrienne Rich so incredibly is and Marjorie Perloff is not.

So, we have three versions of the problem of American poetry and how the problem might be dealt with. Why does McGrath's position seem like the most humane and intelligent, for certainly a poetry that dramatized our public lives, that made poetic our roles as citizens, would be worth possessing? This may be because McGrath is a humane and intelligent person. It may be because McGrath is a poet of enormous experience, a poet at times of greatness. It may also be because McGrath is not a critic in the Clement Greenberg mode with a stake in the making and unmaking of reputations. Neither Vendler nor Perloff is a stupid woman; it would be a mistake to assume so merely because the one, Vendler, writes so badly, and the other, Perloff, is totally unable to hear a poem, or because both have such limited tastes and defend them and themselves so fiercely. So many of our critics have chosen the roles of King and Queen makers, or what others have rudely termed "star fuckers," a phrase I would never apply to academics. Unburdened by this role, McGrath need not defend any poetry that is worthless or damn any that delights him; he is free to love poetry, to allow it to work on him, even to have greater hope for it than it merits. Thus McGrath urges on those who write it that most ambitious of tasks he can imagine, the writing of a powerful, authentic, politically relevant poetry. One thanks him for this in somewhat the same way one thanks Plato for banishing poetry from his ideal republic, for believing poetry is unreliable, dangerous, necessarily seditious, and above all potent enough to change lives. So I thank McGrath for so large a vision of poetry, but I must in fact ask, employing his own words, is this "the problem of poetry"?

What actually happens when a poet of genius makes the effort to "socialize the private vision"? I choose to examine Miguel Hernández, one of the great talents of the century. Born in 1910 in the village of Orihuela, west of Alicante, he attended school less than three years and worked before, during, and after his school years as a goatherd. Fortunately he found the public library and there read voraciously and indiscriminately until he discovered the poets of Spain's Golden Age. While still in his teens he was writing a thorny, private poetry in the strict forms of the past. His first book was published when he was twenty-two, and before he was discovered by the modern poets or indeed had himself discovered those poets—García Lorca, Machado, Jiménez, Guillén. The second book, published three years later, is far richer, combining as it does his delight in contemporary poetry, his extraordinary control of traditional forms, and a natural fluency. Except for a few longish poems, the book is made up entirely of sonnets, perhaps because Hernández in his isolation had not heard that this was no longer a valid form.

Your Heart?—It Is a Frozen Orange

Your heart—it is a frozen orange,
inside it has juniper oil but no light
and a porous look like gold: an outside
promising risks to the man who looks.

My heart is a fiery pomegranate,
its scarlets clustered, and its wax opened,
which could offer you its tender beads
with the stubbornness of a man in love.

Yes, what an experience of sorrow it is
to go to your heart and find a frost
made of primitive and terrifying snow!

A thirsty handkerchief flies through the air
along the shores of my weeping,
hoping that he can drink in my tears.

Think of being able to write at age twenty-four a poetry that can survive not only fifty years but also the translation of Robert Bly, and even in that translation can seem fresh and startling. Little wonder he was quickly discovered and taken up by the poets of that era. The year was 1936, and by July the generals and the Falange (the Fascist party) had risen to overthrow the Republic, and Spain had begun that long terrible civil war that would murder some of her poets and scatter most of the surviving ones to Europe and the Americas. Hernández volunteered immediately, and before the year was over he was fighting on the northern front and later in the defense of Madrid. Perhaps because of his sense of solidarity with the people's army, perhaps because he sensed the desperate nature of the struggle, Hernández turned away from his early poetry and toward exactly that kind of poetry we find McGrath urging upon us. He may even have taken some of his impetus from a remarkable letter he received from García Lorca in response to the gift of his first book, a letter full of brotherly advice:

Your book stands deep in silence like all first books, like my first, which had so much delight and strength. Write, read, study, FIGHT! Don't be vain about your work. Your book is strong, it has many interesting things, and to eyes that can see makes clear *the passion of the man*, although, as you say, it doesn't have any more *cojones* than those of most of the established poets . . . I wish you'd get rid of your obsession, that mood of the misunderstood poet, for another, more generous public minded obsession. . . .   (*Poems*, 3–6)

Well he surely did that, and for a time we who love his poetry were the losers.

Not all the poems from *Vientos del Pueblo* (Winds of the People) are as bad as the title poem, but those which strain to take a public position, which serve as rallying cries in the fight against Franco's armies, are. Needless to say, they became the most popular poems he ever wrote and were and still are performed at public readings; some have even been put to music and sung in the manner of Latin American *Nuevo Canción*. Here is the most celebrated of them:

> *Winds of the People*
>
> This air I breathe
> is the wind of the people,
> a wind that lifts me, tugs
> at my heart, crashes in my voice.
>
> Oxen lower their heads
> impotent, meek,
> before their beaters.
> Lions rise up
> and strike back
> in a fury of claws.

I'm not of a people of oxen,
I'm of those who claim
the lion's hunting grounds,
the cliffs of the eagle,
and the hard path
of the bull of proud horns.
The ox cannot endure on
the windswept plains of my country.

Does anyone talk of yoking
the neck of the Spaniards?
Has he shackled the hurricane?
Has he caged
the ray of light?

You brave Asturians,
you Basques of iron and stone,
Valencianos of joy,
and solemn Castilians
worked like the fields
yet buoyant as air;
Andalusians of lightning
born among guitars
and hammered on the torrential
anvil of tears.
Rye fields of Extremadura,
Galicia of rain and peace,
steady Cataluña,
pure blood of Aragon,
Murcia of dynamite
as common as fruit.
From Leon and Navarra,
you masters of hunger,
sweat, and of the axe,
kings of the mines
and lords of the ploughed ground—
down among the roots
you dig like roots yourselves,
from life to death,
from nothing to nothing.
They, of the ruined fields,
they want to break all of you
under the yokes that must
be broken across their backs.

This new dawn breaking
darkens the last days of the oxen.
Robed in the frank smell
of the stables, the oxen die:
the eagles, the lions,

the bulls of pride
do not shudder, and beyond them
the sky is clear.
The agony of the oxen
passes unnoticed,
that of the full male
swells all creation.

If I have to die, let it be
with my head high.
Dead, and twenty times dead,
my mouth closed in the goat grass,
my teeth still clamped,
my beard bristling.
I wait for my death, singing,
for there are nightingales
above the rifle fire,
there where our fight is, singing.

Certainly in the original it has its virtues, among them an extraordinary rhythmic drive, marvelous formal control, and the fierce expression of anger. To get a full sense of how bad it is at its worst, it might be helpful to adapt it to a more familiar landscape: "Does anyone talk of yoking / the neck of Canadians? / Has he shackled the hurricane?" Or "You brave Michiganders, / you Californians of sun and surf, / New Yorkers of stocks and bonds, / and solemn Georgians / with your crackers and peanuts . . ." It's no better, but it's not a lot worse either, and of course we know the poem failed utterly to predict the course of events, for whether they were lion-like or ox-like, the Spaniards were broken and for over thirty years bowed their heads to an extraordinarily harsh regime. Hernández did not die there above the battle with his head held high, with a war song on his lips. Lacking the proper documents he was refused entry into Portugal, and in 1939 he surrendered with the other survivors of his regiment—that was in May; by the end of the summer the war was over and Hernández was in prison, where a year later he came down with TB. He died there in 1942 at the age of thirty-two. The poems written from prison are among the most touching, private, and authentic he ever wrote; they represent a turning back to the sources of his greatest power and genius, his own unique vision of a world in which human love battles for survival against the armies of hunger and death. The need for a socialized poetry had passed; one might even suppose that the need for poetry itself would have passed, but this was a poet destined to write his way into greatness.

Lullabies of the Onion

*(Dedicated to his son, after
receiving a letter from his
wife saying that all she had
to eat was bread and onion.)*

The onion is frost
shut in and poor.
Frost of your days
and of my nights.
Hunger and onion,
black ice and frost
large and round.

My little boy was
in hunger's cradle.
He suckled on
onion blood.
But your blood is
frosted with sugar,
onion and hunger.

A dark woman dissolved
into moonlight
spills, thread by thread,
over the cradle.
Laugh, child,
you can drink moonlight
if you have to.

Lark of my house,
laugh freely.
Your laughter in my eyes
is the world's light.
Laugh so much
that hearing you, my soul
will beat through space.

Your laughter frees me,
gives me wings.
It banishes loneliness,
tears down these walls.
Mouth that flies,
heart that flashes
on your lips.

Your laughter is
the supreme sword,
conqueror of flowers
and larks.
Rival of the sun.

Future of my bones
and of my love.

The flesh flutters
as sudden as an eyelid;
life, as never before,
takes on new color.
How many linnets,
wings beating, take off
from your body!

I woke from childhood:
don't you ever.
I wear my mouth sadly:
always laugh.
Stay always in your cradle
defending laughter
feather by feather.

You are a flight
so high, so wide,
that your flesh is heaven
just born.
If only I could climb
to the origin
of your flight!

In the eighth month you laugh
with five orange blossoms.
With five little
ferocities,
with five teeth
like five young
jasmine buds.

They will be the frontier
of kisses tomorrow
when you feel a gun
in your mouth.
When you feel a burning
past the teeth
searching for a center.

Fly, child, on the double moon
of her breast:
it is saddened by onions,
you are satisfied.
Never let go.
Don't ever know what's coming,
what goes on.

An individual case is small evidence, you might say, to throw against a summons to enlarge our poetry; the point is that all cases would be individual cases. I could have chosen Antonio Machado; the only bad poems he ever published were written as part of this same war effort. Or to get closer to home, we could look at the poems we wrote as rallying cries against the Vietnam War. I'm talking about a body of poetry written only twenty years ago, most of which is now hopelessly dated. The point is again that each case is an individual case, and when McGrath urges all of his fellow poets to socialize the private vision he is simply not thinking like a poet, he is thinking much more like a school marm or a Republican delegate or an academic critic or a commissar. (Heaven forbid we should look at the art the "Social Realist" imperative has given us.) I take my cue from Lawrence, who urges us to trust the creative writer only when he or she is being a creative writer and never when he or she is being a parson or an editorialist or a politician. In fact Lawrence goes even further, for he urges us to trust the poem and not the poet, the novel and not the novelist, and he has convinced me, not that I needed much convincing, having spent the last forty years largely with poets and their poems.

What is so terribly wrong with American poetry today that it could be improved by a massive dose of Neruda-like hymns to Reagan (Neruda's were to Stalin, an even greater swine)? Do we truly need another "brave little soldier poet" who will tell us from the safety of an American campus exactly what it is like to watch the prisoners being minced, the peasants being raped? Are such poems any better than the hymns to the artistic glories of Rome parodied all those years ago by I. M. Baroque in Bly's magazine *The Sixties*? Is what I did on my Guggenheim a worse subject than what Uncle Moe said to Aunt Molly on the night of my Bar Mitzvah seventy-two years ago? Why not accept the range of the actual and not ask James Merrill to become Vallejo or Richard Howard to be Neruda or shun the work of Louise Glück because it has the artistry and good sense never to suggest the jeremiads of Ernesto Cardenal?

It strikes me that our poetry is enormously varied at present and in very good health and should not be judged by what it's like at its worst; it also strikes me that it is foolish to demand constantly that it be great. All of Latin American poetry in this century has given us only two giants who socialized the private vision and did it with genius, and the work of one of them, Neruda, is, to my way of reading, at its best when it is private, nearly impenetrable, and unkillably romantic (that is in *Residencia en la Tierra*). If we do not currently have among us someone with the genius and force of that other giant, César Vallejo, or our own Frost,

Dickinson, or Whitman, this is nothing new nor surprising; it is a condition we have come to accept and live with. Such poets are rare eruptions on the artistic landscape, and to expect them every ten years is idiotic.

This is not to deny that we have our problems. The truth is that each of us has his or her own problems, each of us fails almost daily to write the poetry we're capable of, and when McGrath urges on us his social cure he is, as I said before, not thinking like a poet.

I know of no description of what it is like to think like a poet that equals in detail and eloquence that which appears in Joyce Cary's remarkable autobiographical novel, *A House of Children*. The following passage occurs just after the young narrator has embarked on his career as poet:

Not only words for feelings, like beauty, love, hate, had taken life and meaning for me; but also concrete substances like mountains, sea, thunder, star, boat, began to have new significances. Of his bones are coral made; it was a chord of strings, a sextet, each singing quietly in the ear of my soul; not only with music but souls of their own. A tune of lonely spirits, the sober and upright bone with the bass voice and rather austere character at one end, and the glimmering sea treasure, living jewel, rolling its merman's song at the other, in perpetual little curling waves of sound, which fell forever on the bright sea floor, made of itself the voice of creation.

. . . this interest in me was chiefly wonder at outside forms, pattern or color, and my sympathy with dolls and wooden horses was an extension of my own self. I assumed that everything was me in some form or other. But now I was wondering at the difference and the mysterious character of things. When I looked at the cliffs and clouds, plenty of which I was bringing into my new epics, I was trying to realise their private selves: as a savage touches some strange object, seeking to know through his fingers, its unique and separate quality. So an African chief, a great religious head in his own country, asked to handle my signet ring, because he had never seen gold, and dandling it in his palm, he looked not at the ring, but into the air, with half-closed eyes, like one waiting for an illumination from heaven. When nothing reached him, he murmured softly like one muttering a prayer: "Da nauyi," meaning, heavy. The prayer was not successful. He handed back the ring with a puzzled and doubtful glance, saying only: "Abin mamaki," a thing of wonder, that is to say, another prayer for enlightenment, but so common in Africa, that it has ceased to have any force. It is used every day by thousands, in face of motors, planes, condenser engines, railway tickets, stainless knives: but it envokes no enlightenment. It expresses only the sense of man's apartness from things, which is also the acknowledgment of his community with everything.

Thirty-five years ago I sat in a small room with Robert Lowell, then my teacher, and asked him how I might lift from its doldrums a particular poem. Lowell had spent about fifteen minutes showing me why this poem was horseshit, something I already knew, for I had come to him not for praise but for help. He had just paused in his steady assault on my poem, when I asked him how I might go about making it better. We sat in silence for over a minute. Then he looked at me, a little resigned smile on his face, and said, "You know, it's damned hard to make sense and keep the rhythm." Nothing was clearer to me than that Lowell was remembering his own experience, and yes, he was exactly right, it is damned hard to make sense, say something worth the saying and not said a thousand times before, and keep the rhythm. That was my problem at the time, and of course it still is, and there would be others down the road, problems more difficult to locate and more impossible to deal with, and there would be no Lowell to go to for help. For these, the lasting problems in my writing life, I had only one person I could go to. As the Buddha said at the end, "You shall be a lamp unto yourself." "A work of art is good if it rises from necessity," writes Rilke to the young poet Mr. Kappus. "In this nature of its origin lies the judgment; there is no other." And how do we arrive at this knowledge? "Nobody can counsel and help you, nobody. Go into yourself," writes Rilke. "This above all— ask yourself in the stillest hour of the night: *must* I write." And of course, *what* must I write? Simple enough? How does one know when the night has reached its stillest hour? How does one go into oneself? How indeed does one go about taking Rilke's advice, even with the best intentions in the world, the most fervent belief in the wisdom of his advice? Believe me, I wanted desperately to take his advice, I believed in it (as I still do), I simply did not speak the same language as Rilke. Nor did I understand that he was doing the best he could to tell me how, but that it would be different for each of us and hence he employed his marvelous diction and imagery; he was speaking like a poet, metaphorically. What he forgot to say was, the news will come to you and not you to it, as the little private tale that follows is intended to illustrate.

In the spring of 1952 in Detroit, I was working at Chevy Gear and Axle, the "abandoned factory" of a poem in my first book, *On the Edge,* and I hated the job more than any I'd had before or have had since, not only because it was so hard, the work so heavy and monotonous that after an hour or two I was sure each night I would never last the shift, but also because it was dangerous. There in the forge room, where I worked until I was somehow promoted to a less demanding, equally boring job, the stock we handled so gingerly with tongs was still red-hot as we pulled it from the gigantic presses and hung it above us on conveyors that carried our handiwork out of sight. Others had mastered the art of handling the tongs loosely, the way a good tennis player handles his racquet as he approaches the net for a drop volley, applying just enough pressure not to let go and not enough to choke it. Out of fear I squeezed for all I was worth, and all the good advice, the coaching I received from my fellow workers, was of no use.

One night just after we'd returned to our machines after the twenty-minute break, the guy I was working with—a squat, broad-shouldered young black man whose energy and good spirits I'd admired for weeks—tapped me on the shoulder and indicated with a gesture that I should step aside. Together we'd been manning a small punch press; he handed me the stock that came along a conveyor, I inserted it in the machine, had it punched, and then hung it on another conveyor. On this occasion he said nothing, though even if he had I wouldn't have heard him over "the oceanic roar of work." He withdrew a short-handled sledgehammer from inside his shirt, and gripping it with both hands hammered furiously at the press's die. He then inserted a piece of stock in the machine, tripped the button that brought the press down, and leaped aside before the press could whip the metal out of his hands. The press froze. I went to summon the foreman, Lonnie, while my partner disposed of the hammer. Lonnie took one look at the machine and summoned two men senior to him, or so I assumed since they arrived dressed in business suits. For twenty minutes they searched the area. I finally figured out that they were looking for the instrument with which the press had been sabotaged. Then they separated us and grilled me. There was no question, they assured me, that the press bore the marks of violence. What had "the nigger" done? I answered that I'd seen nothing out of the ordinary, the machine just broke down, almost tore my hands apart. Oh, they looked at each other, I wanted it that way. Well, they could certainly accommodate me. Before the night was over, I was back on the "Big Press," handling those red-hot sections of steel, my hands stiffening and kinking inside the huge gauntlets. Within a few days I was once again dreaming of fire as my hands gnarled even in sleep. I lasted a few more weeks, and when it became obvious that the "Big Press" was mine forever, I quit.

Five years later, while living in Palo Alto, California, on a writing grant from Stanford University, I received an article clipped from a Detroit newspaper and mailed to me. It told of the closing of Chevy Gear and Axle; its functions had been moved to a new, highly automated plant near Pontiac. I had already tried at least a dozen times to capture the insane, nightmarish quality of my life at Chevy: that epic clanging of steel on steel, the smell of the dead rats we poisoned who crawled off into their secret places and gained a measure of revenge, the freezing winds at our backs as winter moved through the broken windows, the awesome heat in our faces, those dreamlike moments when the lights failed and we stood in darkness and the momentary silence of the stilled machines. In the springlike winter of 1957, sitting in the little poetry room of the Stanford library, which was mine alone each morning, half a country and a universe away from Chevy, I could recall almost without hatred that old sense of utter weariness that descended each night from my neck to my shoulders, and then down my arms to my wrists and hands, and how as the weeks had passed my body had changed, thickening as though the muscles and tendons had permanently swelled, so that I carried what I did with me at all times, even when I lifted a pencil to write my poems. It was not the thickening heaviness of myself I tried to capture in my abandoned factory poem—I only managed a glimmer of that—for I was determined to say something about the importance of the awfulness I had shared in and observed around me, a worthy aim, certainly, but one that stopped me from writing the poetry of what I had most deeply and personally experienced.

Seven years later, in the spring of 1964, I was living in a large, airy house in Fresno, California, a house of beautiful slow dawns. Each morning I would waken early, before six, and watch the light—yellow and pale green as it filtered through the leaves of the sycamore outside my bedroom—transform the darkness into fact, clear and precise, from the tiled floor to the high, sloping, unfinished wooden ceiling. It was a real California house. I would rise, toss on a bathrobe, and work at my poems for hours seated at the kitchen table, work until the kids rising for school broke my concentration. To be accurate, I would work unless the morning were spoiled by some uncontrollable event, like a squadron of jet fighters slamming suddenly over the low roofs of the neighborhood, for we lived less than a quarter mile from a National Guard airfield.

One morning in April of that year I awakened distressed by a dream, one that I cannot call a nightmare, for nothing violent or terribly unpleasant had occurred in it. I dreamed that I'd received a phone call from a man I'd known in Detroit, Eugene Watkins, a black man with whom I'd worked for some years in a grease shop there. Eugene was a tall slender man, ten years older than I, and although he had his difficulties at home he rarely spoke of them. In fact he rarely spoke. What I remember most clearly about working beside him was that I never liked schlepping or loading or unloading in tandem with him because he had a finger missing on his left hand, and I had some deep-seated fear that whatever had caused that loss could easily recur, and I didn't want the recurrence to take some treasured part of myself. The dream was largely a phone conversation, one in which I could see Eugene calling from a phone booth beside U.S. 99 in Bakersfield, 120 miles south of where I lived. He'd called to tell me he was in California with his wife and daughter. They'd driven all the way from Detroit and had just arrived. They wanted to know what they should do and see while they were in the West. As I babbled on about the charms of Santa Monica, L.A.'s Miracle Mile, the fashionable restaurants neither they nor I could afford, the scenic drive up U.S. 1 to Big Sur, I knew that what Eugene was actually seeking was an invitation to visit me. I even mentioned the glories of Yosemite and King's Canyon National Park—neither more than an hour from where I lived—and yet I never invited him. Finally he thanked me for all the information I'd given him, said goodbye, and quietly hung up. In the dream I saw him leave the phone booth and shamble, head down, back to the car, exactly as I would have in his place. I awakened furious with myself for my coldness, my lack of generosity, my snobbery. Why, I asked myself, had I behaved this way? Was it because Eugene was black? Several black friends had visited my house. Because he was working class? I was living in a largely working-class neighborhood. (Who else has an airfield at the end of the block?) Did I think I was so hot with my assistant professorship at a second-rate California college, with my terrific salary that was probably no more than Eugene earned? Was I trying to jettison my past and join the rising tide of intellectuals, car salesmen, TV repairmen, and bank managers who would make it to the top? What the hell was I becoming?

It finally occurred to me that I had not rejected Eugene, my past, the city of my birth, or anything. I had had a dream, and that dream was a warning of what might happen to me if I rejected what I'd been and who I was. The kids were up and preparing for school, so I climbed back in bed with my yellow legal pad and my pen. I was in that magical state in which nothing could hurt me or sidetrack me; I had achieved that extraordinary level of concentration we call inspiration. When I closed my eyes and looked back into the past, I did not see the blazing color of the forges of nightmare nor the torn faces of the workers, I didn't hear the deafening ring of metal on metal, or catch under everything the sweet stink of decay. Not on that morning. Instead I saw myself in the company of men and women of enormous sensitivity, delicacy, consideration. I saw us touching each other emotionally and physically, hands upon shoulders, arms across backs, faces pressed to faces. We spoke to each other out of the deepest centers of our need, and we listened. In those terrible places designed to rob us of our bodies and our spirits, we sustained each other.

The first lines I wrote were for Eugene Watkins. I imagined us together in the magical, rarified world of poetry, the world I knew we would never enter. Although it's snowing there, when we leave the car to enter the unearthly grove, no snow falls on our hair or on the tops of our shoes because "It's the life of poems; / the boughs expensive, our feet dry." But of course that was not the world I was returning to; I wanted to capture in my poetry the life Eugene and I had shared, so before the poem ("In a Grove Again") ends, the grove transforms itself into any roadside stop where two guys might pause to take a piss:

> Meanwhile back in the car there are talismen:
>
> A heater, the splashed entrails of newspapers,
> A speedometer that glows and always reads o.
> We have not come here to die. We are workers
> And have stopped to relieve ourselves, so we sigh.

I remained in bed much of that week. The poems were coming, and for reasons I couldn't explain, I felt my inspiration had something to do with the particular feel and odor of the bed. While there I wrote most of the Detroit poems that appear in my second book, *Not This Pig*. I believe they were the first truly good poems I'd written about the city. They are by no means all sweetness and light. There was and still is much that I hate about Detroit, much that deserves to be hated, but I had somehow found a "balanced" way of writing about what I'd experienced; I'd tempered the violence I felt toward those who'd maimed and cheated me with a tenderness toward those who had touched and blessed me.

The Soul of Brevity

As for the aphorism, the maxim, the wisecrack, the Bartlett's entry, the epigram (with, as Martial had it, a sting in its tail), they have their places. They're portable and memorable, and none of us wishes literature were longer or heavier.

Good ones give us the pleasing, if illusory, sense that something has been said right, for once and for all. They have the last word, at least for a while.

But when a good epigram seems most conclusive—and a good one is nearly all conclusion—and thus most fixed and certain, it is most volatile.

"One's real life is often the life that one does not lead," wrote Oscar Wilde, who built into his witticism the instability of "often." A reader first concurs with Wilde because he has said it well, and because, after all, he said so many things well it would be a likely mistake not to linger thoughtfully with his sentence. "How often?" a thoughtful reader might wonder, exercising a wary and amused scepticism like the one that prompted Wilde. Little has been concluded and much begun.

A very alert reader might even discover in this particular aphorism a Best-in-Show example of a characteristic Wilde trope. "Only a man with a heart of stone could read the death of Little Nell without laughing," Wilde quipped, simply substituting "laughing" for the anticipated "weeping" and thus offering a more psychologically acute sketch of the insensate heart. But that wisecrack is easy, especially for Wilde. Saying the opposite of what's usual in "One's real life is often the life that one does not lead" is wiser by far, and Wilde's practiced formula—the reversal of the expected—fills up with wry and provoking ambiguity.

Of course there are aphorisms that pull shut like doors. "Three may keep a secret, if two of them are dead." Benjamin Franklin.

Some depend on their context. What compilation of quotations is complete without Emerson's "I hate quotations"?

Others depend on being lifted from context. I found this sentence in an Elizabeth Bowen novel: "Fate is not an eagle, it creeps like a rat." And the retired relief pitcher Dan Quisenberry was quotable enough that there were usually reporters around his locker waiting for something like this: "I have seen the future and it looks a lot like the present, only longer."

And there are aphorisms that depend on forgotten contexts for the ways they are commonly misremembered. Ulysses's famous "One touch of nature makes the whole world kin" (*Troilus and Cressida*, III, 3) is usually quoted as a lofty sentiment. But in its original context it is part of Ulysses's attempt to rouse sulky Achilles from his tent, for the fickle world has forgotten what Achilles can do and has the name of Ajax on its every tongue.

> One touch of nature makes the whole world kin—
> That all, with one consent, praise new-born gawds,
> Though they are made and molded of things past,
> And give to dust, that is a little gilt,
> More laud than gilt o'er-dusted.
> The present eye praises the present object . . .

"What," Ulysses is asking Achilles, "have you done for us lately?"

Whatever incites us to misremember Ulysses's shapely line in a nobler context needs deflating, and that's motive enough for a whole class of epigrams.

Bishop Lancelot Andrews: "The nearer the Church the farther from God."

Or, here's one of Martial's acid poems saying exactly what the Roman patronage system rewarded clients to suppress. The poem is XII, xl, and the translation is mine.

> You lie and I concur. You "give"
> a reading of your wretched verse
> and I applaud. You sing and I
> too lift my blowsy voice.
>
> You drink, Pontificus, and I
> drink up. You fart; I look away.
> Produce a cribbage board; I'll find
> a chance to lose, to pay.

There's but one thing you do without
me and my lips are sealed. Yet not
a minim of your money's trickled
down to me. So what?

You'll be good to me in your will?
No doubt you'd bounce a check from hell.
So don't hold back on my account;
if die you must, farewell.

The best epigram, like the endings of great poems, shimmer and twist. Little is ended. There's more to think and feel. The rhetorical pleasure of an epigram may be its conclusiveness and concision, but the soul of its brevity is a long thoughtfulness.

"If you are afraid of loneliness, don't marry," Chekhov wrote. If the reader stops where the rhetorical momentum does, this wisecrack requires no Chekhov. Two guys and some beer will do. But Chekhov is friendlier to loneliness than the lazy reader thinks, and friendlier to marriage.

"Wit is the epitaph of an emotion," wrote Nietzsche, but it would be dull to mistake him as arguing against the chill of wit on behalf of emotion's heat. An emotion has a natural lifespan, and in order for a next one to come along the incumbent needs a death and an epitaph. Of course reading Nietzsche is not for one who thinks wit and emotional life are different.

And it will take a very good reader indeed to match wits and emotions with Callimachus: "A great book is like great evil."

Beginnings

I confess I must rely for the truth of what follows by calling almost totally on memory now. First of all, there's the matter of the lost letters, letters I wrote home to my mother some thirty-three years ago, during the year I spent at the Marianist Preparatory in Beacon, New York, as a postulant seeking entrance into the priesthood. Those letters, sent home at the rate of one or two a week, I long ago saw cut to shreds and thrown away by my poor mother, during one of her low points. In the work of a single afternoon, she made a sacrifice of whatever symbols of her past she could lay hands on, which on this occasion unfortunately included not only many old family photographs but the letters I wrote her from Beacon. Years ago I came to the realization that that loss was one of the chief reasons I have spent the past twenty years as a biographer poring over the letters of other writers and why as a poet I find myself preoccupied with trying to retrieve segments of my past from the cold ash of history.

Images, then, of the old Marianist Preparatory in Beacon, New York, a third of a century ago. The large recreation room off the study hall, with its two Ping-Pong tables, its stacks of metal foldaway chairs, its comfortable, seedy old lounger. I can still see in my mind's eye the four-square, four-storied Victorian structure with its oversized drafty rooms, its high ceilings, its tall dusty windows overlooking Mount Beacon and a rising Easter moon. Upstairs were the cream-colored classrooms where we learned Latin and English and History and—on the top floor—the large dorm with its ancient, public porcelain washing troughs and its tiny infirmary off to one side. Thirty to forty boys, aged thirteen to eighteen, all testing the wings of their fledgling vocations.

The building is gone now, along with the chapel, the rectory, the tool sheds, the dining hall down the road that housed the handful of German nuns who fed us. Even the chlorine-leaking pool, surrounded by its green wooden dressing stalls, is gone now. I spent a year in this place from September 1956 until the following July as a postulant in the Society of Mary, the Marianists, and since my name was so cleverly embedded in the order's, I took it as a youthful, onomastic sign that I was destined not only for the religious life and the priesthood, but to spend my allotted span in this particular order.

The last time I visited Beacon, seventeen or eighteen years ago, I was married and the father of three sons. I had stopped at the Prep on my way home to western Massachusetts after lecturing on literature to the assembled freshmen cadets at West Point. By then there was a new bridge across the Hudson, so that Beacon was almost on the way home. In truth, even if the bridge had not been there, I felt the need to go back to Beacon and see the place again. By then, however, except for the macadam road and the expanse of elms and maples that had dotted the old estate, everything had changed. The buildings themselves had been razed and a new public school stood now in its place. My only consolation that midmorning was seeing Mount Beacon shimmering in the distance like the shadow of God, and even that had been denuded of the old funicular railway I had once ridden to the top of the world.

For thirty years and more, images from those ten precious months at Beacon periodically flood my memory, rising with a frequency and vividness out of all proportion to the relatively short time I spent there. Most of the memories are peaceful beyond belief—low clouds hanging beneath Mount Beacon, bobsledding through a rush of pure white powder, robins jack-hopping across an acorn-studded patch of field. Perhaps it is merely the nostalgia of youth, but I seemed to live closer then to the changing seasons, and can still summon the smells of late summer, the awesome cracking of boughs all through the long night following a powerful winter ice storm. But I also know from the few surviving letters that I wrote others at the time that there were also moments of intense loneliness, moments when I would have given anything to be back home with my family and friends.

I do not know what exactly happened to my religious calling, whether it died or whether it underwent a transformation into something else. But I do know that when I returned home in late July I still believed I was going on to the Marianist novitiate at Mount Marcy, New York, in September, though already something in the smell of roses and the translucent honey of those golden oldies, Presley's "Love Me Tender" foremost among them, taken together with the promise of dating girls from the local high school, became temptations against which I no longer cared to struggle. So, when the time came to get on with my vocation, after a short, intense struggle with myself, I decided not to return.

Whatever happened to my religious vocation, I still count that year at Beacon as the real beginning of my abiding love of writing. The Marianists were—are—a teaching order, and with hindsight I can see that even then I was fated to be a teacher. I can actually date that knowledge to an overcast November afternoon in the fall of 1956, while I stood on the frozen playing field guarding a soccer goalpost. I remember that time so vividly because it is linked in my memory with those black and white images tacked up on the study hall bulletin board from *Life Magazine* of the bodies of the dreaded NKVD spattered with lime to help them decompose, and other images of Hungarian freedom fighters, some no older than myself, holding machine guns as they fought to realize a new order.

For a moment that afternoon, the noisy surge of youthful energy following the soccerball had collected at the other end of the field and I was suddenly left alone to daydream. Then, out of nowhere, apparently, an image possessed me, an image so powerful and seductive that I am still able to call it up with the weird uncircumscribed passions of my youth. The vision is of a spirited cheerleader replete with ponytail. She keeps her eye on me as she goes through her cheering exercises, and I find myself following her every move, at the same time promising *le bon Dieu* that, when I finally leave the order, I will bring the same dedication to teaching that I would have given to the priesthood.

I can see now that what I was doing then was making a bargain in the crassest manner possible, but, as the old religious brother explained, when his false teeth suddenly fell out of his mouth in the middle of his lecture so that he had to force them back in without further ceremony, with the single terse comment that necessity knows no law, so too with the bargain I made that November afternoon. With me, too, my "necessity" seemed outside the Law.

I can still recall that daydream and the youthful promise I made that afternoon, when there was no one to witness but God, and I still find myself checking to see if I've kept that youthful covenant. Since that fall when the first Kennedy was shot, seven years after my boyish daydream and covenant, I have been teaching university students, and, though the world has undergone its own massive metamorphoses politically, culturally, and economically in those twenty-five years, I think I have kept to the heart of my promise.

But Beacon was also the place, as I've said, where I first knew, my heart pounding in my throat, that I wanted to be a writer. It was here that I learned things that now seem idealistic to the point of the delusional and the banal, as if a young Don Quixote had set off to conquer the world and its recalcitrant words for the greater glory of the Word, armed only with a leaky pen. To begin with, ours was not what you would call a literary family. Work, hard work, was what was wanted and demanded at home, at least by my father. There were six kids when I was at Beacon, and the seventh and last arrived two weeks after I returned home that July. My mother named my new sister Regina Maria, since, splendid dear romantic that she was, she believed she had just sacrificed her oldest child to the Marianists and saw my sister as a gift from God to replace her first loss.

During the war—the Big One, as he called it—my father had risen to the rank of technical sergeant. He spent most of his tour of duty at the Aberdeen Proving Grounds in Maryland, instructing others in the repair of heavy equipment and testing the new Sherman tanks that were about to be shipped overseas. Whatever else he may have learned, he certainly learned order and discipline, a discipline he early passed on to his children, so that to this day I find myself "policing the area," i.e., the yard, of my Victorian house for stray litter and cigarette butts before walking through the door.

In our family, outside of the ubiquitous comic books and the daily newspapers, to read was to read textbooks as a way of educating oneself for landing a good job, preferably—as my father hoped, Depression child that he was—a safe civil service job with a pension. The novel, short story, or the rare poem I read were those assigned in class, pored over not for themselves but as a way of getting on. I laughed to myself when I read somewhere that Robert Frost thought the real descendants of the New World Puritans were the New World Catholics, with their strong sense of duty and responsibility. How, I wondered, had Frost found out our secret? For even into my thirties, I had difficulty with Wallace Stevens's dictum that good writing must give pleasure. Did that mean that pleasure was an end in itself? And wasn't that suspiciously like engaging in sex without having children, something, as the old schoolmen had taught, *contra naturam*?

And yet my father was an avid reader of history, especially biographies of church figures like Cardinal Spellman and Pius XII, or political figures like Churchill and Eisenhower and Senator McCarthy; the last my father firmly believed had tried to save his country from the Red Peril. My mother's reading habits were both simpler and more complex, and since she held a full-time position at the Doubleday Book Company's offices in Hempstead, she often brought home books for me to read. Rudyard Kipling's *Jungle Book* was one, Thomas Merton's *Seven Storey Mountain* another. Besides her monthly perusal of *Reader's Digest*, she read every one of James Michener's novels, as well as romantic novels by the carton, and sometimes she read even riskier things. Once, around the time I came back from Beacon, I found on her dresser in a brown-wrapped plain cover a paperback copy of Henry Miller's *Tropic of Cancer*.

I still remember lecturing to my brother, Walter, not then eighteen, for wasting his time reading Jack Kerouac's *On the Road* instead of something more uplifting, like the moral writings of Epictetus, as I was then doing. That was back in 1959, at the end of my freshman year at Manhattan College, and I still shudder when I think of what a pompous ass I was for doing what I did. But for the most part, my family hardly ever discussed with each other the books we read. The most I ventured, being first ever in my immediate family to go to college, was to rehash some of the ideas my tired professor of philosophy had lectured us on in class. I'd spin out some idea, such as Plato on the ideal of Justice, and, when the talk threatened to become esoteric, my father, at the other end of the long table, would fix me with a summarizing stare and pontificate that there was nothing right or wrong but thinking made it so, a signal that the college bullshit session was about to come to an end.

So much for reading. To write meant writing letters, preferably business letters, or a *curriculum vitae* for a job. In our family there was no precedent for writing in order to "express oneself." That was something I did not even begin to take in until I started teaching at UMass-Amherst in the late sixties, by which time I had a Ph.D. and three kids. By that point, having already taught Hunter and Lehmann undergraduates, as well as rookie cops and homicide detectives from among New York's finest and—in my spare evenings—tired stenographers and bank clerks who took continuing ed. classes, I felt I could at least write *about* literature, and I did, including baroque essays on Carlyle and Conrad and Austen, *explications de texte* of Chaucer, Donne, and T. S. Eliot, and—eventually—a dissertation on Hopkins.

But, except for a one-semester course in creative writing in my senior year at Manhattan College, a course I took with John Fandel, a gentle and patient poet, I did not dare to spend time writing anything more creative than literary essays until I was in my early thirties. Writing about literature, and—better—teaching it, was acceptable because I could defend it as having a social purpose. Moreover, from my father's perspective, it did put bread and butter on the table. One did what one had to to survive. In the meantime, the dialogue with literature, like my earlier dialogue with God, continued to bide its time, patiently, as it waited in the wings.

This "accommodation" to literature did not change substantially until 1973, when the Italian poet, Giovanni Giudicci, having read my handful of unpublished poems, told me in his inimitable way that it was time I stopped playing the altar boy before the altar of art and became a priest of the imagination. That, of course, links up almost too neatly with my experience at Beacon, and the only thing in favor of this anecdote is that it is true. But Beacon was still the real beginning, though there is not much in the way to mark the beginning. Perhaps there is something of the maternal about all such modest beginnings: a harboring, a nurturing, the sense of a disembodied smile hovering over an author's infant word. It is not unlike the Christmas story, perhaps, which in retrospect forms the first act in the later retelling of the story of our lives; our preconscious life retold later by our mothers seems to be the only time when history itself takes second place to our mewling, princely egos, which insist on taking stage center from the instant they arrive.

I wish I could remember the name of the outdated navy-blue-covered literary anthology that the brothers gave us high school seniors to read that year or find the notebook I so meticulously kept, outlining the introductions to the various historical periods of English literature with such meticulousness that it can fairly be said that, like one of the assiduous monks in *A Canticle for Leibowitz*, I wound up virtually transcribing the entire text to my notebook, page by page exact, believing the physical act of copying would help embed those literary "facts" on my brain. Or so I seem to remember now those innumerable hours in the darkening study hall, panning the ore of that old text in the hopes of discovering gold.

There was something very special as well about the books I pored over that year, including not only Books I and II of the Aeneid, but a scholarly life of my namesake, St. Paul, as well, which I studied for months, mysteriously delighted with the figure of Christ's burning disciple seated at the feet of that wise Jewish scholar, Gamaliel. For my seventeenth birthday, my mother—at no small sacrifice—bought and sent me, along with a pair of imitation leather shoes, a copy of Mackinlay Kantor's just-published Civil War novel, *Andersonville*. This I read greedily, a piece each day during my few free moments, until Brother Clyde, skimming it for objectionable material, discovered a passage about pigfucking, I think it was, and suggested I turn my attention to other books for the next few years.

As an antidote to Kantor, he suggested that I read the Catholic apologist, G. K. Chesterton, with excursions into Hilaire Belloc. Belloc I found vicious and half mad and quickly abandoned, but I did manage to read several dozen of Chesterton's Father Brown detective stories, his life of St. Francis, and dabbled in *The Everlasting Man*. I even read most of Chesterton's biography and expressed such an interest in this Catholic writer that I eventually managed to get a pass into the town of Beacon, situated about a mile away, in order to do research at the public library. The freedom of that was so novel as to feel like freedom itself, and I spent part of that afternoon just walking the streets of the town. Thinking of that afternoon still arouses in me the half-formed image of a girl rising phoenixlike above the smoke of autumn leaves burning in small, tended piles on those impossibly innocent streets.

The history of the American Revolution is also tied in with these memories, for General Washington and the Continental Army had been sequestered around this region nearly two hundred years earlier. Beacon is a river town, located on the eastern shore of the oil-stained, still-majestic Hudson, with Newburgh—Washington's headquarters—directly across from us (in 1957 it was still reached by ferry) and with West Point twenty miles to the south. On a brilliantly cold mid-February day around Washington's birthday, the entire Prep rode the ferry as its huge, antiquated engines churned the boat through large, virginal white ice floes, taking us to visit Washington's headquarters. I remember how engrossed I was as I stood near the prow, rudely braced by the anti-Catholic pamphlets I'd found in the ferry station, published by some fundamentalist sect out of Tampa, which asked in a heady, terrifying, and quasi-illiterate style how any right-thinking American could actually believe in some wafer God or pay allegiance to the scarlet whore of Babylon.

It is the iambic chuff Chuff chuff Chuff of the straining ferryboat's pistons vibrating through the floorboards and up through the soles of my shoes that I can feel now even as I write about it, and that brings to mind my first effort ever to write a poem. It was the beginning of Lent, and a call from a local convent had gone out for poems on a Lenten theme. The prize for the best poem was ten dollars, and I was intent on winning so that I could buy something nice for my mother's thirty-fourth birthday. But how *did* one go about writing a poem, anyway, I wondered.

At a loss, I went up to Brother Clyde at his desk at the front of the study hall and asked him. In the appendix to my literature textbook, he explained, was a glossary of literary terms with a definition of the various feet and a discussion of line lengths and rhymes. No matter that someone named Allen Ginsberg was making history in San Francisco with his long, unrhymed Blakean verse lines and had already caused a mild stir with something called *Howl*. In any event, I do not believe anyone at the Prep had yet heard of Ginsberg or his *Howl*, and in any event I would no more have been allowed to read that poem than I'd been allowed to read *Andersonville*. In any event, in the province in which I lived, poems, as even my tattered textbook informed me, should rhyme.

Poems, I learned, were also marked by lines of metrically recurring feet, usually in units of four or five, but could have as few as one to as many as seven or eight. If my textbook spoke of metrical shading and variation, I paid no attention, and wouldn't have understood the meaning of these nuances anyway. For in truth, I'd just been pressed into service as an auxiliary drummer for the Marianist Prep's ragtag Marching Band and at the moment I had percussion on the brain. Like the atom in my physics textbook, the foot was the essential building block of the world of the poem, and was made up of a stressed syllable linked at either end to one or two (relatively) unstressed syllables. Leaving aside the problematic issue of the double-stressed spondee, no doubt invented by some troublemaker who couldn't leave well enough alone, there were four possible kinds of feet, and out of these the poet strung together his poems the way a jeweler strung pearls on a string. There was the rising iambic foot, which went dah-DUM, and the mirror image of this called the trochee, a falling rhythm which went DUM-dah. Then there was the galloping anapest—dah-dah-DUM dah-dah-DUM—and, finally, the lugubrious chant stroke of Longfellow's dactyls that had informed his ubiquitous *Hiawatha*. This one went DUM-dah-dah DUM-dah-dah and was somehow faintly epic and heroic.

For my Lenten poem I chose the iambic foot strung together seven times. This combination, I could not help feeling, would give my effort a certain nobility and epic expansion and, since seven was a sacred number, it would gain by that as well. I would also employ rhyming couplets, seven of them, which would add up to fourteen, in imitation of the fourteen Stations of the Cross, which the poem meant to commemorate. What I did not know at the time was that I was using the old fourteener or poulter's measure, whose long lines naturally break into breath units of four feet and three. In other words, I was using the four-three ballad or hymnal form.

The lines themselves would march smartly across the page, exactly as we did whenever we postulants went off to mass or to the refectory for meals. In spite of my best intentions, however, the poem spent itself after only twelve lines, and these I soon regrouped into three squads of four, each of which displayed about as much subtlety as a Roman pha-

lanx. At the top of the page I wrote the obligatory dedication, "J. M. J.,"
followed by the title, "Forgive Me," and this was in turn followed by the
mini-phalanx of my poem. In spite of its curtailed length, I was anxious
to have the poem follow the course of the Via Dolorosa, and filled out
the long lines with as many baroque and redundant modifiers as my
piety and zeal could muster, meanwhile trying to remember all the while
to look into my heart and write. Here was what I wrote:

> I help to beat and scourge Your back a bloody crimson red
> And place a crown of prickly thorns upon your regal head.
> Your sacred name and character I mock and ridicule.
> O Lord each time I flee your love I prove myself a fool.
>
> I hurt and help to make You fall along the Dolor's way,
> And scorn Your mother and the others as they watch and pray.
> I strip Your garment from Your limbs and from your whip-lashed skin.
> Yes, all of this I do to you when I commit a sin.
>
> I help to drive the ugly nails into Your feet and wrists,
> And mock Your kingly deity with sland'rous waving fists.
> Each time I sin against Thee, Lord, I help to break Your heart.
> Lord, help me hate my sins and evermore from them depart!

In the course of writing those lines, the beat of which I kept tapping
out on my desk to make sure it conformed, I managed to evoke most of
the traditional images of the Passion, on which the entire community
had been daily meditating for weeks, plus a touch of Poe's "The Raven,"
all wrapped neatly into the rhythms I see now I'd gleaned from my careful reading over the years of various store-bought birthday cards. I can
see too that the poem's logic is not unlike an Ignatian meditation made
specifically for someone with the attention span of a Peter Quince: the
composition of a particular place—a Grand Guignol version of the Via
Dolorosa, trombone crescendos and all—followed by a meditation on
the significance of place, and ending with a petition.

I cannot help noticing too that the verb "help" is there five times,
turning with a jackknife spring at the end as the help shifts from the
youthful torturer to the Victim, no doubt an encoded cry for help from
that Victim in getting through the poem. Is it any wonder that, five years
later, as a college senior, I fell instantly and irrevocably in love with the
alternating stress and feather-light modulations of Fr. Hopkins's sprung
rhythms, whether in the hammering opening of "Thou mastering me
God," or the heartbreaking rhythms I caught in his elegy to a dead black-
smith, cut down in his thundering, boisterous prime, when he prayed
that the Lord would "rest him all road ever he offended."

The poem completed, I submitted it (that is the precise word one wants) to my superiors, who in turn sent it on to the local convent, and about a month afterward I learned that I had been awarded first prize. From our little religious store I bought a very modest gift for everyone in my family, and a very good (plastic) rosary for my sometime Lutheran, sometime Baptist mother. I had looked in a book, much as my father had taught me to look in his automotive books to change the spark plugs or the oil filter on anything from a '55 Chevy to a Nash Rambler, and I had learned how to write a poem. Better still, it had paid off in cash. Everyone, except perhaps the poor nuns, were winners.

That it would take a lifetime of listening to the play of the wind through the shagged pines, the arrhythmia of one's self breathing, and the phrasal modulations that constitute another's unique voiceprint, as well as attending to the shifts and jagged countershifts present in all sorts of music, from country to Buddy Holly to Bessie Smith to Mozart and Debussy and back to Charlie Bird Parker, as well as in Catullus and Virgil, Dante and Chaucer, Keats and Whitman, Williams and Berryman and Lowell, could not then have occurred to me. In the beginning, I could only hear and register the percussive strokes of the snare and marching drum, or the tic-tic-tic of an engine's valves and pistons, both as sharp and as defined as all ethical and moral issues then seemed to me, as they seemed to repeat their anapestic and comforting imperatives of "thou shalt, thou shalt *not*."

That May I entered my second and last contest, this one held by the Marianists themselves for the best poem and the best short story about the Order's founder, Father Chaminade. This time, with the hubris of the as-yet-unbested, I entered both contests, writing nothing less than a poetic epic, again in fourteeners—the poem has mercifully disappeared forever—that focused on Fr. Chaminade's rooftop escape while the Girondist forces of revolutionary Paris sought to guillotine him; I then wrote an eleven-page biographical novella centering on the entire life of the founder. As it turned out, I was co-winner in both contests, which for me had the antiseptic feel of kissing one's grandmother. Worse still, I had to swallow the bitter aspic that competition even among the forty of us could be more formidable than I had been led to expect.

Reading over one's juvenilia, Stevens has written, can give one the creeps. Still, we have to begin somewhere, impelled forward as we are from nothing but a hope that turns out to be ninety-nine percent illusion. It is like trying to outline the aurora borealis as it flutters across the deep heavens on a summer's night. Angels cheer us from those vast heights, and at first we dream they are performing fiery cartwheels for every fresh copulative we add to noun. Or, if it is not angels we can see, then perhaps a cheerleader going through her paces on a field rampant of dun gold.

As we feel the loss of our bodies press upon us, we are sometimes compensated by old daydreams that seem to become fresher and more vivid even as they—and we—recede into the past. It may be merely a light, after all, that we end up following, a light continually riding across the chalkboard of the mind, on which are scrawled huge symbols in a language we cannot read. We look again, and the light is bouncing gaily now across a silvered screen on which the words of some old song have been written, as with those old sing-alongs we watched on holidays in the old study hall that long ago disappeared. It was a light by which we learned to stitch words together once—dah-dee-DUM dah-dee-DUM—until such time as we could teach ourselves to sing.

Excerpts from a Journal

10 July 1989

. . . Plot: the aesthetic approximation of gravity.

. . . What are our efforts of fiction and poetry but codified explorations (akin to those signals radio astronomers send out into space in the hope of receiving signals in return: proof of "intelligent life" elsewhere in the universe) of what it *is*, what it might *mean*, to exist as these individuals, these unique men and women standing here, at this time. As folklorists and anthropologists have concluded, despite the universality of their to-poi, folk tales/legends/ballads reflect the *mentalité* of a particular epoch. Thus are we all involved in a grand collective effort: familial: sometimes rivalrous. But collective.

. . . The necessary resistance to fixed forms. The challenge of regenerating "fixed" forms.

. . . Why is there a direction to Time? Is the structure we impose upon our lives, as on world history, even cosmological history, merely that— an imposition? Or is it coherently generated from within? And if so, *why* should this be so? Why for instance "chronology"—"causality"— "logic"?

. . . Time is the most mysterious element in which we live. We sense that for the writer of perfect miniatures no less than for the writer of large, complex, ambitious, imperfect novels, each effort of writing represents that codified metaphorical definition of the self-in-progress; the heart's measurement of a certain irretrievable chunk of Time.

. . . Art too as a counterworld to the "real" world. A strategy of retreat, appraisal, analysis, judgment. Which is why all art is political, despite the effort of some artists to deny the fact. But its "political" quality may simply be the fact of its obdurate existence: *I stand here,* the artist declares—*the State stands there.* In any case, art is not an escape from experience, still less from reality: it *is* experience, it *is* reality, in its own inviolable terms.

. . . The Swiss novelist and playwright Max Frisch tells the story of an ambassador's visit to the Hermitage in Leningrad: "He wanted to see the art known to be hidden in the Hermitage and not shown to the public. Works of the old Russian avant-garde. The museum functionary—a woman who is a connoisseur—showed him this and that. His last wish: *The Black Square* of Malevich. Why that? Because it exists, said the ambassador, and it's here, in the Hermitage. . . . And the two of them stood, thrilled, before Malevich. Why don't you go and hang it right next to the paintings of social realism in which the Soviet people recognize themselves at work for society, and people would see—Malevich is baloney! The woman listened. Seriously, though, said the ambassador, you don't have to hide Malevich in the cellar; nobody would look at it. The woman laughed: You're wrong, she said. People wouldn't understand the point of a black square, but they would see that something else exists beside the society and the state."

. . . *Something else exists beside the society and the state.*

. . . Emily Dickinson: "Dare you see a Soul *at the White Heat?*"

. . . For the Postmodernist writer of fiction and poetry the dilemma might be stated: how to be intelligently faithful to what we know of the world, of the universe, of the fluidity and unreliability of "fixed" forms; how to work around the seeming folly of the orderly text in which chronology is the measurement of plot—5 follows 4 follows 3 follows 2 follows 1 follows the convention of the "title." How to assimilate knowledge and instinct. Robert Frost's famous dismissal of what he perceived as anarchic free verse (playing tennis without a net: lovely homey image) revealed not so much the elder poet's blindness to newer experimental poetry as an instinctive conservatism: that to channel one's vision through seemingly fixed, even classical forms is in fact the supreme challenge.

. . . *Why write?* To read what I've written. *Why read what you've written?* Because, for all its possible flaws and omissions, no one else could have written it.

. . . All of us, writing now, are Postmodernists, whether voluntarily or in-.

You can't escape your era: can't pretend to not know what is known, what is in the very air. The curse of Postmodernism is this self-consciousness: this inability to not-know what is known. (The image of Magritte's canvas imposed upon a "natural" landscape scene: the artist *is* his canvas, the canvas is only the canvas, not the "natural" subject nor even its precise representation. The danger in the public's collective response: If your canvas is only your canvas, telling us solely about you, of what value is it?—why should we attend to it?)

23 July 1989

. . . The antagonism between the individual and the collective; between the Artist and the State. Simply, most succinctly put: *Something else exists.*

. . . In Washington, D.C., as I write this, an old debate is being energetically/politically rekindled: Should federal funds be used to support controversial ("indecent and offensive") works of art? Should taxpayers' money be used to support works of art many, if not most, citizens would find incomprehensible, if not frankly repulsive? All subtleties and ambiguities are flattened out, for this is the way of politics, the way of media-displayed passion. As with the related issue of abortion (should federal funds be used, etc., etc.) there is a dramatic polarization of energies; little room for subtlety, ambiguity, neutrality.

. . . Flaubert, 1852: "What seems beautiful to me, what I should like to write, is a book about nothing, a book dependent upon nothing external, which would be held together by the strength of its style. . . . From the standpoint of pure Art one might almost establish the axiom that there is no such thing as subject, style in itself being an absolute manner of seeing things."

. . . Yet the attraction of "subject": even of seemingly fixed forms: for there *is* after all natural movement, inevitable movement, causal movement, in even cosmological time. Energy certainly shifts from one plane to another; fundamentally conserved, it's said, throughout the (infinite?) universe, yet it transforms itself ceaselessly, there are numberless clocks ticking and all in one direction. Disequilibria: dying out here, emerging there. Dissolution of identity. Gravity. As my astrophysicist friend says, "Gravity can impose and maintain order (low entropy) in defiance of nature's tendency toward chaos (high entropy) only by compelling matter to fall toward some density concentration. . . . The initial explosion of space and time had just the proper vigor to fling matter so far apart that now the time required for it to collapse back to a point, its so-called free-fall time, exceeds the age of the universe." Thus that chronological trajectory of events we so glibly denote as "plot" is but the aesthetic approximation of gravity.

. . . In a letter, to me, just now, one of the three or four most famous and most honored writers of our time says, and not even modestly, "I can't take my 'literary estate' seriously when I'm still trying to learn to write."

24 July 1989

. . . So: why doesn't everything in the universe happen at once? Why is Time moving forward in a single implacable motion like an army of robots?

. . . Bereft these days of a piece of my heart. This queer "miniature novel" I'd been working on for what seemed to me far too long, and now it's finished, and I miss it terribly, the odd unrepeatable voice of it, its interior rhythms, the very alienness of the landscape (much of it in Detroit Metropolitan Hospital: a fictitious approximation of the real hospital), most of all the strange heroine, murderer/murdered, one of the "insulted and injured" . . . The idea of a miniature novel, not a novella, though of about the length of a novella (90–100 pp.), with brief chapters, pages smaller than the usual, cover smaller, and so forth: in every respect a real novel except its *size*. Where these notions come from, whimsical and unworkable, wholly uncommercial, I don't know.

. . . Hauntedness: about which writers don't seem to have written.

We work in the dark—we do what we can—we give what we have. Our doubt is our passion and our passion is our task. The rest is the madness of art.   (Henry James, "The Middle Years")

. . . The phenomenon of being haunted. Akin somehow to love; that is, loving; being "in love." What means most to us, what has lodged most deeply in us, must then be measured by the degree of loss (often surprising) we suffer afterward.

. . . Theory: the life-of-the-work-in-progress mimics or recapitulates or perhaps parodies the life-of-the-writer-in-progress. In an oblique/codified/unarticulated way. Thomas Mann: *Art strides on . . . through the medium of the personality.* But the personality too strides on, unfolds, evolves, or simply survives, through the medium of art.

. . . In John Updike's meticulously written *Self-Consciousness* Updike speaks of the random bits of words, music, images that sift through his consciousness; thus help to define it. For instance, the lyrics of an old popular song, "The Old Lamplighter," sung by Bing Crosby, filter through his head frequently. Why is it that we are so haunted by certain things, and not by others: why certain bars of music, and not by others?—why do we forget most works of art we see, yet retain, sometimes with mesmerizing eidetic force, certain others? . . . These riddles we carry about with us, wholly incapable of comprehension.

. . . The insomniac: the eclipsed self/the buried self/the wiser self: anticipating the future as if from a vantage point exterior to time; or, and this futilely, rethinking the past as if rehearsing it, wanting this second time to get everything right—the right syllable in the right place, the perfect punctuation.

. . . In Olive's, the other evening, discussing poetry with Dan and Jeannie Halpern. And I said how much I loved C. K. Williams's poetry because of its radiant madness; that glimmer of something fiery around the edges of the lines as if in the margins of the book; the man's willingness to do so much, crazily much, yes and to fail too, which many of our poet-friends draw back from. And Dan and Jeannie said that the madness is in the poetry, but confronted, assimilated. Whereas the poetry of [X] whose work I like too, though like less than Williams's, is virtually unchanging; uniform; the absolute denial of madness in the service of a spurious order, sanity. And it is the second poet who is neurotic, in his private life: a problematic drinker, often out of control.

. . . The insomniac, like a victim of a proprioceptive imbalance, experiencing the absence of a presence. Most absences are merely absent; but some manifest themselves as presences, the loss so deep it stuns. (Yet who would, or should, feel anything like pity, let alone sympathy, for the writer grieving for his/her completed work . . . of course not. These are not true losses as the world grants us losses!)

. . . The writers who are lacerated by their work are the writers who love it most. There is no contradiction here. (Though perhaps madness.)

. . . *Writing* the preliminary effort, *reading* the event. This is a discovery I believe comes belatedly. I mean—it is not a realization that a young writer is likely to have. (By young I suppose I mean those who plunge head-on, rarely rereading, impatient with even the immediate past— wasn't John Cheever said to be that way? or was, at least, when in fact young? And I too, certainly.) Yet it's a countryheaded truth, so simple it can be overlooked, that we *write*, with whatever varying degrees of effort or ease, dread or hope, resignation or expectation, in order to *read* that text which only we, and only at this time in our lives, can have written. The unique text, the inviolable text, the sacred text toward which all previous effort has drawn us.

. . . The moment of illumination, that one does not "own" one's imagination exactly. The soul *at the white heat*. Incandescence which alters the materiality of its very being. This is the point that must be reached, even as it seems problematic it *can* be reached. I was trying to explain to my friend Elaine Showalter who once wanted to write novels, did in fact write a novel while in her twenties, that the anxiety/excitement of writing was the attraction; that, if you begin writing at nine o'clock in the morning and are still writing, granted interruptions, at eleven o'clock in the evening, the "voice" will have undergone such transformations, taken you to such unexpected alien places of the soul, skidded you along the continuum of what you'd imagined your "plot," you might stand amazed, even humbled by the journey. That other sorts of activities, writerly activities too, of a discursive nature, certainly of a "critical" nature, simply cannot provide this experience. There is a plateau, and you walk upon it. In prose fiction and poetry you are plunged onward.

. . . Very difficult for a novelist to have "opinions." To see only one side of an issue and to stay with it. The world of the novel is always inhabited by aspects of the self that relate in dialectical ways, the movement of beings in time and in flux, a kaleidoscope of mirror-selves. Splinters, shards. All things persisting in their being: the exercise of will in contention with will. But the novelist contains them all, thus it's a mirror of the larger organic "real" world where we are obliged to see that even those who imagine themselves our enemies, distinctly not in love with us, have still their own truth; their truths; their angles of vision that are legitimate. To be politically effective one can't be subtly inclined. I mean, inclined to be subtle. Or ironic. (Irony: "glancing on both sides," as Thomas Mann said. Irony being that which is lost in translation/lost in any crowd/lost sometimes even on the printed page where you had supposed it would be obvious.) (As in my *New York Times* pieces on Gorbachev and Salman Rushdie.)

. . . Yet we have to grant to our enemies even their willful distortions of us, and of what we say. For these distortions probably contain a truth. As a funhouse mirror, distorting, always contains a painful truth.

... Practicing the piano, it's practicing the fingers. Tissue, muscle, bone. "Tissue-memory." Of course it's in the brain—it must be in the brain— yet when you play the piano, playing for instance a piece you have not so much as glanced at nor thought of in many years, the notes define themselves by an eerie unconscious *fingering* of the keys: a spatial move- ment not even related to the actual keys but to—well, space. So with writing: the sharpening of the sensibility that confronts the world and the world-of-language by way of practice. Fidelity to practice. Rehearsal/ revision/apprentice work/throwing away much in order to retain some.

... The almost greedy pleasure in destroying a manuscript: 600 pages: and this despite my archivist's/appraiser's insistence that this unpub- lished manuscript is "valuable." (It was a novel written in the 1970s. Bought by Henry Robbins at Dutton when I left Vanguard, so belatedly, for Dutton; scheduled to be published in 1980; but supplanted by a more ambitious novel, *Bellefleur*, and then supplanted by another ambitious novel, and another; until finally I asked for it to be returned. And reading through it the other day I came to the conclusion that I wanted it simply vanished from the face of the earth—the material too raw, unassimi- lated, yet the core of the story still "exciting" to me so that I might be seduced into rewriting it entirely, and I don't want to rewrite it, I refuse to rewrite it, revisiting that period in my life when I'd needed to write that particular novel because of a particular convulsion of the soul, but I am another person now and I want the record of it, simply, gone.) What is "valuable," I might have asked—can it be defined in terms of money?

25 July 1989

... The hauntedness of "The Rise of Life on Earth." Like the hauntedness of *You Must Remember This* and *Because It Is Bitter, and Because It Is My Heart.* The loss palpable as any presence.

... The writer/poet: excited by/thrown into a state of dread by the an- ticipation of: that eerie moment when consciousness is altered by an apprehension of structure. The final image for instance. The final words. Always I ask my novelist friends what is the first line of your new novel, and what is the last line, and a significant look flashes between us, yes this is what writing is about: the uncanniness of being overtaken by structure. Russell Banks's *Affliction* was originally to end, "—and he shot him." By *Because It Is Bitter, and Because It Is My Heart* was to end, " 'Do you think I will look the part?' " as a young white woman in a white wedding dress stands before a mirror. Russell had to push past his original idea of an ending because, arriving there, or in revising, he discovered it wasn't after all quite right: this happens to us most often. *But we need the false solace of an ending* as workers need scaffolding for high buildings. Usually, my posited endings recede before me like mirages on a hot asphalt road but, this time, I kept it: a ventriloquist's bemused query, here in Princeton, New Jersey, that is so dazzlingly far from the upstate New York of my early life: "Do you think I will look the part?"

. . . Masks do not merely, or exclusively, hide faces. They shape faces too.

. . . Why, for most writers, is the writing-self the supreme self? The social self—the familial self—the lover-self—the professorial self—even the journal-self: why undervalued? These numerous selves are not fictions, they may in fact be the heart's purest expression, but they seem to possess less value because not so finely and obsessively honed. We may not grant to "naturalness" a measure of respect because it is so effortless.

. . . A theory: some of our writing is in fact a dialogue with our (earlier) selves. Yes you once believed this but now you believe *this*. Sharon Olds explaining before reading a fastidiously written poem that years ago she would not have allowed herself to write so mandarin a poem for "political" reasons: now, she writes what she pleases.

. . . Norman Mailer remarking ruefully that he'd had the "sour" realization that nothing less than transforming the consciousness of his era would please him, as a writer. And so certainly he has failed—who could not fail?—given such outlandish premises? Perhaps Mailer really meant the transformation of his own consciousness, in which he has succeeded.

. . . Writing the screenplay, for Martin Scorsese, of *You Must Remember This*. Bemused by having to resist suggestions (not from Marty so much as from a studio executive) that the ending be given a distinctly male focus. (The chauvinism/sexism is absolutely unconscious. The "innocent" sort, amenable to discussion.)

. . . Donald Barthelme died only yesterday aged 58. A friend whom I had not seen in a few years but thought of frequently; having heard he'd had cancer, but not having heard that he was critically ill. Don was a very fine person; very friendly; more at ease, I'd thought, with Ray than with me, but not really uneasy with me (though I found it easier to talk with his lovely wife Marian than with Don: perhaps this was true of others?). Rereading some of Don's stories . . . prose-poems . . . "not to bore myself" Don said was his primary impetus for writing . . . the leap of language, images, turning clichés inside-out, the art of collage which he believed to be the technique of the twentieth century. Exquisite little stories, many of these prose pieces. (Another cancer death. So many. Where once death struck us as an aberration, a novelty, a rent in the fabric of plausibility, now it begins to seem, for my generation certainly, the tolling of a bell that is going to toll at regular intervals from now on until finally you cease hearing it which doesn't mean it ceases tolling only that you cease hearing it.)

. . . Richard Ford remarking over the telephone that he still missed Ray Carver so much. "Ray was able to make me laugh." Everyone misses Ray Carver, not excluding those who never knew him; or, like us, knew him only slightly. Like John Gardner, whom I knew perhaps to the same degree, if one could speak with confidence of "knowing" a man of such seething complexity, Ray Carver in his absence exudes a palpable absence-of-presence.

. . . These parallel lives. Our parallel lives. In an inch of history. Choral/communal/familial. Even the old rivalries, feuds—the arguments of kin. (Yet I remember one of the first things Don B. said to me. At lunch in a Cuban restaurant on Sixth Ave. near Don's and Marian's apartment. Nabokov had died a few days before, perhaps that very day. Don said, "That raises us all a notch higher," and I had to ask him what he meant, and he told me, and I was a bit shocked, yes in fact I was embarrassed and shocked, that he should think either of us, either *Barthelme* or *Oates* might be in such a position as to be enhanced by the death of magisterial *Nabokov*. But what I said, what words I'd managed to say, whether deflecting the remark with humor, or challenging it, whatever, I don't recall. And the other day seeing Don's obituary in the *Times* the first thing I thought of was Ray Carver's photograph and obituary some months ago in the same place; and the second thing I thought of was Nabokov, Don's remark about Nabokov.) (And how unfair, to Barthelme. After all. As if, to me, let alone to others, he had not said many things, and many of them generous/good/kindly/memorable.) ("Fragments are the only form I trust.")

26 July 1989

. . . What we love in those writers we love, and in those works of our own we love, or are still mesmerized by, is of course rarely content/subject matter but voice. Voice/rhythm/pulse/beat. The indefinable/unmistakable *beat*.

. . . (Being fingerprinted, the other evening. At the Hopewell Township Police Headquarters. And learning to our surprise that, in fact, fingerprints aren't permanent; they fade, in some people, especially people who handle paper a good deal—bank clerks most obviously, said the policeman. The sophistication of forensic science to the contrary, getting a "good" print from most surfaces is no easy task.) (And why were Ray and me fingerprinted by Hopewell police? What a good question.) (So the voice-beat/voice-print is less violable than the fingerprint so far as identity is concerned.)

. . . Not content/subject matter but *beat.* Think of Jean Toomer's *Cane.* Think of Faulkner from *The Sound and the Fury* onward. Think of Virginia Woolf not only in the formal prose fictions but in the diaries and letters. Think of Dickinson, of Whitman, of Philip Levine; of Wm. Carlos Williams, Adrienne Rich in much of her prose as well as her poetry, D. H. Lawrence in both poetry and prose (though not in his polemics). The very (comic) belaboredness of certain of the legalistic passages of Kafka, and of Borges, through which the irony glints like mica. (Though these are translations. Yet seemingly very fine translations.) What we love in our friends' voices is that *beat.* I would not say really that I can write about anything (still less, like Flaubert, that I can write about nothing) but it's true that subject matter interests me far less than the establishment of a voice; the phenomenon too that some subjects, and not others, have the curious power of generating a voice, a beat, a certain inevitable rhythm. A way of saying our imagination is not our own.

. . . (Why? How is this? The writer is sometimes overcome with the desire to memorialize certain subjects, settings. Certain people. Even as these are finite, are fading and dying, they are being established in the imagination. As if fastidiously engraved in stone. "With each death," says Wm. Carlos Williams, "dies a piece of the old world." *Thus* the impetus to write, to memorialize. This is not the sole impetus but it is perhaps the most powerful.) (Virtually faint with yearning, sometimes. An inchoate yearning. Memories of upstate New York, especially Lockport and the Erie Canal and the surrounding countryside where I grew up; the windy gritty streets and sulphurous air of Detroit, Michigan; isolated settings here and there in the United States, for wayward reasons. Not Princeton: to write of Princeton, as in fact I have done, I had to very nearly reinvent myself as a person who might write of Princeton. Whereas with these other settings, the need is to rein in the emotion, the "white heat." How to comprehend romance? (For surely this is the very pulse of romance: the writer mesmerized by the contents of his/her imagination.) Even the writer who appears to the world as icy-cold, inhospitable to romance, let alone sentiment, is of course romantic at heart; for all writers are romantic, idealizing their subject matter, hoping to memorialize their very voices.

. . . Yet the writing of prose would not interest me if it didn't move, or give the impression of moving, along a "realistic" continuum. How to create fictitious worlds of words that nonetheless give the impression of being "real": not merely style, or gesture: not mere Postmodernist display.

. . . *Is there a distinctive female voice?* the (woman) writer is asked repeatedly. And the answer is *No, there are as many distinctive female voices as there are female writers.*

. . . *Your writing departs from traditional feminist subjects,* the (woman) writer is asked repeatedly—*why is this?* And the answer is, *Since I am a feminist, whatever I write about is in fact a "traditional feminist subject."*

. . . Why the universe, why the biological world, should be so governed by rhythm, by pulsations, by beat: what a mystery. Thus the powerful appeal of poetry and music. These deep physiological impulses. It's said that despite enormous differences in size, not to mention styles of life, mammals live through about the same total numbers of breaths and heartbeats in their lifetimes: whether these lifetimes cover a period of weeks or years, many years. (With the exception of our species. The approximate two hundred million breaths/eight hundred million heartbeats allotted to mammals is *multiplied by three* for us. We can expect to live three times as long as a comparably sized mammal but why this is so, we can't expect to know.) The secret life of a soul in its/our sequential adventure in Time: a matter of (heart)beats.

. . . Creating language to communicate our visions to one another, we are engaged in creating rhythms that have to please us first, excite us sufficiently to grant us the strength for sustained periods of effort: these periods, as the veteran writer well knows, containing many days of frustration, disappointing work, lacunae that must nonetheless be traversed. To get *there* you must start from *here* since there is no other starting point but *here.* The beat/beat/beat of a private language that might mimic the prenatal beat of the mother; unnamed as Mother of course but commonly renamed as God (the Father). Thus Godhead/Logos/patriarchal language vis à vis the maternal, the wordless solace of flesh. But it is the maternality, if such a word exists, of the original language-

beat, that inspires us. Mesmerizes us. Pulsations preceding content. The famous anxiety of the writer, or do I mean the anxiety leavened by euphoria, is that, waking up tomorrow, we will have lost the *beat*; will have been expelled from it prematurely.

. . . For of course one day we must be expelled. Prematurely, or precisely on time.

27 July 1989

. . . Years ago, in August 1977, in the suburb of Birmingham, Michigan, in the lovely home of friends (the woman a writer-friend of mine, the man, since deceased, a high-ranking executive at Gulf & Western), there sat my parents in that splendidly furnished living room, my father Frederic making us all laugh by telling one of his droll farmer tales (he who worked for forty years at Harrison's Radiator in Lockport, New York, a city boy with no natural talent for country living though forced by economic necessity to live with his in-laws on their diminished farm), his funniest/saddest tale of that season he tried to raise pigs for meat, how the pigs burrowed under the fence one day; how the pigs ran squealing out onto Transit Road and were nearly struck by cars and trucks; how he had to chase after them and catch them one by one by hand—by tackling them in his arms; how after much effort, far too much effort to be described, he managed to get them all back in their pen, all six or seven of them, frantically struggling smelly creatures weighing about one hundred pounds each, how as he threw them back over the fence they landed heavily on their sides and the "earth shook" (for some reason this odd expression made us all laugh harder). And shortly after that my father killed the pigs, and slaughtered them, the first time in his life he'd attempted such a thing, and a horror it was, an unimaginable horror it was, and then he "cured" the meat with some sort of salt-gun injection; and hung up the meat in the barn; and the meat rotted. "Oh no," the company cries, "—oh *no*! After all that!" And it's so wildly funny, this horror in retrospect, aided of course by my father's understated manner, his handsome face expressing a look of profound and innocent bafflement as if, even now, he doesn't quite comprehend how he could have done such things, and is depending upon the present company of sympathetic listeners to help him which of course they do, we do (for I, Frederic's daughter, hearing this familiar story in more painful detail than I'd ever heard before, am part of the audience of listeners: if I remember pigs from my childhood, actual pigs, they have been supplanted now by these far more vivid creatures, these comic-malevolent creatures so graphically evoked by my father that they seem very nearly to exist in the Grahams' impeccable living room): is this part of the point of the story? That, in 1977, we might help Frederic Oates who is sixty-three years old understand the Frederic Oates who was once so much younger, so much less in control of his life? I know of course that the episode of forty years before was not amusing in the slightest. When it happened, it made no one laugh. My father was trying to raise pigs to supplement his income just as he tried other things, other country things, or city jobs (like commercial sign painting, for which he had a good deal more aptitude), he tried what he could because we were poor; not desperately poor but, yes, poor; for only a man beset by money worries tries such things, a fact one must gloss over in the Grahams' living room in Birmingham, Michigan, on this perfect summer day. It was not an experience intended to be recounted as an anecdote, raising the pigs/chasing the pigs/slaughtering the pigs/discovering one day that their meat had rotted, it was a kind of domestic tragedy; a profound humiliation—for Frederic Oates must have known himself, for all his farmer's ineptitude, superior to such endeavors. But now the domestic tragedy is long since dissolved, just as the old farmhouse and the old barns are gone; the humiliation is forgotten as if it had never been; my father tells this story as effectively as anyone might have told it, and we are all laughing, and we are all sympathetic, and I sat there for some minutes struck to silence, seeing how, for us, for the Oates family, yes but for all of us, what is Past is retrieved only by way of language selected for a specific purpose; the Past is in fact the consequence of a sequence of Presents palimpsestically overlaid upon it; and that by degrees erased, abandoned, as reality yields gratefully to myth, as serrated edges are blurred to smoothness, raw experience to family legend. And now that my parents' lives—and mine—have so changed, have been so transformed as if by magic, perhaps we are ready to surrender the past to anecdote, past griefs to present laughter, I sat thinking these things, disturbed, yet not seriously, for in such affable gregarious social situations one can't be seriously disturbed by much, and it was impressed upon me how, if you survive, everything in time becomes a narrative, an artful structure of words, words that do your bidding, a way of proclaiming not *This happened to me* but, in triumph, *I did this*. If you survive.

The Magic Show

As a kid, through grade school and into high school, my hobby was magic. I enjoyed the power; I liked making miracles happen. In the basement, where I practiced in front of a stand-up mirror, I caused my mother's silk scarves to change color. I used a scissors to cut my father's best tie in half, displaying the pieces, and then restored it whole. I placed a penny in the palm of my hand, made my hand into a fist, made the penny into a white mouse. This was not true magic. It was trickery. But I sometimes pretended otherwise, because I was a kid then, and because pretending was the thrill of magic, and because for a time what seemed to happen became a happening in itself. I was a dreamer. I liked watching my hands in the mirror, imagining how someday I might perform much grander magic, tigers becoming giraffes, beautiful girls levitating like angels in the high yellow spotlights, naked maybe, no wires or strings, just floating.

It was illusion, of course—the creation of a new and improved reality. What I enjoyed about this peculiar hobby, at least in part, was the craft of it: learning the techniques of magic and then practicing those techniques, alone in the basement, for many hours and days. That was another thing about magic. I liked the aloneness, as God and other miracle makers must also like it—not lonely, just alone. I liked shaping the universe around me. I liked the power. I liked the tension and suspense when, for example, the magician displays a guillotine to the audience, demonstrating its cutting power by slicing a carrot in half; the edgy delight when a member of the audience is asked to place his hand in the guillotine hole; the hollow silence when, very slowly, the magician raises up the blade. Believe me, *there* is drama. And when the blade slams down, if it's *your* hand in the hole, you have no choice but to believe in miracles.

When practiced well, however, magic goes beyond a mere sequence of illusions. It becomes art. In the art of magic, as opposed to just doing tricks, there is a sense of theater and drama and continuity and beauty and wholeness. Take an example. Someone in the audience randomly selects a card from a shuffled deck—the Ace of Diamonds. The card is made to vanish, then a rabbit is pulled out of a hat, and the hat collapses into a fan, and the magician uses the fan to fan the rabbit, and the rabbit is transformed into a white dove, and the dove flies into the spotlights and returns a moment later with a playing card in its beak—the Ace of Diamonds. With such unity and flow, with each element contributing as both cause and effect, individual tricks are blended into something whole and unified, something indivisible, which is in the nature of true art.

Beyond anything, though, what appealed to me about this hobby was the abiding mystery at its heart. Mystery everywhere—permeating mystery—even in the most ordinary objects of the world: a penny becomes a white mouse. The universe seemed both infinite and inexplicable. Anything was possible. The old rules were no longer binding, the old truths no longer true. If my father's tie could be restored whole, why not someday use my wand to wake up the dead?

It's pretty clear, I suppose, where all this is headed. I stopped doing magic—at least of that sort. I took up a new hobby, writing stories. But without straining too much, I can suggest that the fundamentals seemed very much the same. Writing fiction is a solitary endeavor. You shape your own universe. You practice all the time, then practice some more. You pay attention to craft. You aim for tension and suspense, a sense of drama, displaying in concrete terms the actions and reactions of human beings contesting problems of the heart. You try to make art. You strive for wholeness, seeking continuity and flow, each element performing both as cause and effect, always hoping to create, or to re-create, the great illusions of life.

Above all, writing fiction involves a desire to enter the mystery of things: that human craving to know what cannot be known. In the ordinary world, for instance, we have no direct access to the thoughts of other human beings—we cannot *hear* those thoughts—yet even in the most "realistic" piece of fiction we listen as if through a stethoscope to the innermost musings of Anna Karenina and Lord Jim and Huck Finn. We know, in these stories, what cannot be known. It's a trick, of course. (And the tricks in these stories have been elevated into art.) In the ordinary sense, there *is* no Huck Finn, and yet in the extraordinary sense, which is the sense of magic, there most certainly *is* a Huck Finn and always will be. When writing or reading a work of fiction, we are seeking access to a kind of enigmatic "otherness"—other people and places, other worlds, other sciences, other souls. We give ourselves over to what is by nature mysterious, imagining the unknowable, and then miraculously knowing by virtue of what is imagined. There are new standards of knowing, new standards of reality. (Is Huck Finn real? No, we would say, by ordinary standards. Yes, by extraordinary standards.) For a writer, and for a reader, the process of imaginative knowing does not depend upon the scientific method. Fictional characters are not constructed of flesh and blood, but rather of words, and those words serve as explicit incantations that invite us into and guide us through the universe of the imagination. Language is the apparatus—the magic dust—by which a writer performs his miracles. Words are uttered: "By and by," Huck says, and we hear him. Words are uttered: "We went tip-toeing along a path amongst the trees," and we see it. Beyond anything, I think, a writer is someone entranced by the power of language to create a magic show of the imagination, to make the dead sit up and talk, to shine light into the darkness of the great human mysteries.

In many cultures, including our own, the magician and the storyteller are often embodied in a single person. This seems most obvious, I suppose, in religion, which seeks to penetrate into the greatest mysteries of all. The healer, or the miracle worker, is also the teller of stories about prior miracles, or about miracles still to come. In Christianity, the personage of Jesus is presented as a doer of both earthly miracles and the ultimate heavenly miracle of salvation. At the same time Jesus is a teller of miraculous stories—the parables, for instance, or the larger story about damnation and redemption. The performance of miracles and the telling of stories become part of a whole. One aspect serves the other. In the culture of the North American Kiowa tribes, the shaman or witch doctor was believed to have access to an unseen world, a world of demons and gods and ancestral spirits, and these spirits were invoked in rites of healing and exorcism and divine intervention. But the shaman also told stories *about* those spirits: their wars, their loves, their treacheries, their defeats, their victories. The shaman's earthly claims upon his people were at once validated and legitimized by heavenly stories.

My point, of course, has to do with the interpenetration of magic and stories. In part, at least, storytelling involves the conjuring up of spirits—Huck Finn or Lord Jim. And those spirits, in turn, make implicit moral claims on us, serving as models of a sort, suggesting by implication how we might or might not lead our own lives. Stories encourage and discourage. Stories affirm and negate. In the tales of the Kiowa shaman, as in those of the modern New York novelist, spirits of virtue struggle against spirits of evil, heroes go up against villains, antiheroes confront antivillains, and in the course of the narrative a spirit's spirit is both defined and refined in moral terms. But these terms are not absolute. Stories are rooted in particulars—this village, this time, this character— and it strikes me that storytelling represents one form of what we now call situational ethics. The spirits in a story cast moral shadow and moral light. By example, through drama, stories display our own potential for good and evil: the range of moral possibility is extended.

There is also, I think, an incorporeal but nonetheless genuine "aliveness" to the characters, or ghosts, that are conjured up by good stories. In *The Sun Also Rises*, Jake Barnes and Brett Ashley and Bill Gorton and Mike Campbell are identities—spirits of a sort—that live between the covers of that book. They are not embodied, of course, and never were. They have no flesh and never did. Yet these characters live in the way spirits live, in the memory and imagination of the reader, as a dead father lives in the memory of his son or in the imagination of his daughter. The storyteller evokes, and invokes, this spirit world not with potions or pixie dust, but, as I suggested earlier, with the magic of language—those potent nouns, those levitating verbs, those tricky little adverbs, those amazing conjunctions, the whole spectacular show of clauses becoming sentences and sentences becoming paragraphs and paragraphs becoming stories. The Kiowa shaman achieves a similar effect by inducing in his tribe a trancelike state, summoning a collective dream with the language of incantation and narrative drama. The writer of fiction, like the shaman, serves as a medium of sorts between two different worlds—the world of ordinary reality and the extraordinary world of the imagination. In this capacity, the writer often enters a trancelike state of his own. Certainly this is my own experience. When I am writing well, invoking well, there is a dreamlike sense of gazing through the page as if it were the thinnest onionskin parchment, watching the spirits beyond, quietly looking on as the various characters go about their peculiar business. This is the sensation I get—both physical and emotional—as a waking dream unfolds into words and as the words unfold into a piece of fiction. Half in the embodied world, half in a world where bodies are superfluous. I realize, as this semitrance occurs, that the page before me is only paper, the typescript only ink, and yet there is also a powerful awareness of those ghostly characters in motion just behind the page, just beyond the boundaries of the mundane. Whatever we call this process—imagination, fantasy, self-hypnosis, creativity—I know from my own life that it is both magical and real. And I think other writers of fiction would offer similar testimony. In any case, to complete the parallel with which I began, it is reported that the Kiowa shaman, too, enters the trance of his own dream, partly as a way of inducing that dream in his tribe, partly to serve as a guide into and through the other, fictional world. The more I write and the more I dream, the more I accept this notion of the writer as a medium between two planes of being—the ordinary and the extraordinary—the embodied world of flesh, the disembodied world of idea and morality and spirit.

In this sense, then, I must also believe that writing is essentially an act of faith. Faith in the heuristic power of the imagination. Faith in the fertility of dream. Faith that as writers we might discover that which cannot be known through empirical means. (The notions of right and wrong, for instance. Good and evil. Ugliness and beauty.) Faith in story itself. Faith that a story will lead, in some way, to epiphany or understanding or enlightenment. In the most practical sense, just to *begin* a story involves a great leap of faith that the first imagined event will somehow lead to the next, that chapter two will somehow follow upon chapter one. Faith that language will continue to serve us from day to day. Faith that a story will take us somewhere—in the plot sense, in the thematic sense—and that the destination will be worth the journey. And just as faith seems essential to me as a writer, and maybe to all of us, it seems also true that crises of faith are common to the vocation of the storyteller: writer's block, lapses of confidence, the terror of aesthetic subjectivity as the final arbiter of excellence. For all of us, I would guess, there is, at least on occasion, a terrible sense of howling in the dark. I would suppose that many of us have experienced more than one crisis of faith—in our talents, in our lives—and yet because we are still at work, still writing, I would also suppose that we have at some point undergone a renewal of that faith.

So far I've been discussing, in a less than systematic way, a set of "mysteries" inherent in the *process* of writing fiction. But it seems to me that the fiction itself—the story, the novel—must ultimately represent and explore those same mysteries. Or to say it bluntly: it is my view that good storytelling involves, in a substantive sense, a plunge into mystery of the grandest order. Briefly, almost in summary form, I want to examine this notion through two different windows of craft—plot and character.

It is my belief that plot revolves around certain mysteries of fact, or what a story represents as fact. What happened? What will happen? Huck and Jim hop on a raft (fact) and embark on a journey (fact) and numerous events occur along the way (facts). On the level of plot, this narrative appeals to our curiosity about where the various facts will lead. As readers, we wonder and worry about what may befall these two human beings as they float down a river in violation of the ordinary social conventions. We are curious about facts still to come. In this sense, plot involves the inherent and riveting mystery of the *future*. What next? What are the coming facts? By its very nature, the future compels and intrigues us—it holds promise, it holds terror—and plot relies for its power on the essential cloudiness of things to come. We don't know. We want to know.

In a magic act, as in a story, there is the reporting (or purporting) of certain facts. The guillotine *is* sharp, it *does* cut the carrot, the man's hand *does* enter the guillotine's hole, the blade *does* slam down. For an audience, the mystery has entirely to do with future facts. What will become of this poor man? Will he lose his hand? Will he weep? Will the stump bleed as stumps tend to do?

Without some concept of the future, these questions would be both impossible and irrelevant. It is the mystery of the future, at least in part, that compels us to turn the pages of a novel, or of a story, or of our own lives. Unlike the animals, we conceive of tomorrow. And tomorrow fascinates us. Tomorrow matters—maybe too much—and we spend a great portion of our lives adjusting the present in hope of shaping the future. In any case, we are driven to care and to be curious about questions of fate and destiny: we can't help it, we're human.

On one level, then, I am arguing in defense of old-fashioned plot—or in defense of plot in general—which is so often discredited as a sop to some unsophisticated and base human instinct. But I see nothing base in the question, "What will happen next?" I'm suggesting that plot is grounded in a high—even noble—human craving to *know*, a craving to push into the mystery of tomorrow.

This is not to argue, however, that plot need give an impression of finality. A good plot does not tie up the loose ends of the future in a tidy little knot. The plot of my own life has not often, so far as I can tell, resolved itself in any neat and final way. Death itself, when it comes, dissolves into enigma. Maybe this, maybe that. But who knows? Who really *knows*? The plot mystery of life—what will happen to us, to all of us, to the human race—is unresolved and must remain that way if it is to endure as a compelling story. As a species, I believe, we are beguiled by uncertainty. It is both a gift and a burden. We crave knowledge, yes, but we also crave its absence, for the absence alone makes possible the joy of discovery. Once the factual curtain falls—for instance, if we were to know beyond doubt that Lee Harvey Oswald acted on his own to assassinate President Kennedy—that ticklish sense of uncertainty vanishes and the puzzle no longer puzzles and the story is both finished and boring. Nothing remains to ignite curiosity. Nothing beckons, nothing tantalizes. As Edmund Wilson suggests in his famous comment, "Who cares who killed Cock Robin," there is something both false and trivial about a story that arrives at absolute closure. With closure, the facts of today have no bearing on the facts of tomorrow. (It seems ironic that most so-called mystery stories conclude with no mystery whatsoever. The killer's methods and motives are exposed. Ah, we think, no *wonder*. All is explicable, all is settled. The case is closed.) A satisfying plot, I believe, involves not a diminution of mystery but rather a fundamental enlargement. As in scientific endeavor, the solution to one set of problems must open out into another and even greater set. The future must still matter. The unknown must still issue its call. One tomorrow must imply the next.

About real people, we sometimes say: "Well, she's a mystery to me," or "I wonder what makes him tick." Such comments represent, I think, a deep and specific desire for the miraculous: to enter another human soul, to read other minds and hearts, to find access to what is by nature inaccessible. A person lives in his own skin. All else is other, and otherness is suspect. If we see a man laugh, for instance, we might guess that he is experiencing elation or giddiness or joy of some sort. But perhaps not. Maybe it's ironic laughter, or nervous laughter, or the laughter of the insane. Again, who knows? In a story called *The Lady With the Pet Dog*, Chekhov has one of his characters muse as follows: "Judging others by himself, he did not believe what he saw, and always fancied that every man led his real, most interesting life under cover of secrecy as under cover of night." It is easy to sympathize with this view. Like Chekhov's character, we can "judge others by ourselves," but we cannot directly experience their loves and pains and joys. We know our own thoughts—we know by the act of thinking—but we cannot think those "other" thoughts. The mystery of otherness seems permanent and binding, a law of the universe, and yet *because* it is a mystery, *because* it binds, we find ourselves clawing at the darkness of human nature in an effort to know what cannot be known. "I love you," someone says, and we begin to wonder. "Well, how much?" we say, and when the answer comes, "With my whole heart," we then wonder about the wholeness of that heart. We probe and probe again. Along with Chekhov, we fancy that there is some secret lodged inside a human personality, hidden as if under cover of night, and that if light could be cast into the darkness of another's heart, we would find there the "real" human being. Such curiosity seems to me both inevitable and misdirected. Judging from what I know of myself, the human "character," if there is such a thing, seems far too complex and fluid and contradictory ever to pin down with much solidity or specificity. To really know a human character, to expose a single "secret," strikes me as beyond reach. In a sense, we "know" human character—maybe even our own—in the same way we know black holes: by their effects on the external world. The source of the light is sucked up by the nature of nature.

My focus here is on the construction of literary character, and my general argument is that characterization is achieved not through a "pinning down" process but rather through a process that opens up and releases mysteries of the human spirit. The object is not to "solve" a character—to expose some hidden secret—but instead to deepen and enlarge the riddle itself. Too often, I believe, characterization fails precisely *because* it attempts to characterize. It narrows; it pins down; it explicates; it solves. The nasty miser is actually quite sweet and generous. The harlot has a heart of gold. The gunfighter is a peaceable guy who yearns to own a small cattle ranch. The failure here is twofold. For me, at least, such solutions do not square with my sense of the immense complexity of man's spirit. The human life seems cheapened. Beyond that, however, this sort of characterization has the effect of diminishing the very mystery that makes us care so passionately about other human beings. There is false and arbitrary closure. A "solved" character ceases to be mysterious, hence becomes less than human. As with plot, I believe that successful characterization requires an enhancement of mystery: not shrinkage, but expansion. To beguile, to bewitch, to cause lasting wonder—these are the aims of characterization. Think of Kurtz in *Heart of Darkness*. He has witnessed profound savagery, has immersed himself in it, and as he lies dying, we hear him whisper, "The horror, the horror." There is no solution here. Rather, the reverse. The heart *is* dark. We gape into the tangle of this man's soul, which has the quality of a huge black hole, ever widening, ever mysterious, its gravity sucking us back into the book itself. What intrigues us, ultimately, is not what we know but what we do not know and yearn to discover.

The magician's credo is this: don't give away your secrets. Once a trick is explained—once a secret is divulged—the world moves from the magical to the mechanical. Similarly, with plot and character, the depletion of mystery robs a story of the very quality that brings us to pursue fiction in the first place. We might admire the cleverness of the writer. But we forget the story. Because there is no miracle to remember. The object of storytelling, like the object of magic, is not to explain or to resolve, but rather to create and to perform miracles of the imagination. To extend the boundaries of the mysterious. To push into the unknown in pursuit of still other unknowns. To reach into one's own heart, down into that place where the stories are, bringing up the mystery of oneself.

On Wording

I. On Wording

No matter how sorrowful the subject matter of one's story or poem, no matter how grim one's vision of human existence, every serious artist brings to his or her creation a similar kind of loving care for detail and form. In this sense all true art is life enhancing, for it affirms the virtues of precision and the goodness of design. If nihilists give themselves over to the absence of purpose and order, artists commit themselves to the structuring of chaos and the filling of the existential *void*.

The love of verbal order, which Yeats describes as "speech wrought of high laughter, loveliness and ease," is at the heart of each artist's motivation to create, and it demands that one's craft be taken as seriously as one's chosen subject. Thus every poem also celebrates itself by demonstrating the power of the human mind to create design, adding to nature where nature is seen as barren of human purpose. When we, as readers, peruse a poem, we regard it as a presence and as an event, as well as consider its meaning. This is what Williams asserts when he says: "A poem which does not arouse respect for the technical requirements of its own mechanics . . . will be as empty as a man made of wax or straw . . . technique means everything. . . . The importance lies in what the poem is. Its existence as a poem is of first importance, a technical matter."

Yeats warns, "The greatest temptation of the artist is creation without toil," and Blake insists, "Invention depends altogether upon execution or organization; as that is right or wrong, so is the invention perfect or imperfect. Whoever is set to undermine the execution of art is set to destroy art."

In a 1945 letter to a friend, Dylan Thomas wrote: "It is only the texture of a poem that can be discussed at all. Nobody wants to talk about how a poem *feels* to him: he finds it emotionally moving or he doesn't: and, if he does, there's nothing to discuss except the means, the words themselves, by which this emotional feeling was aroused." In the same sense, an experienced writer cannot instruct a beginner in how to be imaginative or how to become inspired. The writer can, however, exhort the beginner to be deliberate in the choice of words, in the conviction that without the right wording, without the appropriate rhythms, without design, an essential aspect of what one feels does not get communicated. It is as if Shakespeare, having written "This thou perceiv'st, which makes thy love more strong, / To love that well which thou must leave ere long," might have expressed what he felt by saying: "You can see that what makes your love stronger is that you must leave life pretty soon." For the artist, the choice of words is not a matter of mere ornament; it is a matter of conveying the *feeling* of what one thinks.

In his poem, "Adam's Curse," Yeats compares the difficulty of writing a poem with the difficulty of making oneself into a humanely beautiful person. The poem's central idea is that art cannot be created without labor and that spontaneity, paradoxically, is something that must be achieved, through discipline, as the effect of the completed poem. Both in art and in love, Yeats claims, the experience of grace comes, not first, but last. In Adam's fallen world only labor and control can liberate instinct. Such is the condition and burden of our inheritance from Adam. Yeats's poem begins:

> We sat together at one summer's end,
> That beautiful mild woman, your close friend,
> And you and I, and talked of poetry.
> I said: "A line will take us hours maybe;
> Yet if it does not seem a moment's thought,
> Our stitching and unstitching has been naught.

Yeats's poem ends convincingly because it creates the *illusion* that its words have flowed naturally and inevitably from the poem's innermost emotion of weariness: Yeats's pessimism about winning the love of Maud Gonne, the woman he addresses. The poem is successful in contriving to express—and thus to relieve—an immediate feeling of emotional failure—a failure redeemed through the very act of its deliberate and organized articulation.

II. On Sincerity and Skill

In his essay "Politics and the English Language," George Orwell states that "the great enemy of clear language is insincerity." There are, I believe, two kinds of insincerity: the insincerity of the scoundrel whose intent is to deceive and manipulate, for whom language is powerful precisely because it can conceal the truth; and the variant of insincerity into which we all slip from time to time, that, while not exactly intentional, is partly unconscious. We might call the latter the insincerity of failed self-knowledge; it comes from laziness or lack of courage. Auden portrays this kind of insincerity deftly in his parody of the social worker who exclaims: "We are all here on earth to help others; what on earth others are here for I don't know." Montaigne says: "If falsehood, like truth, had only one face, we would be in better shape. For we would take as certain the opposite of what the liar said. But the reverse of truth has a thousand shapes and a limitless field. . . . We are men, and hold together only by our word."

Good writers need good readers, and good readers must be good listeners. Caring listeners must be as sensitive to rhythm and voice tone as they are to image and to meaning. Robert Frost declared in a letter to E. A. Robinson: "Good writing is good speaking caught alive. The speaking tones are all there on the printed page."

Whatever claims we might conjecture or dispute for the political or moral effects of literature upon society, we would agree, I assume, that literature must perform the essential cultural function of keeping the language "alive," rescuing it from abstractions that are devoid of image or feeling. Orwell goes on to say that "in our time, political speech and writing are largely the defense of the indefensible," yet Orwell's modest political optimism was rooted in his further statement that "the present political chaos is connected with the decay of language; and one can probably bring about some improvement by starting at the verbal end." Language is most effective *and* truthful when it refers concretely to the physical world of common experience and when it evokes a human voice whose intonation conveys the nuances of emotion.

The poet James Wright told the story of a candidate for mayor who promised his potential voters that under his administration the city would rise to "new platitudes of achievement." Wright's remark in response to this political promise was that he could almost hear the language crying out: "Save me! Save me!" We must continue to try to listen to each other and to learn to use words precisely, so that heartfelt and imaginative writing, free of sloppiness and quackery, will not become merely an oddity of our civilization like the duck-billed platitude.

As writers and readers we share a love for language, for how words sound, for the rhythms they can dance out, for the patterns they can be made to form; but we also share the unending responsibility for guarding language so that it remains accurate as a means by which human truths may be sought and expressed in order that we can hold together. If the enemy of honest language is insincerity and if even the writer of the most firm integrity can lie a little, out of the human weakness that desires attention or influence, then it follows that we need each other not just as audience, but as critics, helping each other to know ourselves better.

Commenting on Shelley's claim that poets are the "unacknowledged legislators of the world," Auden says that the "unacknowledged legislators of the world" describe more appropriately not the poets, but the secret police. He is right. There are limits to what artists can do through their art to improve the human condition. Were this not so, Shakespeare surely would have cured us many griefs ago. Perhaps the beginning of artistic integrity is simply humility: a poem is, first and last, merely a poem. As Yeats admits; "We do not have the gift to set a statesman right." I do not think I am being pessimistic in suggesting that all that literary art can do is help keep our language fresh, heartfelt, and honest, and rescue discourse from excessive abstraction and propaganda. Human history, as I imagine its mythic origin, begins with the serpent's lie to Eve in the Garden of Eden. The fork-tongued devil—the principle of deception for the sake of power and self-deception for the sake of pride— still contends for the ownership of the world. We need each other's support in the endeavor to tell a further truth than the comfortable indignations that confirm our own self-righteousness. Telling the complex truth requires skill as well as sincerity. Or perhaps, I might say, it requires the patience to develop skill as a necessary aspect of sincerity.

Theodore Roethke describes himself as a "perpetual beginner." And Yeats, in the last year of his life, wrote to Dorothy Wellesley: "I am beginning to learn how to write." The talent to learn how to write honestly and well demands the patience to accept limited success and to endure failure. In a hundred years, most current writers are likely to be forgotten. What keeps us trying against the odds must be our belief in the power of language: the value of verbal design can add to the world it describes. William Carlos Williams asserts his poetic commitment to the creating of design: "The birds twitter now anew, but a design / surmounts their twittering. / It is a design of man / that makes them twitter. It is a design." If such lasting design—design that both enhances and surmounts nature—is difficult to achieve, at least we may choose to feel with Robert Frost that "what is worth succeeding in, is worth failing in." Our best hope, of course, is that our sincere failures will be instructive, that we will grow in skill by acknowledging and understanding them.

III. On Experience

For every literary artist the impulse to write derives, at least in part, from something rooted in his or her own experience. Some element of that originating impulse will become manifest in the work of art, though it may be transformed significantly in the process of creation and revision. And yet the activity of creation must include its own emotion, independent of the artist's initiating subject. Every true poem contains and expresses the delight of its own creation, thus possessing what Wallace Stevens calls the "gaiety of language."

Because of this aspect of the poem, in which the poem celebrates itself as a model of the human power of artistic creation, the effect of the poem differs radically from the emotion that the poem is about. No matter how sorrowful their subjects, all good poems bring pleasure. A bad poem about a beautiful landscape leaves an impression of ugliness. No poetic attempt can be redeemed by the poem's worthy subject or the poet's sincerity. Because poems often are complex, they may puzzle us at first and reveal their emotional force upon contemplation. Gutsy emotions may be evoked by a poem, but no poem is written directly from the gut. A poet does not write about death at his father's funeral, nor about desire when aroused to make love. A human statement may be directly and deeply moving, but we do not value it as a poem, no matter how affected we are, unless it has the passion of poetic design as well as the passion appropriate to its own chosen subject. Ultimately, we love poems for being poems, though we demand that they be serious and intelligent in the way they bear witness to human emotion and behavior.

An entry in Yeats's diary of September 1909, preparatory to his writing the poem, "The Fascination of What's Difficult," reads as follows:

Subject: To complain of the fascination of what's difficult. It spoils spontaneity, and pleasure, and wastes time. Repeat the line ending difficult three times and rhyme on bolt, exalt, colt, jolt. One could use the thought that the winged and unbroken colt must drag a cart of stones out of pride because it is difficult, and end by denouncing drama, accounts, public contests and all that's merely difficult.

This passage is revealing in its self-consciousness; it is hardly language conveying the immediacy of experience or even conviction of belief. Although it does allude to the experience of getting his plays produced, Yeats needed to relive that experience in the imaginative process of writing his poem before the completed poem could convey his feelings of anger, before he could find in the poem itself a voice with the energy to utter a real curse:

> The fascination of what's difficult
> Has dried the sap out of my veins, and rent
> Spontaneous joy and natural content
> Out of my heart. There's something ails our colt
> That must, as if it had not holy blood
> Nor on Olympus leaped from cloud to cloud,
> Shiver under the lash, strain, sweat and jolt
> As though it dragged road-metal. My curse on plays
> That have to be set up in fifty ways,
> On the day's war with every knave and dolt,
> Theater business, management of men.
> I swear before the dawn comes round again
> I'll find the stable and pull out the bolt.

Yeats's "curse on plays / That have to be set up in fifty ways" indeed expresses his frustration; yet poetic inspiration, symbolized by the horse, Pegasus, has been liberated into flight within the poem's formal design.

There is a story about Pablo Picasso, perhaps apocryphal yet, like a parable, convincing in conveying a danger inherent in the artistic process. An art dealer owned three paintings attributed to Picasso, but he was only sure that one of them had been painted by Picasso. And so he arranged a test by inviting Picasso to his gallery to assign dates to the paintings. "That's a fake," said Picasso when shown the first painting. "That too is a fake," Picasso said when shown the second; again with the third Picasso asserted, "That also is a fake." The puzzled art dealer stated that he knew for certain that the third painting had indeed been painted by Picasso himself. "Let me assure you," Picasso replied, "that I can paint a fake Picasso as well as anyone." Imitating one's own success may be the most subtle form of artistic fakery. The experience of writing, no matter what one's poem or story is about, always must include the experience of venturing anew into the fresh possibilities of verbal design, the gaiety of language, even in the face of the most profound sorrow.

IV. On Prowess and Revision

Form both controls and releases energy in literary art and in sports. Frost is right, I believe, in arguing that these talents—what he calls "prowess"—are alike whether one is disciplining the mind or the body.

Frost describes prowess as the "ability to perform with success in games, in the arts and in battle." Sometimes, possessed no doubt by the Muse of Poetry, athletes, not usually eloquent, burst into metaphor. I offer two favorite examples: when asked what it was like to face the great hitter, Rod Carew, one pitcher replied, "Trying to get a fast ball past Rod Carew is like trying to sneak the sunrise past a rooster"; when a running back was asked what it was like to be tackled by the crushing linebacker, Dick Butkus, he replied: "Butkus is an accident looking for a place to happen." The theme is always energy and its marvelous transforming power. Blake tells us that "Energy is eternal delight."

All sport lovers know that the poet laureate of baseball is Yogi Berra, for the ordinary laws of linguistic logic never have been able to inhibit Yogi—as when he proclaimed, transforming what was once a cliché, that "90 percent of the game of baseball is one-half mental." And when manager Casey Stengel instructed Yogi to swing only at balls within the strike zone, after which advice Yogi fanned on three straight pitches, he complained: "Casey, I can't think and hit at the same time." The literary translation of that remark might be found in one experienced writer's reply to a novice: "Yes, I do think about craft much of the time—except when I'm writing." One may begin with literary potential, but real "prowess" comes through achieved control: discipline is needed to release power and give energy its focus in performance.

There is a cartoon in which Patrick Henry, having just declared "Give me liberty or give me death!" is sentenced by the judge to be shot. As two sergeants are about to lead him from the courtroom, Henry turns to the judge and says, "Your Honor, let me try rephrasing that." This cartoon, of course, is a parable of the writer's special prerogative—his or her liberty to revise a poem even at the last minute. In this respect the consequences of actual life most differ from the consequences of writing. We are not free to revise historical events. The closest we come in life to the artist's ability to revise is through the power to forgive and to ask for forgiveness. In "Asphodel that Grey Flower," William Carlos Williams says: "What power has love but forgiveness? In other words / by its intervention / what has been done / can be undone." The artist's freedom to revise, to begin again, to try to do better, is a kind of grace—the special privilege of the life of the imagination.

Revision means learning through the acknowledgment of limitation and failure. Creation in its largest sense, then, must be thought of as a process of creation, destruction, and re-creation. In this process we may become aware of powers we did not know we possessed. In a practical sense—since the human mind is agile in its capacity for rationalization—whenever a friendly critic says to us, "That poem can be improved; its language can be more precise, more visual, more musical; its structure can be more dramatic, more expressive," he can help us overcome the powerful wish to have completed the poem. The critic, or his interiorized admonishing voice, can help us find the strength to destroy what has been only partially realized, and to begin again. Such self-discipline, incorporating the critical and revising intelligence into a larger creative enterprise, is expressed in Picasso's advice to a young painter:

When you begin a picture, you often make some pretty discoveries. You must be on guard against these. Destroy the thing, do it over several times. In each destroying of a beautiful discovery, the artist does not really suppress it, but rather transforms it, condenses it, makes it more substantial. What comes out in the end is the result of discarded finds. Otherwise, you become your own connoisseur. I sell myself nothing.

A famous American poet offered his audience of aspiring poets the following formula for composition: "First idea, best idea," he said. How could they possibly go wrong by following such advice? Successful writing must be easy if one can count on the Muse, on instant inspiration, to do the work. But how does one know the first idea is the best idea if one does not have a second idea with which to compare it? In a perverse mood, one might imagine Galileo declaring: "First hypothesis, best hypothesis, and so of course, the sun must revolve around the earth." The rationalizing wish to write without revision belies the deeper delight of sustained concentration, of accumulating detail and shaping particulars into an informing design. Artistic pleasure requires the fidelity to return and reconsider. Yeats claimed in his autobiography: "Is it not certain that the Creator yawns in earthquake and thunder and other popular displays, but toils in rounding the delicate spiral of a shell?" Such toil frees the imagination to consider the further possibilities of its own designs and, of equal importance, it rewards the artist's consideration of the reader in the meticulously communicated sharing of a vision.

V. On Grace

In 1932, Sidney Cox, Frost's intimate friend, sent Frost his biography of him in which Cox took pains to relate what he knew about Frost's life to his poetry. Cox's assumption was that a direct connection was to be found between Frost's historical experience and his art. With a severity that risked destroying their friendship, Frost wrote back to Cox: "To be too subjective with what an artist has managed to make objective is to come on him presumptuously and render ungraceful what he in pain of his life had faith he had made graceful."

No biographer can describe the leap an artist makes between his or her life and art. That particular transformation is the very mystery of art. The ability to fabricate is, in part, a power we create out of pure potentiality. This power to create grace from disorder derives from the cultivation of a discipline, the learning of a skill; its potential is inherent, but its realization must be earned. No aspect of craft is beneath the concern of the serious artist—as suggested by the cartoon that shows a novelist working at his desk, apparently in frustration, who looks up to see the Muse descending, harp in hand. She smiles benevolently and says: I before E except after C." The commitment to achieve graceful form, to master a craft, and thus to be worthy of the Muse, always has needed the reinforcement of a tradition that honors serious art and of a community that supports the process of learning. The love of words and of patterns of words and the belief in the reality of the illusion that words can create constitute the writer's essential bond with the reader.

It is difficult to define what Frost meant when he spoke of giving to words a form that possesses "grace." Perhaps grace comes when the mind holds onto something precious, when the distraction of "getting and spending" falls away and we achieve a clarification of what we value or what we love. Or perhaps grace comes when performance is in harmony with intention, and, paradoxically, we feel free of the limitation of being a singular individual bound by a single life. As artists, we become more than ourselves; we become what we have made. "All that is personal soon rots," Yeats said, knowing that the artist's inevitable argument against nature is to preserve his or her words of shared caring, words carved into graceful form from what time would obliterate.

We do not invent language; we inherit it. Language has its own genius that re-creates itself through our use of it. We are the means by which it grows and keeps itself alive. Like a god, it speaks through us and survives us. Our minds are created by language; our thinking is made possible by the structure it provides, just as our bodies know only what our senses are capable of perceiving. And if we give ourselves to the language, embracing it, cherishing it word by word, laughing as we name the world, we may take on something of its grandeur and its majesty. I want to say that we receive its "grace," for we enter into the community of mind that crosses time and place, containing them. Every true poem, by its very nature, is a celebration of its inheritance—the language—which is never ours, though we, in our passing, partake of its ongoing grace.

VI. On Fame

Two events—a remark at breakfast by my younger son and a dream I had—teased me into thinking about fame. Trying to prepare himself for school, but still sleepy and distracted, my son asked me: "Dad, was it you or the other Vermont poet who wrote 'Birches'?" I reminded him that "Birches" was written by Robert Frost. My moment of fame had come and gone, and I went to my study, wondering if the wish to be remembered is indeed an essential aspect of a writer's motivation—as if in some psychological sense the fear of death and oblivion could be mitigated by the thought that something we have made survives us in our culture.

Last May, having taught my final class and turned in my grades, I was seized with what Frost calls "a springtime passion for the earth." I did not need another metaphor to connect me to my place, my Vermont landscape; I needed the earth itself—the actual touch of things, and so I decided on the project of expanding my rock garden. This work involves hauling the largest rocks I can lift and arranging them in curves and circles within which flowers and shrubs can be planted. The rocks must be placed so as to support and hold each other as if they had been destined to fit together. For the whole month rocks were the center of my thoughts and the sufficient pleasure of my days. Having completed my work, seeing that it was good, I had the following dream. I was sitting in a familiar auditorium, and we were waiting for the speaker to arrive at the podium. A distinguished, white-haired man—perhaps it was William Butler Yeats himself—glided to the microphone and said: "Will Robert Pack please come up from the audience?" Amid great applause, I left my seat, and with firm strides I walked along the aisle, up the steps to the platform where Yeats awaited me. He took my hand, held it, and then announced: "I am proud to inform all of you gathered here tonight that Robert Pack is this year's recipient of the Nobel Prize for outstanding achievement—in the building of rock gardens." The shocking aspect of the dream was the exquisite clarity of my awareness of disappointment. Yes, I was delighted to have won fame, and yet I knew that it was not exactly the fame I had hoped for.

In thinking about this dream, it seemed apparent to me that a sense of specific accomplishment could be separated from the wish for approval and public reward. As much as I love my rock garden, I do that work, not to connect myself with someone else or with an audience, but for its intrinsic pleasure. The element of intrinsic pleasure is no less in the fitting together of words to make a poem; but the further criteria of wishing to be understood, to reach into another's life, defines, for me, what is essential to the desire for artistic accomplishment. This definition is important in its practical emphasis on communication, touching through words, sharing a sense of human worth with an actual audience of caring listeners.

Literary communication, however, includes more than ideas and conscious structures; it also includes the feelings that accompany ideas and the knowledge both of things and of people. For such communication we need more than accurate description; we need metaphors and stories, and thus indirection—Dickinson's "Tell all the Truth but tell it slant." In his sequence of dream songs, where Berryman declares, "these poems are not meant to be understood, you understand," he is seriously joking (another form of indirection). And when Stevens states that "a poem must resist the intelligence almost successfully," he, too, is reminding us that poems speak from mysterious or unconscious depths, yet finally they must be gathered into the structures of consciousness through the discipline of craft. Out of the poet's silences, into his or her words, and finally into the reader's silences, might be one way of charting the process of artistic reaching out. Such a process does not need the validation of fame, for it bespeaks the universal human need to touch and be touched. Wherever an audience chooses to assemble, art takes on the quality of holiness—not because it is divine, but because it issues from the endless struggle against separation and loneliness. It matters only a little now who wrote "Birches." What does matter is that such a poem has become part of our collective inheritance, for also we need art in order to be more compassionately conscious of the sources of our own joys and sorrows. Perhaps in a thousand years, after who knows what wars and cataclysms, "Birches" will still survive in some anthology under the heading "Circa 1900, author anonymous." If so, not knowing the name of the author will be a bearable loss to the living.

VII. On Looking

Robert Frost asserted in a letter that "poetry is a fresh look and a fresh listen." The cadences implied by the sequences of words on a page is what Frost meant when he said, "I can't keep up any interest in sentences that don't *shape* on some speaking tone of voice." The willingness to listen constitutes the literary bond that holds us together, and the shared love for the names of things. For example, in August in Vermont the fields and woods will be brimming with flowers in bloom: fireweed, black-eyed Susans, purple vetch, bird's-foot trefoil, tiger lilies, hawkweed, asters, chickory, thistle, purple loosestrife, daisy fleabane, small sundrops, joe-pye-weed, wood sorrel, and jewelweed. The names themselves are a cornucopia of delights. And on Bread Loaf Mountain, following the constellations of the zodiac on a clear night, one can become dizzy with stars. Chances are good at this time of the year that we will get our first display of northern lights. The sense of awe, both wonder and dread, that comes from the feeling of human finitude in the presence of cosmic space ties us to our first ancestors and reminds us of our mere creaturehood, our vulnerability, and thus our need for language to assert our momentary presence on this planetary stage. This world of lights and images, witnessed and named, is indeed the theater, as Stevens says, in which we play out the obscure dramas of our lives:

> It is a theater floating through the clouds,
> Itself a cloud; although of misted rock
> And mountains running like water, wave on wave,
> Through waves of light. It is of cloud transformed
> To cloud transformed again, idly, the way
> A season changes color to no end,
> Except the lavishing of itself in change,
> As light changes yellow into gold and gold
> Into its opal elements and fire's delight,
> Splashed wide-wise because it likes magnificence
> And the solemn pleasures of magnificent space.

Surely, at the heart of literary ambition, there lies the wish to name things in their passing, cherishing them more powerfully, precisely because they *are* passing. We are most centered in our lives when we apprehend ourselves in our own vanishing—as Shakespeare's Antony does in a passage that is the literary source of Stevens's description above of the northern lights. Shakespeare's key word "pageant" becomes Stevens's key word "theater."

ANTONY: Eros, thou yet behold'st me?
EROS: Ay, noble lord.
ANTONY: Sometimes we see a cloud that's dragonish;
A vapor sometimes like a bear or lion,
A towered citadel, a pendant rock,
A forked mountain, or blue promontory
With trees upon't that nod unto the world
And mock our eyes with air. Thou hast seen these signs;
They are black Vesper's pageants.
EROS: Ay, my lord.
ANTONY: That which is now a horse, even with a thought
The rack dislimns, and makes it indistinct
As water is in water.

EROS: It does, my lord.
ANTONY: My good knave, Eros, now thy captain is
             Even such a body: here I am Antony,
             Yet cannot hold this invisible shape . . .

As Shakespeare's vision informs Stevens's poem, so, too, Stevens's words become part of the natural landscape, part of the spectacle of the northern lights, and those words enable us to see more clearly, more humanely, what already is there in the physical world, our home, our place.

Samuel Butler quipped that "a chicken is an egg's way of producing another egg," and, likewise, for us, creatures of culture as well as of nature, it is probably meaningless to assign priority to the things of this world over our names for them. We are now preceded both by trees and by the names of trees—Oak, Maple, Ash, Poplar, Birch, Basswood. Throughout recorded looking, the place we inhabit is always being expanded as the natural fact of the newly rooted poems becomes, in its turn, both precedent and cause for the worded nature that follows in the flare of its inevitable passing.

VIII. On Humility

There is a story about Albert Einstein that reads as a parable of artistic, as well as scientific, ambition. A promising physicist was described to Einstein as a very humble young man. Einstein reputedly replied: "How can he be humble? He hasn't discovered anything yet!" Humility, like modesty, is a dangerous virtue, for, as Einstein suggested, one must have some accomplishment to be modest about. And if one's modesty exceeds one's achievements, one risks being hypocritical—one's humility becomes an invitation to flattery. The parable also implies that a physicist probably needs a measure of presumptuous ambition if he or she sets out to do original work. So, too, the serious artist must venture forth against discouraging odds in the attempt to create a poem, a story, or a novel that will survive and become part of an enduring tradition. In effect, every artist must prepare himself, through trial and repeated effort, to wake up one morning and say, "Today I will begin work on my masterpiece that, perhaps, I will call *Paradise Lost.*" There can be no substantial ambition without arrogance in the face of the task to be accomplished, and, of course, such animating arrogance—"I have presumed," Milton confesses—carries with it, inevitably, the fear of unworthiness: humility, not as a manifestation of virtue, but as a form of uneasiness. Most serious writers will acknowledge *worry* as a symptom of ambition, but the anxiety inherent in ambition may be regarded as both necessary and good; anxiety need not result in the denial or distortion of influences.

And yet to argue in behalf of the healthy and grateful aspect of tradition and influence necessitates also the acknowledgment of the anarchic wish for the breaking of constraints that are associated with parental power. At a public reading, a Vermont poet recited a poem in which he shoots Robert Frost so that his own poetic style would supersede the supposedly old-fashioned diction of Frost. The audience nervously applauded, though one saucy wit remarked afterward that he thought Frost would have been faster on the draw than his would-be assassin. Yes, the Oedipus and the Electra complexes have their equivalents in the arena of literary ambition. But it is also possible that sons can reconcile with their fathers, daughters with their mothers, and that gratitude for what the parents have embodied—tradition seen as a gift, an enabling inheritance—can become the bond that replaces an adversary sense of generational competitiveness. Thus, also, the compulsive pursuit of the eccentric and the new may give way as an *avant-garde* aesthetic to a more stable emphasis on substance and quality.

All writers must celebrate what Yeats called "monuments of unaging intellect," the society of readers and writers that forms when literary values and ambitions are shared. The conception of quality and literary seriousness, as exemplified in models of past achievement, should strengthen a writer's resolve to do his or her best, without diminishing the sense of self or individual style. In his late poem, "Under Ben Bulben," Yeats writes his own epitaph and leaves his inheritance to the next generation of poets, exhorting them: "Irish poets, learn your trade, / Sing whatever is well made, / Scorn the sort now growing up / All out of shape from toe to top, / Their unremembering hearts and heads / Baseborn products of base beds." The devoted reader of Yeats may feel that Yeats has earned the right to indulge in his own grouchiness that derives both from defiance of death and from generational tension, but the dominant passion of Yeats's poem that moves us here includes his injunction to preserve the commitment to artistic excellence and the personal wish to be remembered. To resent the past is to repress the certain knowledge that the present generation—for all our innovations and reforms—soon becomes the past. A serious writer's only hope lies in the power of a literary tradition that remains relevant and alive, in which the bond between parent and child is a source of power, rather than a threat to individuality.

Another parabolic story tells of a monk who is lying on his deathbed, hoping that he will be inspired with some final words for his fellow monks to remember. The grieving monks circle about him, enumerating his talents and his virtues: "He had the truest tenor voice in our choir," said one. "He was the best interpreter of the philosophy of Aquinas," said another. A third added: "You could always count on him for a sympathetic look and a kindly word." "His poetry flowed so gracefully within the constraints of sonnet form" said the literary monk among them. The dying monk managed to lift his head a little from his pillow as they bent to catch his final words: "Don't forget my humility!" he whispered. One can imagine a pious gasp suppressed collectively by the surviving monks, yet one also can imagine that in their official decorum they fail to notice the dying monk's exaggerated wink as he points across the room to the desk where, later, they will find his poems, meticulously inscribed, carefully arranged by theme, and bound in the finest Florentine leather to be preserved for his posterity as his legacy.

On Being Prolific

One night recently I woke my wife with a nudge. "*Now* what is it?" she asked. The question I had for her, urgent though it seemed to me, was a little anticlimactic under the circumstances. But I forged ahead. "Darling," I said. "Do you consider me . . . prolific?" Her response will not bear repetition in these pages.

I think I'm not unlike many writers in worrying about my productivity. Indeed, across the nation, writers everywhere are talking to their shrinks about this very thing. Like the rest of them, I know in my heart of hearts—I *really* know—that quantity and quality must never be confused. I remind myself that Chidiock Tichborne, the Elizabethan poet, wrote—or is survived by—only *one* poem, his famous "Elegy for Himself," written in the Tower of London on the eve of his execution for treason. I would rather have written that single poem than the "Collected Poems" of most other poets. But the kind of worry I'm talking about goes well beyond reason.

It's probably natural that writers should dwell on this subject, even be obsessed by it. Shoemakers—if any still exist—must take seriously into account the number of shoes they make in a given period as well as their quality. Literature is the last great cottage industry. Every poem or novel is a one-of-a-kind thing, made at home, by hand. Not even the word processor can change this. And since quality is less easily measurable than quantity, is it any wonder writers like to tot up the number of words or pages—and books—they have written?

When writers get together, the subject often turns to productivity. How does Joyce Carol Oates—whose name is synonymous with productivity—do it? What about Stephen King or Anthony Burgess? Or—among literary critics—Harold Bloom? (The story circulates in academe that a graduate student once telephoned Mr. Bloom at home in New Haven. His wife answered, "I'm sorry, he's writing a book." "That's all right," the student replied. "I'll wait.")

The great nineteenth-century writers, of course, set the standards by which we judge productivity. I grow anxious when I think of them: titanic figures like Scott, Dickens and Balzac, they tortured themselves harnessing themselves to the desk for painful hours, pushing against the natural rhythms of creativity. The wonder is how good their work is, given the amount of it.

Sir Walter Scott, the Wizard of the North, is the first British writer for whom productivity became an issue. His son-in-law and biographer, John Gibson Lockhart, spoke of his "ceaseless pen." Scott's works include a four-volume collection of Scottish ballads, editions of Dryden and Swift, a large *Collected Poems*, twenty-seven massive novels, numerous shorter tales, a nine-volume biography of Napoleon, twelve volumes of collected letters and a journal that runs to more than 700 pages in print. Much of this frenzied writing activity was undertaken to finance a publishing company that Scott partially subsidized (shades of Mark Twain and the typesetting-machine company that bankrupted *him*). Scott was also devoted to his house, called Abbotsford. This mock-medieval monstrosity on the banks of the Tweed grew year by year, turret by turret, requiring endless outlays of hard cash. (I have a picture of it on the wall of my own study—as a warning.)

The centerpiece of the house is Scott's baronial study, which features a desk of immense proportions with two working surfaces. The ferociously driven author always had at least two projects in the works at any given time, and the two desktops helped to keep them separate. "Whatever he wrote met with great acclaim," writes his modern biographer, Edgar Johnson. "At Abbotsford he rose at five, wrote till noon, and crowded the rest of the long day with physical activity. Plagued with stomach cramps, anxious about debts, teeming with ideas that must somehow be gotten onto paper, he was a hero at his desk—as gallant as Rob Roy or Ivanhoe." A Scottish poet, Iain Chrichton Smith, recently attended an exhibition of Scott's manuscripts and wrote an affecting poem about the experience that, for me, goes to the heart of the issue here:

> Walking the room together in this merciless
> galaxy of manuscripts and notes,
> I am exhausted by such energy.

What love he must have lost to write so much.

I associate overproductivity with pain, the anguish of expression (from the Latin *ex-pressus*—pushing something deep inside out into the open air). It hurts. But it heals, too. This seems clear in the case of Honoré de Balzac, who poured out a torrent of books between 1822 and 1848, publishing eight books in 1842 alone! An overweight, ugly man with an overwhelming sense of social inferiority, he would don his monk's gown and write through the wee hours and, sometimes, into the next afternoon. He describes his routine in a letter to a friend:

"I must tell you that I am submerged in excessive labour. The mechanics of my life have altered. I go to bed at six or seven in the evening, like the hens. I am awakened at one o'clock in the morning and work till eight. At eight I sleep for an hour and a half. Then I have something light to eat, and a cup of black coffee, and harness my wagon until four. I receive callers, I take a bath or I go out, and after dinner I go back to bed. I have to live like this for months on end if I am not to be overwhelmed by my obligations. The profits accrue slowly; the debts are inexorable and fixed. It is now certain that I shall make a great fortune; but I need to go on writing and working for another three years."

There is a sad, wonderful optimism in the certainty that he is about to "make a great fortune."

To spur himself on, Balzac used heavy doses of coffee that he prepared for himself in the Turkish fashion, infusing the grounds in cold water, then heating them; he gradually used less and less water, creating a brew as thick as mud—a caffeine riot. Taken on an empty stomach, the effects were astounding, causing ideas (in Balzac's own words) to "pour out like the regiments of the Grand Army over the battlefield, and the battle begins. Memories come charging in with flags flying: the light cavalry of comparisons extends itself in a magnificent gallop; the artillery of logic hurries along with its ammunition train, and flashes of wit bob up like sharpshooters." In this agitated, unnatural way he composed the vast cathedral of his *Comédie Humaine,* a multivolume invocation of French society that is also an anthology of human emotions and situations.

Dickens, for me, is the quintessentially productive writer. He has much in common with Balzac, his contemporary: lower-middle-class origins, an overexcitable imagination, a restless nature and a capacity for inhuman labor. He had no will to resist taking on new projects. Since his novels sold exceedingly well, publishers were only too willing to get him to sign on the dotted line. At several points in his career, he worked simultaneously on two or three novels for serial publication while editing a journal and managing the affairs of a vast extended family. His energy level was such that he often took long late-night walks to cool his nerves.

Generally speaking, his early novels came more easily than the later ones, but he almost always wrote at breakneck speed, entranced by the vivid creations teeming from his brain. A visitor once recorded for posterity an indelible image of Dickens at work. Henry Burnett writes: "One night in Doughty Street, Mrs. Charles Dickens, my wife and myself were sitting round the fire cosily enjoying a chat, when Dickens, for some purpose, came suddenly into the room. 'What, you here!' he exclaimed; 'I'll bring my work.' It was his monthly portion of 'Oliver Twist' for Bentley's. In a few minutes he returned, manuscript in hand, and while he was pleasantly discoursing he employed himself in carrying to a corner of the room a little table, at which he seated himself and recommenced his writing. We, at his bidding, went on talking our 'little nothings,'—he, every now and then (the feather of his pen still moving rapidly from side to side), put in a cheerful interlude. It was interesting to watch, upon the sly, the mind and the muscles working (or, if you please, *playing* in company, as new thoughts were being dropped upon the paper). And to note the working brow, the set of mouth, with the tongue tightly pressed against the closed lips, as was his habit."

With age, it became harder and harder for Dickens to write quickly. During the composition of "Little Dorrit," for instance—written in his forties—Dickens recalls the agony of "prowling about the room, sitting down, getting up, stirring the fire, looking out of the window, tearing my hair, sitting down to write, writing nothing, writing something and tearing it up, going out, coming in, a Monster to my family, a dread Phaenomenon to myself." On and on, churning through *Bleak House, Hard Times, Our Mutual Friend,* right up to the unfinished *Mystery of Edwin Drood,* Dickens refused *not* to write in bulk. Haunted by the specter of bankruptcy, which had sent his father to debtor's prison, he may have wanted to insure that nothing similar could happen to him. Much like Scott and Balzac, he was driven to possess the outward signs of success, too, such as Gad's Hill Place, the magnificent house in Kent that he, as a child, had often admired. More generally, Dickens wrote because writing—lots of writing—was what being Charles Dickens was all about. The pressure of his imagination required the myriad shapes and forms that emerge in his fiction.

Anthony Trollope, by contrast, was a milder—and probably happier—man. I love to contemplate Trollope, who wrote for only three hours a day but was no less prolific than Dickens or Balzac. His forty-seven novels, several of which—*The Warden, Barchester Towers, Framley Parsonage*—might be called masterpieces, are a testament to the fruits of discipline. But the aura of genius that clung to Balzac, Scott and Dickens was alien to Trollope. In his wonderfully honest and charming autobiography (1883), he pretty much did himself in with the critics once and for all by describing his working methods. "All those I think who have lived as literary men," he wrote, "will agree with me that three hours a day will produce as much as a man ought to write." He goes on, describing his working methods in midcareer: "It had at this time become my custom—and it still is my custom, though of late I have become a little lenient to myself—to write with my watch before me, and to require from myself 250 words every quarter of an hour."

A servant awakened Trollope each morning at 5, seven days a week, bringing him a hot cup of coffee (tea came later in the morning). In an English country house, in midwinter, this early rising was not an attractive prospect, especially in the age before central heating and electric light. But Trollope had his demons. By 5:30 he was at his desk, rereading the previous day's work and making small corrections for roughly half an hour. By six, he was clocking himself at the usual thousand words per hour. He completed his daily quota of 2,500 words (in today's terms, ten double-spaced typed pages) by 8:30, when he got himself dressed for breakfast. After eating a hearty meal, he went off to work in the Post Office, where he was a high official. Two weekdays, instead of going to the office, he would spend the day on horseback, hunting foxes. Evenings were spent with his family or at his club. This routine almost never varied throughout his long life.

American writers of the period—Mark Twain, James Fenimore Cooper and Henry James, for instance—were no slouches when it came to productivity, but somehow productivity does not emerge as a *defining* characteristic. James, for instance, was astonishingly productive—the New York Edition of his work contains twenty-three volumes, in self-conscious imitation of Balzac's standard edition—but he did not make productivity a point of honor.

Trollope's calmly professional attitude toward writing, however, remains a kind of unspoken ideal for contemporary British writers like Graham Greene, Anthony Burgess, Iris Murdoch and A. N. Wilson—all of whom regard productivity as a virtue. Iris Murdoch has gone so far as to chide E. M. Forster for his *lack* of productivity: "Six novels?" she remarks in an interview. "Come on, Forster, you can do better than that!" She herself has published a novel almost every year without pause since her first novel appeared. When asked what she does when she gets stuck, she replied, "I just keep writing."

And there is A. N. Wilson, who makes me nervous. He is younger than I am, by a couple of years, but I will never catch up to him. (Why should I *want* to? Don't ask.) Born in 1950, Mr. Wilson has published twelve novels, biographies of Scott, Milton, Belloc and Tolstoy; he recently completed a life of C. S. Lewis and, I dare say, another novel. A former book editor of the *Spectator*, he contributes countless reviews and essays to major British periodicals. Worse yet, the writing is good. He comments: "Writing a book is a full-time occupation. You are thinking about it all the time. Sometimes you will wake up in the morning and realize that the book's problems have been with you even in sleep. Before conscious thought has dawned, even before you opened your eyes in the morning, you realize exactly what is wrong with that chapter you were struggling to finish the day before. Or so it has been with me. Until a typescript is actually out of my hands, and with the printer, I am mulling over it ceaselessly. For this reason, the question of how long it takes to write a book is an unanswerable one, particularly in the case of novels, where years of meditating upon a particular theme will suddenly bear fruit. 'It didn't take long to write that,' someone will say, upon hearing that the actual *penning* of a story took only a matter of weeks. Well, no it didn't: only about twenty-seven years."

By contrast, contemporary American writers—Saul Bellow, Mary McCarthy, William Styron, Norman Mailer and Thomas Pynchon—often harbor long silences, publishing in gigantic, well-publicized spasms. A few of our best writers—J. D. Salinger, Ralph Ellison, Grace Paley and Harold Brodkey—have fashioned whole careers out of the sound of one hand clapping. Their silences seem . . . productive. But then we have Joyce Carol Oates, Gore Vidal and John Updike, who seem more British than American in their attitudes. "The British tradition of the man of letters insists that writers write a lot, including book reviews," said Joyce Carol Oates. "I think a writer has a responsibility to comment on the culture, to read other writers. I don't know why so many of our writers refuse to write book reviews." Of her own working methods, she said: "I take endless notes before I begin writing a novel, often when I travel. I write on the backs of envelopes, in the margins of magazines, on theater programs."

Alas, Ms. Oates—whose work I deeply admire—has paid a price for her prolificacy. Mary Gordon said this recently in the March 2, 1986, issue of The *New York Times Book Review*: "We punish Joyce Carol Oates for the crime of her productivity. A book a year, in some years two—we respond as if she did it just to make us look bad, the A student who hands in for a geography assignment not only a weather map of the Hawaiian Islands, but a paper-mâché model of a volcano as well." Apart from the obvious question about whether or not a writer can keep to a high standard while writing so much, there is also the fact that Ms. Oates is a woman. Does the prospect of a wildly prolific woman frighten away male readers?

Two writers whose productivity has intrigued me are John Updike and Gore Vidal; they have both written as much as Joyce Carol Oates, though reviewers rarely call attention to this aspect of their careers. Mr. Updike's frequency of publication is somewhat masked by the sameness of his novels and stories in texture and theme. This kind of productivity makes sense. But Mr. Vidal is unpredictable and, worse, his books really *sell*! Beginning as a war novelist at the age of nineteen, with *Williwaw*, he has written everything from historical fiction (*Julian, Burr, Lincoln*) to contemporary satire (*Myra Breckinridge, Duluth*)—with twenty-two novels to date. He has also had hits on broadway (*Visit to a Small Planet, The Best Man*) and hits on the silver screen (*Ben Hur, Suddenly, Last Summer*). During the 1950s he wrote nearly a hundred television plays. And then, of course, I mustn't forget to mention the six volumes of essays, which many critics regard as his best work. "Yet the reviewers tend to treat every one of my books as though it were my first," said Mr. Vidal, talking to me on the telephone from Ravello, Italy. He refers to this country as "the United States of Amnesia."

Unfairly, I somehow expect writers of genre fiction—Isaac Asimov, Stephen King, Danielle Steel, Louis L'Amour—to churn out lots of books, since they write to something like a formula. (When asked in a recent interview about the key to his productivity, Stephen King replied: "Nothing in particular. I don't take notes. I don't outline, I don't do anything like that. I just flail away at the thing.") But "real" writers aren't supposed to churn them out. They must agonize. (Do *I* agonize? Sometimes. But the level of agony seems unrelated to the quality of the work.)

What seems true is that serious writers who write a lot of books and who experiment with different kinds of writing will suffer for it. The critics won't keep up with them. Their books will be reviewed in isolation from previous works, and their careers will resist categorization. Overproduction can also damage the quality of a writer's prose. Anthony Burgess, one suspects, would have been well advised to slow down; there is a frenetic, distorted quality to many of his novels that broadcasts the haste of their composition. Virtually every prolific writer has dull passages, even whole books worth tossing out. Nevertheless, telling these writers to slow down is like telling a bird not to fly. "I write a lot because I'm a writer," Mr. Vidal said in his lofty, mandarin voice. "That's what I do."

Writing about Writing

Pictures and writings are portraits of their authors," Gauguin tells us in his notebooks. And the artist and photographer Alexander Liberman writes in his book, *The Artist and his Studio*, "Rembrandt in his old age studied himself, painted himself . . . Van Gogh sought in his many self-portraits the secret of himself. Memory is haunted by the questioning eyes of the painters looking at themselves in the mirror, looking into us as if we were mirrors that could answer their questions." He ends this book with the 1927 etching by Picasso titled "The Painter and his Model," in which Picasso, almost as nude as the model herself, is at his easel hard at work.

This has been a year of looking at pictures for me, and I have started to notice, in fact have become obsessed by, self-portraits of artists with the paraphernalia of their art: Velasquez at his easel in "The Maids of Honor," showing us the artist's studio as seen by himself in a mirror; the Poussin self-portrait in which the horizontal lines of stacked-up canvases draw the viewer's eye to the artist's head; Vermeer's "The Allegory of the Art of Painting"; Ben Shahn's "The Artist," in which the painter's hands are nearly as large as his head and hold dozens of paintbrushes. Perhaps the culmination of these pictures for me was at a recent exhibit at the National Gallery of Art in Washington. In "The Peale Family," painted by Charles Peale in 1771, the artist himself turns from his easel to watch his brother, also an artist, sketching, while from a ledge in the background a classical sculpture looks down at the rest of the family, all of them busily eating even as they pose. I would also like to mention here a painting by Mark Leithauser called "Dromedary." This is a portrait not of the artist, but of a camel. It was painted, I am told, with a camel's hair brush, and this brush itself appears in the painting, a kind

of emblem of the theme I am talking about, though the painter himself
has disappeared from the picture.

It was clear to me almost from the beginning that my involvement
with these artists' self-portraits with paintbrush or easel was connected
to my increasing awareness of writers writing about writing. I have been
told that a *New Yorker* editor warned a young fiction writer that she
could use the exclamation point only three times over the course of a
lifetime. This reminded me of another so-called rule I heard once that
each poet was allowed to write just three poems titled "Poem." And last
year I had a poem returned to me from a magazine with a note from a
young editor chiding me that poems should never be written about poetry. Yehuda Amichai, a poet with whom I agree about most things, is
on the young editor's side about this one. In a talk at the Folger Shakespeare Library, he said that he utterly disliked poems about writing poetry, although he confessed to have written one himself. He compared
the matter to going to a restaurant hungry and having the chef come out
of the kitchen and talk about how he cooked the soup. "You just want
to eat the soup," said Amichai. As the mother of a chef, I confess that I
like to listen to talk about cooking. I also like to write poems about
writing. And so, it seems, do many other poets I know and read.

There are first of all the poems that can be roughly grouped together
as *ars poetica*, or How To Do It poems. Probably the most famous of
these is Archibald MacLeish's poem by that title in which we are told
that "a poem should not mean but be." And then there is "Poetry" by
Marianne Moore, also familiar, where we are told to be "literalists of the
imagination—above insolence and triviality" who should be able to
"present for inspection, imaginary gardens with real toads in them."

A less didactic but wonderfully effective example of this genre is
Charles Simic's "Dismantling The Silence," which begins: "Take down
its ears first / Carefully so they don't spill over. / With a sharp whistle
slit its belly open. / If there are ashes in it, close your eyes / And blow
them whichever way the wind is pointing." Clearly he is talking about
how to write a poem.

I think my own favorite *ars poetica* may be the one by Milosz that has
a question mark following its title. The subject matter of the Milosz
poem is not so much aesthetic as it is philosophical, even political. What
should a poem concern itself with, what is its function? In fact, when
should we attempt to write poetry? Here are the last two stanzas of that
poem.

> The purpose of poetry is to remind us
> how difficult it is to remain just one person,

for our house is open, there are no keys in the doors,
and invisible guests come in and out at will.

What I'm saying here is not, I agree, poetry
as poems should be written rarely and reluctantly,
under unbearable duress and only with the hope
that good spirits, not evil ones, choose us for their instruments.

Another obvious category of poems about poetry is what I call "writer's block poems." Bill Stafford became famous for, among other things, saying that "there is no such thing as writer's block if your standards are low enough." I try to follow his instructions, to sit at my desk and unselfconsciously allow the poem to take me where it will. But when that becomes totally impossible I occasionally write myself out of a slump by writing about what is obsessing me, i.e., the slump itself. Here is a short poem of mine actually called "Block."

Block

I place one word slowly
in front of the other,
like learning to walk again
after an illness.
But the blank page
with its hospital corners
tempts me.
I want to lie down
in its whiteness
and let myself drift
all the way back
to silence.

I have written other poems, one called "Letter," one called "Eyes Only," that are on the same subject but in a veiled way. In disguising the true subject of these poems, I have fooled even myself out of whatever it was that was blocking me.

Then there are the invocations to the muse, the oldest, most traditional category of poems that call attention, right up front, to the fact that they are about to be poems. "Sing in me Muse, and through me tell the story," begins the *Odyssey*, an invocation once considered necessary for the successful completion of a work.

My own particular muse is canine and sleeps at my feet while I write. So far I have only written one poem to him, and I don't think anyone would know, unless told, that a dog inhabited that particular poem.

The more traditional muse resembles Sir Philip Sydney's, who, like a good creative writing teacher, told Sydney, "Fool! . . . look in thy heart, and write." Sydney's muse is a metaphoric descendent of Homer's, though surely recognizable. Contemporary muses come in many disguises.

Roland Flint has a poem called "The Gift," in which he is about to read one of his earlier poems called "Still" to several friends. One of them, a young woman named Nancy, asks to lie down on the couch the better to listen.

> Without ever knowing it,
> All my obscure scribbler's life
> I have wanted to write one poem
> A woman beautiful as Nancy
> Would want, like that, to lie down for.
> I thank her for revealing this,
> For liking my poem about whiskey
> And for meaning it,
> But most for lying down.
>
> When I go to the writer's last place
> I will say for credentials,
> I am Flint: I wrote one poem
> Nancy the muse lay down for.

The poem that ends James Wright's book, *Shall We Gather By The River*, is called "To The Muse," and in it his muse is also a particular and real woman. Here is just a bit of that complex and moving poem.

> I wish to God I had made this world, this scurvy
> And disastrous place. I
> Didn't, I can't bear it
> Either, I don't blame you, sleeping down there
> Face down in the unbelievable silk of spring,
> Muse of black sand,
> Alone.

Anne Sexton, in "Flee On Your Donkey," speaks from inside a mental hospital where poetry is one of the instruments she uses to try to save herself.

> Today an intern knocks my knees,
> testing for reflexes.
> Once I would have winked and begged for dope,
> Today I am terribly patient.
> Today crows play black-jack
> on the stethoscope.
>
> Everyone has left me
> except my   muse,

that good nurse.
She stays in my hand,
a mild white mouse.

Though most of us love our muses, the muse is not necessarily benign. This is not only because it is too often faithless, as in Don Justice's poem, "The Telephone Number of the Muse," that ends: "I call her up sometimes, long distance now. / And she still knows my voice, but I can hear, / Beyond the music of her phonograph, / The laughter of the young men with their keys. / I have the number written down somewhere." Let me interject here that poets have also been known to be the faithless ones, as in verse 55 of "Astrophel and Stella," where Sydney tells his muses that he is giving them up for a particular woman.

Writing does have its dark side, as I try to make clear in my own poem, "Voices," where my muse, like Joan of Arc's, exacts a price, in this case future silence or even madness.

Voices

Joan heard voices,
and she burned for it.
Driving through the dark
I write poems.
Last night I drove through
a stop sign, pondering
line breaks.
When I explained
the policeman nodded,
then he gave me
a ticket.
Someone who knows told me
writers have fifteen years:
then comes repetition,
even madness.
Like Midas, I guess
everything we touch turns
to a poem—
when the spell is on.
But think of the poet after that
touching the trees
he's always touched,
but this time nothing happens.
Picture him rushing from trunk
to trunk, bruising
his hands on the rough bark.
Only five years left.
Sometimes I bury

my poems in the garden,
saving them
for the cold days ahead.
One way or another
you burn for it.

In a portrait not of the artist at his easel but of the poet at his desk, Larry River's picture of Frank O'Hara includes the text of a poem about a young poet "full of passion and giggles" who "brashly erects his first poems / and they are ecstatic / followed by a clap of praise / from a very few hands. / Where is the castle he should inhabit on a promontory / while his elegies are dictated to him by the divine prosecutor? / it is a bank on 14th Street." Surely a contemporary muse, or anti-muse, if ever there was one.

I want to mention just briefly poems written to or about other poets; sometimes these poets serve as kind of muses themselves. These poems can also be elegies to poets who have died, Shelley's "Adonais," for example, or Wordsworth to Milton, or, for that matter, Tennyson to Milton. There is Auden's "In Memory of W. B. Yeats" and Anne Sexton to Sylvia Plath and Maxine Kumin to Anne Sexton, and so on and on, down through the long history of poetry.

One way that poets used to call attention in their poems to the fact that they were writing poems has largely disappeared. Perhaps that is because not many people still write sonnets, or more likely it is because we no longer are confident that our poems or any poems or indeed any writings will be immortal. "So long as men can breathe, or eyes can see, / So long lives this, and this gives life to thee," wrote Shakespeare in his eighteenth sonnet, echoing, among others, Spenser, who wrote in his seventy-fifth sonnet: " 'Not so,' quoth I, 'let baser things devise / To die in dust, but you shall live by fame; / My verse your virtues rare shall eternise, / And in the heavens write your glorious name.' "

When I started thinking about this subject, I thought I would have to search fairly hard to find enough good poems about poetry to use as illustrations. On the contrary, I could scarcely open a book without finding another one. If, as Wallace Stevens says, the imagination is the only reality, perhaps there is nothing else to write about, and indeed the received wisdom is that all of Stevens' poems are about writing. So, in its way, is Adrienne Rich's poem "Diving Into the Wreck," as is an early poem of mine called "Skylight," in which nothing specifically about writing ever appears. There is also a whole category of poems that seem, at least to some degree, to be about writing but are really using writing itself as a metaphor for, among other things, the imagination. One of the best poems about the imagination is Robert Hass's "Heroic Simile."

Just as that long and complex poem brings us at the end to a human truth about a man and a woman, Richard Wilbur's poem "The Writer," with its nautical imagery and its picture of two generations of writers, is really about a more universal truth concerning fathers and daughters, whether or not they write, though the difficulties of writing become a perfect metaphor for what Wilbur is getting at.

There is an enormous range to poems in which writing is used as subject or metaphor or simply in a peripheral way. Here, first, is "The Self and the Mulberry," one of my favorite poems by Marvin Bell, which I take to be, among other things, a poem about the limitations of metaphor.

The Self and the Mulberry

I wanted to see the self, so I looked at the mulberry.
It had no trouble accepting its limits,
yet defining and redefining a small area
so that any shape was possible, any movement.
It stayed put, but was part of all the air.
I wanted to learn to be there and not there
like the continually changing, slightly moving
mulberry, wild cherry and particularly the willow.
Like the willow, I tried to weep without tears.
Like the cherry tree, I tried to be sturdy and productive.
Like the mulberry, I tried to keep moving.
I couldn't cry right, couldn't stay or go.
I kept losing parts of myself like a soft maple.
I fell ill like the elm. That was the end
of looking in nature to find a natural self.
Let nature think itself not manly enough!
Let nature wonder at the mystery of laughter.
Let nature hypothesize man's indifference to it.
Let nature take a turn at saying what love is!

I felt so strongly about this poem when I first read it that I wrote a poem called "The Mirror" in response to it. My poem ends, "Ask nature what love is. / Silence is answer enough." In fact, there is a whole genre of poems written in response to other poems; one of the best practitioners of this genre is Bell himself who, with William Stafford, published a book called *Segues: A Correspondence in Poetry*.

Next I'm going to cite "The Waters" by William Matthews, a poem I had pinned up over my desk for years. There are contradictions in this poem between muteness and language (the waters, after all, don't feel the need to break their long syllable into music). The very real pain it evokes about poetry as a calling is redeemed for the reader by the beauty of the poem itself, and so in a way it exemplifies its own subject.

The Waters   *for James Tate*

If you stare out over the waters
on a bright day when the wind is down
and the waters move only to groom
themselves, turning their beautiful faces
a little to guess how the light looks
on them this way, and that. . . .

If you hear them, contented as they seem
to be, and quiet, so that they seethe,
like a slow fire, and their long syllable
is not broken into music. . . .

And if you should carry them with you
like the memory of impossible errands
and not know what you carry, nor how,
so that you feel inelevably mute,
as if from birth, then you will be apt
for speech, for books, and you'll be glib

though it torment you, and you'll rise
to the sacraments of memory and lie down
unable to forget what you can't name,
and the wine in your glass will be ink.

In a very different mood, but also in its way a poem that defines what it is to be a poet, is Nancy Willard's "In Praise of ABC."

In Praise of ABC

In the beginning were the letters,
wooden, awkward, and everywhere.
Before the Word was the slow scrabble of fire and water.

God bless my son and his wooden letters
who has gone to bed with A in his right hand and Z in his left,
who has walked all day with C in his shoe and said nothing,
who has eaten of his napkin the word Birthday,
and who has filled my house with the broken speech of wizards.

To him the grass makes its gentle sign.
For him the worm letters her gospel truth.
To him the pretzel says, I am the occult

descendant of the first blessed bread
and the lost cuneiform of a grain of wheat.

Kneading bread, I found in my kitchen half an O.
Now I wait for someone to come from far off
holding the other half, saying
What is broken shall be made whole.
Match half for half; now do you know me again?

Thanks be to God for my house seeded with dark sayings
and my rooms rumpled and badly lit
but richly lettered with the secret raisins of truth.

A house seeded with dark sayings but richly lettered with the secret raisins of truth—a kind of definition of poetry right there.

One of my favorite Robert Pack poems has always been "After Returning from Camden Harbor," though I didn't realize until rereading it again that it dealt not only with the trick of the computer-made poem but on some level all along it suggested the contrasts between chaos and the order inherent in the act of poetry itself.

After Returning from Camden Harbor

With the idea of water still in mind,
I say these words out loud and know, therefore,
that I am not asleep; furiously
my mind seizes on green things to assert
its wakefulness: a plain, translucent pitcher,
quiet with milk, on a yellow tablecloth
brightened by morning sun. I observe my lawn,
as if asleep, hazy and steaming with dew
like a white sea sparkling green, according
to the soothing words of my idea of water,
though thunderclouds gathered furiously
over Camden Harbor with sailing boats
rearing like horses against the flat slap
of foaming waves. What stirs my wakefulness
is my idea of you who challenge me
to break free from my tightening mind
that furiously defends itself with words—
on Saturday when water, green as my anger
slobbering like horses, whinnied and surged
from my mind's depths: the nightmare sea where words
are forever wakening, forever asleep.
And though I spoke them, they were not my words;
because my anger toward you at Camden Harbor
snorted and roiled like foaming water,
it seemed as if I stood there still asleep
repeating an idea someone else's green mind

furiously had brought forth. I did not
say what I wanted then to choose to say,
and so I could not feel what furiously
I wanted to feel, according to the idea
that love means choice or that we live asleep—
as beside the water shaking the dock
I failed to will to compose the words
that could free me from the sea-dream of my anger
into a chosen yellow breakfast scene
with a flowered cup and a green pitcher of milk
casting its shadow as you pour for me.
Leaving next dawn, awed from high Camden Hill,
the stilled bay water seemed asleep, and we
drove on in sullen silence homeward
through shifting sea-green light of crowded pines
until, as if from nowhere, you explained
that a computer—given six random words
and the idea each sentence must include them,
all repeating in the final line—
composed a poem that furiously made sense.
Still angry, and yet wanting to please you,
a pitcher on a yellow tablecloth in mind,
I asked you what the six words were; you said
idea   water   asleep   furiously   green   words.

It says something about the effect of this poem that when I remembered it, years after reading it for the first time, what I remembered was a perfectly peaceful scene with a quiet pitcher of milk on a yellow tablecloth.

"Early Poems" by Donald Justice also left me, over the years, with a sense of perfect tranquility. Though this poem gently scoffs at itself, starting with "How fashionably sad those early poems are," it manages to laugh at nostalgia while perfectly and movingly embodying it, a kind of lovely joke on itself but even more on us, who have forgotten the music of rhymes and meters and must be reminded.

Early Poems

How fashionably sad those early poems are!
On their clipped lawns and hedges the snows fall.
Rains beat against the tarpaulins of their porches,
Where, Sunday mornings, the bored children sprawl,
Reading the comics before their parents rise.
—The rhymes, the meters, how they paralyze.

Who walks out through their streets tonight? No one.
You know these small towns, know all traffic stops
At ten. Idly, the street lamps gather moths,
And the pale mannequins wait inside dark shops,

Undressed, and ready for the dreams of men.
—Now the long silence. Now the beginning again.

Here now, in a very different mood, is Ellen Voigt's poem, "Dancing With Poets."

Dancing With Poets

"The accident" is what he calls the time
he threw himself from a window four floors up,
breaking his back and both ankles, so that walking
became the direst labor for this man
who takes my hand, invites me to the empty strip of floor
that fronts the instruments, a length of polished wood
the shape of a grave. *Unsuited for this world—*
his body bears the marks of it, his hand
is tense with effort and with shame, and I shy away
from any audience, but I love to dance, and soon
we find a way to move, drifting apart as each
effects a different ripple across the floor,
a plaid and a stripe to match the solid navy of the band.
And suddenly the band is getting better, so pleased
to have this pair of dancers, since we make evident
the music in the noise—and the dull pulse
leaps with unexpected riffs and turns, we can hear
how good the keyboard really is, the bright cresting
of another major key as others join us: a strict
block of a man, a formidable cliff of mind, dancing
as if melted, as if unhinged; his partner a gift of brave
elegance to those who watch her dance; and at her elbow,
Berryman back from the bridge, and Frost, relieved
of grievances, Dickinson waltzing there with lavish Keats,
who coughs into a borrowed handkerchief—all the poets of exile
and despair, unfit for this life, all those who cannot speak
but only sing, all those who cannot walk
who strut and spin until the waiting citizens at the bar,
aloof, judgmental, begin to sway or drum their straws
or hum, leave their seats to crowd the narrow floor
and now we are one body, sweating and foolish,
one body with its clear pathetic grace, not
lifted out of grief but dancing it, transforming
for one night this local bar, before we're turned back out
to our separate selves, to the dangerous streets and houses,
to the overwhelming drone of the living world.

I don't want to argue that this poem is about anything other than what it seems to be about: an ordinary bar where some poets had a good time dancing. If, for a moment, that "borrowed" handkerchief made me believe that Keats was actually present, don't think that it's easy to make me suspend my disbelief. But I do want to point out that in "Dancing With Poets," Ellen Voigt manages to slip in at least two fine definitions of what poetry, at its best, can do: "we make evident the music in the noise," she tells us, and later the dancers are "not lifted out of grief but dancing it."

In my own poem "Prosody 101," I don't try to describe what a poem can do or even, for all my talk of iambic pentameter, how it should be made. What I want to show is how a poem can make us feel, and I do this with a series of comparisons that are designed to make the reader forget that the subject at hand is poetry so that he can be surprised when he comes back to that subject at the end of the poem.

Prosody 101

When they taught me that what mattered most
was not the strict iambic line goose-stepping
over the page but the variations
in that line and the tension produced
on the ear by the surprise of difference,
I understood yet didn't understand
exactly, until just now, years later
in spring, with the trees already lacy
and camellias blowsy with middle age
I looked out and saw what a cold front had done
to the garden, sweeping in like common language,
unexpected in the sensuous
extravagance of a Maryland spring.
There was a dark edge around each flower
as if it had been outlined in ink
instead of frost, and the tension I felt
between the expected and actual
was like that time I came to you, ready
to say good-bye for good, for you had been
a cold front yourself lately, and as I walked in
you laughed and lifted me up in your arms
as if I too were lacy with spring
instead of middle-aged like the camellias,
and I thought: So this is Poetry.

There are too many fine poems about poetry to even list, so I will simply name a few more of my own favorites: Yeats's "The Coat"; Dylan Thomas's "In My Craft Or Sullen Art"; Howard Nemerov's "Writing"; Seamus Heaney's "The Diviners"; Elizabeth Bishop's "Visits To St. Elizabeth's"; Josephine Jacobsen's "The Chinese Insomniacs"; "Talking Back" by William Meredith.

Each poem by each poet had a distinct reason for being written, and it isn't easy to yoke them together simply because in part at least they are poems about poetry. But during the time that I gathered these poems together, I did come to some tentative conclusions about why we poets break the so-called rule against writing this kind of poem. The most obvious reason, of course, is that writers tend to choose as subjects those things they care most passionately about. And it occurred to me that a mention of craft within the body of a poem might sometimes be a kind of secret invocation to the muse, a whispered call for help. But there are other things at stake as well.

Let me quote from an essay by Delmore Schwartz called "The Vocation of the Poet in the Modern World." He is writing, here, about T. S. Eliot, but it could just as easily be James Joyce he was describing, whose wish to purify the language of the tribe is the central theme of *Portrait of the Artist as a Young Man*. The implication here is that calling attention to language will somehow in itself be beneficial. Writes Schwartz: "In the modern world, the poet who has been truly called cannot respond as poets did in idyllic and primitive periods, when merely the naming of things, as Adam named the animals, was enough to bring poems into existence. On the contrary, he must resist the innumerable ways in which words are spoiled, misused, commercialized, deformed, mispronounced, and in general degraded. We can see clearly how much this resistance is part of the vocation of the poet if we consider the recurrent references to language itself in the poems of that truly modern poet, T. S. Eliot."

Here is the passage from *Four Quartets* that he quotes:

> So here I am, in the middle way, having had twenty years—
> Twenty years largely wasted, the years of l'entre deux guerres—
> Trying to learn to use words, and every attempt
> Is a wholly new start, and a different kind of failure
> Because one has only learnt to get the better of words
> For the thing one no longer has to say, or the way in which
> One is no longer disposed to say it.

This picture of the writer, starting and failing and starting again, must be familiar to all writers, and I suppose we must take a kind of comfort from the fact that we are not alone in our struggles. "From the sweat of your brow you shall gain your bread," said God to Adam, who had perhaps had too easy a time with those first poems of his: the names of the plants and animals. The writer is not so different from the farmer toiling in his fields or any other laborer. I am a "gloomy woodcutter in the forest of words," writes Charles Simic in his poem, "Ballad." In fact, when we let the tools of our craft show in our work, we are not unlike the farmer bringing mud on his shoes into the house, the woodcutter leaking saw-dust from his pockets. I try to capture this concept of writing as being an integral part of ordinary life in a poem that I call "The Myth of Per-fectibility."

The Myth of Perfectibility

I hang the still life of flowers
by a window so it can receive
the morning light, as flowers must.
But sun will fade the paint,
so I move the picture to the exact center
of a dark wall, over the mantel
where it looks too much like a trophy—
one of those animal heads
but made up of blossoms.
I move it again to a little wall
down a hallway where I can come upon it
almost by chance, the way the Japanese
put a small window in an obscure place,
hoping that the sight of a particular landscape
will startle them with beauty as they pass
and not become familiar. I do this all day long, moving
the picture or sometimes a chair or a vase
from place to place. Or else I sit here at the typewriter,
putting in a comma to slow down
a long sentence, then taking it out,
then putting it back again
until I feel like a happy Sisyphus,
or like a good farmer who knows
that the body's work is never over,
for the motions of plowing and planting continue
season after season, even in his sleep.

Because I started this piece talking about painting, I'm going to end it now with a passage from Van Gogh's letters to his brother Theo that brings together, in a tangible way, painting and writing: "I still have in my heart a desire to paint a bookshop with the frontage yellow and rose, at evening," wrote Van Gogh, "it is such an essentially modern subject. Because it seems to the imagination such a focus of light—I say, there is a subject that would go well between an olive grove and a cornfield, the seedtime of books and prints. . . ."

Learning from Chekhov

This past year I taught at a college two and a half hours from my home. I commuted down once a week, stayed overnight, came back. Through most of the winter I took the bus. The worst part was waiting to go home in the New Rochelle Greyhound station. The bus was un-reliable, as was the twenty-minute taxi ride I took to get there, so I wound up being in the station, on the average, forty minutes a week.

One thing you notice if you spend any time there is that although the bus station is a glassed-in corner storefront, none of the windows open, so the only time air moves is when someone opens the door. There is a ticket counter, a wall of dirty magazines, a phone, a rack of dusty candy. It's never very crowded, which is hardly a comfort when half the people who *are* there look like they'd happily blow your brains out on the chance of finding a couple of Valiums in your purse.

Usually I bought a soda and a greasy sugar cookie to cheer myself up and read *People* magazine because I was scared to lose touch with reality for any longer than it took to read a *People* magazine article. Behind the counter worked a man about sixty and a woman about fifty, and in all the time I was there I never heard them exchange one personal word. Behind them was a TV, on constantly, and it will give you an idea of what kind of winter I had when I say that the first ten times I saw the *Challenger* blow up were on the bus station TV. I was having a difficult time in my life, and every minute that kept me from getting home to my husband and kids was painful. Many of you who have commuted will probably know what I mean.

Finally the bus came; the two drivers who alternated—the nasty younger one who seemed to slip into some kind of trance between New-burgh and New Paltz and went slower and slower up the thruway, and the older one who looked like a Victorian masher and had a fondness for some aerosol spray which smelled like a cross between cherry Lifesavers and Raid. The bus made Westchester stops for half an hour before it even got to the highway.

As soon as I was settled and had finished the soda and cookie and magazine from the bus station, I began reading the short stories of Anton Chekhov. It was my ritual and my reward. I began where I'd left off the week before, through volume after volume of the Garnett translations. And I never had to read more than a page or two before I began to think that maybe things weren't so bad. The stories were not only—it seemed to me—profound and beautiful, but also involving, so that I would finish one and find myself, miraculously, a half hour closer to home. And yet there was more than the distraction, the time so painlessly and pleasantly spent. A great sense of comfort came over me, as if in those thirty minutes I myself had been taken up in a spaceship and shown the whole world, a world full of sorrows, both different and very much like my own, and also a world full of promise, an intelligence large enough to embrace bus drivers and bus station junkies, a vision so piercing it would have kept seeing those astronauts long after that fiery plume disappeared from the screen. I began to think that maybe nothing was wasted, that someday I could do something with what was happening to me, to use even the New Rochelle bus station in some way, in my work.

Reading Chekhov, I felt not happy, exactly, but as close to happiness as I knew I was likely to come. And it occurred to me that this was the pleasure and mystery of reading, as well as the answer to those who say that books will disappear. For now, books are still the best way of taking great art and its consolations along with us on the bus.

In the spring, at the final meeting of the course I was commuting to teach, my students asked me this: if I had one last thing to tell them about writing, what would it be? They were half joking, partly because by then they knew me well enough to know that whenever I said anything about writing, I could usually be counted on to come up—often when we'd gone on to some other subject completely—with qualifications and even counterexamples proving that the opposite could just as well be true. And yet they were also half serious. We had come far in that class. From time to time, it had felt as if, at nine each Wednesday morning, we were shipwrecked together on an island. Now they wanted a souvenir, a fragment of seashell to take home.

Still it seemed nearly impossible to come up with that one last bit of advice. Often, I have wanted to somehow get in touch with former students and say: remember such and such a thing I told you? Well, I take it back, I was wrong! Given the difficulty of making any single true statement, I decided that I might just as well say the first thing that came to mind—which, as it happened, was this: the most important things, I told them, were observation and consciousness. Keep your eyes open, see clearly, think about what you see, ask yourself what it means.

After that came the qualifications and counterexamples: I wasn't suggesting that art necessarily be descriptive, literal, autobiographical or confessional. Nor should the imagination be overlooked as an investigational tool. Italo Calvino's story, "The Distance of the Moon," about a mythical time when the moon could be reached by climbing a ladder from the earth, has always seemed to me to be a work of profound observation and accuracy. If clearsightedness—meant literally—were the criterion for genius, what should we do about Milton? But still, in most cases the fact remains: The wider and deeper your observational range, the better, the more interestingly and truthfully you will write.

My students looked at me and yawned. It was nine in the morning, and they'd heard it before. And perhaps I would not have repeated it, or repeated it with such conviction, had I not spent the year reading and rereading all that Chekhov, all those stories filled and illuminated with the deepest and broadest—at once compassionate and dispassionate—observation of life that I know.

I have already told you what reading the Chekhov stories did for me, something of what they rescued me from and what they brought me to. But what I have to add now is that after a while I started noticing a funny thing. Let's say, for example, that I had just come from telling a student that one reason the class may have had trouble telling his two main characters apart is that they were named Mikey and Macky. I wasn't saying that the two best friends in his story couldn't have similar names. But, given the absence of other distinguishing characteristics, it might be better—in the interests of clarity—to call one Frank, or Bill. The student seemed pleased with this simple solution to a difficult problem, I was happy to have helped. And then, as my bus pulled out of New Rochelle, I began Chekhov's "The Two Volodyas."

In that story, a young woman named Sofya deceives herself into thinking she is in love with her elderly husband Volodya, then deceives herself into thinking she is in love with a childhood friend, also named Volodya; in the end, we see her being comforted by an adoptive sister who has become a nun, and who tells her "that all this is of no consequence, that it would all pass and God would forgive her." What I want to make clear is that the two men's having the same name is not the point of the story;

here, as in all of Chekhov's work, there is never exactly "a point." Rather, we feel that we are seeing into this woman's heart, into what she perceives as her "unbearable misery." That she should be in love— or not in love—with two men named Volodya is simply a fact of her life.

The next week, I suggested to another student that what made her story confusing was the multiple shifts in point of view. It's only a five-page story, I said. Not *Rashomon*. And that afternoon I read "Gusev," one of the most beautiful of Chekhov's stories about a sailor who dies at sea. The story begins with the sailor's point-of-view, shifts into long stretches of dialogue between him and another dying man. When Gusev dies—another "rule" I was glad I hadn't told my students was that, for "obvious" reasons, you can't write a story in which the narrator point-of-view character dies—the point of view shifts to that of the sailors burying him at sea and then on to that of the pilot fish who see his body fall, to the shark who comes to investigate, until finally—as a student of mine once wrote—we feel we are seeing through the eyes of God. What I have found—what I've just proved—is that it's nearly impossible to *describe* the end of this story with any accuracy at all. So I will quote the last few marvelous paragraphs. What I want to point out—what needs no pointing out—is how much would have been lost had Chekhov followed the rules.

He went rapidly towards the bottom. Did he reach it? It was said to be three miles to the bottom. After sinking sixty or seventy feet, he began moving more and more slowly, swaying rhythmically, as though he were hesitating, and, carried along by the current, moved more rapidly sideways than downwards.

Then he was met by a shoal of fish called harbor pilots. Seeing the dark body the fish stopped as though petrified, and suddenly turned round and disappeared. In less than a minute they flew back swift as an arrow to Gusev, and began zig-zagging round him in the water.

After that another dark body appeared. It was a shark. It swarmed under Gusev with dignity and no show of interest, as though it did not notice him, and sank down upon its back, then it turned belly upwards, basking in the warm transparent water, and languidly opened its jaws with two rows of teeth. The harbor pilots are delighted, they stop to see what will come next. After playing a little with the body the shark nonchalantly puts its jaws under it, cautiously touches it with its teeth, and the sailcloth is rent its full length from head to foot; one of the weights falls out and frightens the harbor pilots, and, striking the shark on the ribs, goes rapidly to the bottom.

Overhead at this time the clouds are massed together on the side where the sun is setting; one cloud like a triumphal arch, another like a lion, a third like a pair of scissors. . . . From behind the clouds a broad green shaft of light pierces through and stretches to the middle of the sky; a little later another, violet-colored, lies beside it; next to that, one of gold, then one rose-colored. . . . The sky turns a soft lilac. Looking at this gorgeous enchanted sky, at first the ocean scowls, but soon it too takes tender, joyous, passionate colors for which it is hard to find a name in human speech.

Around this same time, I seem to remember myself telling my class that we should, ideally, have some notion of whom or what a story is about—in other words, whose story is it? To offer the reader that simple knowledge, I said—I must have been in one of my ironic moods—wasn't really giving much. A little clarity of focus cost the writer almost nothing and paid off, for the reader, a hundredfold. And it was about this same time that I first read "In the Ravine," perhaps the most heartbreaking and most powerful Chekhov story I know, in which we don't realize that the peasant girl Lipa is our heroine until almost halfway through. Moreover, the story turns on the death of a baby—just the sort of incident I advise students to stay away from because it is so difficult to write well and without sentimentality. Here—I have no pedagogical excuse to quote this, but am only including it because I so admire it—is the extraordinarily lovely scene in which Lipa plays with her baby.

Lipa spent her time playing with the baby which had been born to her before Lent. It was a tiny, thin, pitiful little baby, and it was strange that it should cry and gaze about and be considered a human being, and even be called Nikifor. He lay in his cradle, and Lipa would walk away towards the door and say, bowing to him: "Good day, Nikifor Anisimitch!"
And she would rush at him and kiss him. Then she would walk away to the door, bow again, and say: "Good day, Nikifor Anisimitch!" And he kicked up his little red legs and his crying was mixed with laughter like the carpenter Elizarov's.

By now I had learned my lesson. I began telling my class to read Chekhov instead of listening to me. I invoked Chekhov's name so often that a disgruntled student accused me of trying to make her write like Chekhov. She went on to tell me that she was sick of Chekhov, that plenty of writers were better than Chekhov, and when I asked her who, she said: Thomas Pynchon. I said I thought both writers were very good, suppressing a wild desire to run out in the hall and poll the entire faculty on who was better—Chekhov or Pynchon—only stopping myself because—or so I'd like to think—the experience of reading Chekhov was proving not merely enlightening, but also humbling.

Still there were some things I thought I knew. A short time later I suggested to yet another student that he might want to think twice about having his character—in the very last paragraph of his story—pick up a gun and blow his head off for no reason. I wasn't saying that this couldn't happen, it was just that it seemed so unexpected, so melodramatic. Perhaps if he prepared the reader, ever so slightly, hinted that his character was, if not considering, then at least capable of this. A few hours later I got on the bus and read the ending of "Volodya":

Volodya put the muzzle of the revolver to his mouth, felt something like a trigger or a spring, and pressed it with his finger. Then he felt something else projecting, and once more pressed it. Taking the muzzle out of his mouth, he wiped it with the lapel of his coat, looked at the lock. He had never in his life taken a weapon in his hand.

"I believe one ought to raise this," he reflected. "Yes, it seems so."

Volodya put the muzzle in his mouth again, pressed it with his teeth, and pressed something with his fingers. There was the sound of a shot. Something hit Volodya in the back of his head with terrible violence and he fell on the table with his face downwards among the bottles and glasses. Then he saw his father as in Mentone, in a top hat with a wide black band on it, wearing mourning for some lady, suddenly seize him by both hands, and they fell headlong into a very deep dark pit. Then everything was blurred and vanished.

Until that moment we'd had no indication that Volodya was troubled by anything more than the prospect of school exams and an ordinary teenage crush on a flirtatious older woman. Nor had we heard much about his father, except that Volodya blames his frivolous mother for having wasted his money.

What seemed at issue here was far more serious than a question of similar names and divergent points of view. For as anyone who has ever attended a writing class knows: the bottom line of the fiction workshop is motivation. We complain, we criticize, we say that we don't understand why this or that character says or does something. Like parody method actors, we ask: what is the motivation? Of course, all this is based on the comforting supposition that things, in fiction as in life, are done for a reason. But here was Chekhov telling us that—hadn't we ever noticed?—quite often people do things—terrible, irrevocable things— for no good reason at all. No sooner had I assimilated this critical bit of information than I happened to read "A Dull Story," which convinced me that I had not only been overestimating, but also oversimplifying the depths and complexities of motivation. How could I have demanded to know clearly how a certain character felt about another character when—as the narrator of "A Dull Story" reveals on every page—our feelings for each other are so often elusive, changing, contradictory, hidden in the most clever disguises even from ourselves?

Clearly Chekhov was teaching me how to teach, and yet I remained a slow learner. The mistakes—and the revelations—continued. I had always assumed and probably even said that being insane was not an especially happy state, that the phrase "happy idiot" was generally an inaccurate one and that, given the choice, most hallucinating schizophrenics would opt for sanity. And maybe this is mostly true, but as Chekhov is always reminding us, "most" is not "all." For Kovrin, the hero of "The Black Monk," the visits from an imaginary monk are the sweetest and most welcome moments in his otherwise unsatisfactory life. And what of the assumption that, in life and in fiction, a crazy character should "act" crazy, should early on clue us into his craziness? Not Kovrin, who, aside from these hallucinatory attacks and a youthful case of "upset nerves," is a university professor, a husband, a functioning member, as they say, of society, a man whose consciousness of his own "mediocrity" is relieved only by his conversations with the phantasmagorical monk, who assures him that he is a genius.

Reading another story, "The Husband," I remembered asking: What is the point of writing a story in which everything's rotten and all the characters are terrible and nothing much happens and nothing changes? In "The Husband," Shalikov, the tax collector, watches his wife enjoying a brief moment of pleasure as she dances at a party, has a jealous fit and blackmails her into leaving the dance and returning to the prison of their shared lives. The story ends:

Anna Pavlovna would scarcely walk. She was still under the influence of the dancing, the music, the talk, the lights, and the noise; she asked herself as she walked along why God had thus afflicted her. She felt miserable, insulted, and choking with hate as she listened to her husband's heavy footsteps. She was silent, trying to think of the most offensive, biting and venomous word she could hurl at her husband, and at the same time she was fully aware that no word could penetrate his tax collector's hide. What did he care for words? Her bitterest enemy could not have contrived for her a more helpless position. And meanwhile the band was playing, and the darkness was full of the most rousing, intoxicating dance tunes.

The "point"—and, again, there is no conventional "point"—is that in just a few pages, the curtain concealing these lives has been drawn back, revealing them in all their helplessness and rage and rancor. The point is that lives go on without change, so why should fiction insist that major reverses should always—conveniently—occur?

And finally, this revelation. In some kind of fit of irritation, I told my class that it was just a fact that the sufferings of the poor are more compelling, more worthy of our attention than the vague discontents of the rich. So it was with some chagrin that I read "A Woman's Kingdom," a delicate and astonishingly moving story about a rich, lonely woman—a factory owner, no less—who finds herself attracted to her foreman . . . until a casual remark by a member of her own class awakens her to the impossibility of her situation. By the time I had finished the story, I felt that I had been challenged, not only in my more flippant statements about fiction but in my most basic assumptions about life. In this case, truth had nothing to do with social justice, or with morality, with right and wrong. The truth was what Chekhov had seen and I—with all my fancy talk of observation—had somehow overlooked: cut a rich woman and she will bleed just like a poor one. Which isn't to say that Chekhov didn't know and know well: the world being what it is, the poor do get cut somewhat more often and more deeply.

And now, since we are speaking of life, a brief digression, about Chekhov's. By the time Chekhov died of tuberculosis at the age of forty-four, he had written—in addition to his plays—588 short stories. He was also a medical doctor. He supervised the construction of clinics and schools, he was active in the Moscow Art Theater, he married the famous actress, Olga Knipper, he visited the infamous prison on Sakhalin Island and wrote a book about that. Once when someone asked him about his method of composition, Chekhov picked up an ashtray. "This is my method of composition," he said. "Tomorrow I will write a story called 'The Ashtray.'" Along the way, he was generous with advice to young writers. And now, to paraphrase what I said to my class, listen to Chekhov instead of me. Here are two quotations from Chekhov's letters, both on the subject of literary style:

In my opinion a true description of Nature should be very brief and have the character of relevance. Commonplaces such as "the setting sun bathing in the waves of the darkening sea, poured its purple gold, etc."—"the swallows flying over the surface of the water twittered merrily"—such commonplaces one ought to abandon. In descriptions of Nature one ought to seize upon the little particulars, grouping them in such a way that, in reading when you shut your eyes, you get the picture.

For instance you will get the full effect of a moonlit night if you write that on the milldam, a little glowing star point flashed from the neck of a broken bottle, and the round black shadow of a dog or a wolf emerged and ran, etc. . . .

In the sphere of psychology, details are also the thing. God preserve us from commonplaces. Best of all is it to avoid depicting the hero's state of mind; you ought to try to make it clear from the hero's actions. It is not necessary to portray many characters. The center of gravity should be in two people: he and she.

You understand it at once when I say "The man sat on the grass." You understand it because it is clear and makes no demands on the attention. On the other hand it is not easily understood if I write, "A tall, narrow-chested, middle-sized man, with a red beard, sat on the green grass, already trampled by pedestrians, sat silently, shyly, and timidly looked about him." That is not immediately grasped by the mind, whereas good writing should be grasped at once—in a second.

Another quotation, on the subject of closure:

My instinct tells me that at the end of a story or a novel I must artfully concentrate for the reader an impression of the entire work, and therefore must casually mention something about those whom I have already presented. Perhaps I am in error.

And here are a number of quotations on a theme which comes up again and again in his letters—the writer's need for objectivity, the importance of seeing clearly, without judgment, certainly without prejudgment, the need for the writer to be, in Chekhov's words, "an unbiased observer."

That the world "swarms with male and female scum" is perfectly true. Human nature is imperfect. . . . But to think that the task of literature is to gather the pure grain from the muck heap is to reject literature itself. Artistic literature is called so because it depicts life as it really is. Its aim is truth—unconditional and honest. . . . A writer is not a confectioner, not a dealer in cosmetics, not an entertainer; he is a man bound under compulsion, by the realization of his duty and by his conscience. . . . To a chemist, nothing on earth is unclean. A writer must be as objective as a chemist.

It seems to me that the writer should not try to solve such questions as those of God, pessimism, etc. His business is but to describe those who have been speaking or thinking about God and pessimism, how and under what circumstances. The artist should be not the judge of his characters and their conversations, but only an unbiased observer.

You are right in demanding that an artist should take an intelligent attitude to his work, but you confuse two things: solving a problem and stating a problem correctly. It is only the second that is obligatory for the artist.

You abuse me for objectivity, calling it indifference to good and evil, lack of ideas and ideals, and so on. You would have me, when I describe horse thieves, say: "Stealing horses is an evil." But that has been known for ages without my saying so. Let the jury judge them; it's my job simply to show what sort of people they are. I write: you are dealing with horse thieves, so let me tell you that they are not beggars but well fed people, that they are people of a special cult, and that horse stealing is not simply theft but a passion. Of course it would be pleasant to combine art with a sermon, but for me personally it is impossible owing to the conditions of technique. You see, to depict horse thieves in 700 lines I must all the time speak and think in their tone and feel in their spirit, otherwise . . . the story will not be as compact as all short stories ought to be. When I write, I reckon entirely upon the reader to add for himself the subjective elements that are lacking in the story.

And now, one final quotation, which given my track record for making statements and having to retract them a week later, struck me with particular force:

It is time for writers to admit that nothing in this world makes sense. Only fools and charlatans think they know and understand everything. The stupider they

are, the wider they conceive their horizons to be. And if an artist decides to de-
clare that he understands nothing of what he sees—this in itself constitutes a
considerable clarity in the realm of thought, and a great step forward.

Every great writer is a mystery, if only in that some aspect of his or
her talent remains forever ineffable, inexplicable and astonishing. The
sheer population of Dickens' imagination, the fantastic architecture
Proust constructs out of minutely examined moments, etc., etc. We ask
ourselves: How could anyone do that? And of course, different qualities
of the work will mystify different people. For me, Chekhov's mystery is
first of all one of knowledge: how does he know so much? He knows
everything we pride ourselves on having learned, and of course much
more. "The Name Day Party," a story about a pregnant woman, is full
of observations about pregnancy which I had thought were secrets.

The second mystery is how, without ever being direct, he commu-
nicates the fact that he is not describing The World or how people should
see The World or how he, Anton Chekhov, sees The World, but only one
or another character's world for a certain span of time. When the characters are less than attractive, we never feel the author hiding behind
them, peeking out from around their edges to say: "This isn't me, this
isn't me!" We never feel that Gurov, the "hero" of "The Lady with the
Pet Dog" is Chekhov, though, for all we know, he could be. Rather we
feel we are seeing his life—and his life transformed. Chekhov is always,
as he says in his letters, working from the particular to the general.

The greatest mystery for me—and it's what, I think, makes Chekhov
so different from any other writer I know—is this matter he keeps alluding to in his letters: the necessity of writing without judgment. Not
saying, Stealing horses is an evil. To be not the judge of one's characters
and their conversations but rather the unbiased observer. What should,
I imagine, be clear, is that Chekhov didn't live without judgment. I don't
know if anyone does, or if it is even possible except for psychotics and
Zen monks who've trained themselves to suspend all reflection, moral
and otherwise. My sense is that living without judgment is probably a
terrible idea. Nor, again, is any of this prescriptive. Balzac judged everyone and found nearly all of them wanting; their smallness and the fe-
rocity of his outrage is part of the greatness of his work. But what
Chekhov believed and acted on more than any writer I can think of is
that judgment and especially prejudgment was incommensurate with a
certain kind of literary art. It is, I believe, what—together with his range
of vision—makes him wholly unique among writers. And why, for reasons I still can't quite explain, his work comforted me in ways Balzac
just simply could not.

Before I finish, I'd like to quote Vladimir Nabokov's summation of his lecture on Chekhov's story, "The Lady with the Pet Dog":

All the traditional rules of storytelling have been broken in this wonderful story of twenty pages or so. There is no problem, no regular climax, no point at the end. And it is one of the greatest stories ever written.
We will now repeat the different features that are typical for this and other Chekhov tales.
First: The story is told in the most natural way possible, not beside the after-dinner fireplace as with Turgenev or Maupassant, but in the way one person relates to another the most important things in his life, slowly and yet without a break, in a slightly subdued voice.
Second: Exact and rich characterization is attained by a careful selection and careful distribution of minute but striking features, with perfect contempt for the sustained description, repetition, and strong emphasis of ordinary authors. In this or that description one detail is chosen to illume the whole setting.
Third: There is no special moral to be drawn and no special message to be received.
Fourth: The story is based on a system of waves, on the shades of this or that mood. . . . In Chekhov, we get a world of waves instead of particles of matter. . . .
Sixth: The story does not really end, for as long as people are alive, there is no possible and definite conclusion to their troubles or hopes or dreams.
Seventh: The storyteller seems to keep going out of his way to allude to trifles, every one of which in another type of story would mean a signpost denoting a turn of the action . . . but just because these trifles are meaningless, they are all-important in giving the real atmosphere of this particular story.

Let me repeat one sentence which seems to me particularly significant. "We feel that for Chekhov the lofty and the base are not different, that the slice of watermelon and the violet sea and the hands of the town governor are essential points of the beauty plus pity of the world." And what I might add to this is: the more Chekhov we read, the more strongly we feel this. I have often thought that Chekhov's stories should not be read singly but as separate parts of a whole. For like life, they present contradictory views, opposing visions. Reading them, we think: How broad life is! How many ways there are to live! In this world, where anything can happen, how much is possible! Our whole lives can change in a moment. Or: Nothing will ever change—especially the fact that the world and the human heart will always be wider and deeper than anything we can fathom.

And this is what I've come to think about what I learned and what I taught and what I should have taught. Wait! I should have said to that class: Come back! I've made a mistake. Forget about observation, consciousness, clearsightedness. Forget about life. Read Chekhov, read the stories straight through. Admit that you understand nothing of life, nothing of what you see. Then go out and look at the world.

LYNNE SHARON SCHWARTZ

Remembrance of Tense Past

I became aware, some years ago, of the spreading use of the present tense in fiction the way one becomes aware of an epidemic of 'flu. So many people you meet are afflicted by it, until not to be hints at some dubious immunity, almost a standoffishness, an unwillingness to partake of the *Zeitgeist*. But while influenza does its worst to old people, the present tense for the most part strikes at the young. In that regard it might be better likened to the mini-skirt in one of its brief flowerings in the late sixties (a time, incidentally, when magazine editors were known to reject present-tense stories for impropriety). Likewise, the present tense has gone beyond stylish to positively *de rigueur*, so that a writer of my age will try it on in the privacy of her boudoir, wistfully regarding her image and thinking: Can I? Should I? Will I pass or simply look ridiculous?

Just when women were refusing to be regarded solely as objects of sexual desire, they began showing more sexy parts. A double and contradictory message? Or maybe an even more difficult challenge, namely: by showing our desirability more than ever, we're making it tougher for you to meet our demands. This ambiguity and quasi-perverseness should be kept in mind while examining the meanings and ramifications of the present tense—not with a view to extirpating it like the 'flu, but to understanding what it implies about fiction and those who write it.

Having grown up on fiction written in the past tense, I would at once notice the present tense, especially in the work of students, as a deviation. I was aware of the writer's immanence, not as narrative voice, which I would have applauded, few things being so appealing as the sound of a human voice, but as technician. It was the auditory jolt that bothered me, not the break with convention, good writing by its nature being a break with convention. Granted that I may be an aesthetic Luddite, yet I was concerned with whether this particular technology was adopted for a conscious reason or was a mindless succumbing to fad. When breaking with convention it is wise to know exactly why you are doing so, and what you may gain and lose, and whether you are simply substituting another convention with new and more disguised disadvantages.

I began asking my students why they wrote—and read—in the present tense. They chorused a short-answer reply: it gave a greater feeling of immediacy. When pressed to define what they meant by "immediacy," they said: that it's happening now, as you read.

What is the notion that the action is happening as one reads? John goes to the window, he parts the curtains and looks out; he sees a neighbor starting his car; his wife enters the room and says she is going to the store, and so on. Barely worth a yawn. However, it is happening as you read, or so we agree to believe, in the tacit contract between reader and writer. This contract asks for a considerable suspension of disbelief: the reader agrees to assume also that what appears on the page has objective truth and merits his time and attention. We all know, of course, that the writer has made it up. She has thought it over and manipulated it, revised it in a calculated fashion, after which it has been set in type, printed, corrected, bound in hard covers, and distributed on trucks or through the mail. But we put aside such knowledge when reading fiction. So in actuality, the use of the present tense requires a further suspension of disbelief: despite all of the above, we are asked besides to believe the story is happening as we read.

Moreover, if a reader is presented with a series of incomplete actions, "happenings-as-he-reads," reflection and evaluation (comprehension) may be suspended indefinitely. In the guise of a spurious immediacy, the action is thrust so close that the reader is overwhelmed, or supposed to be overwhelmed, anyway, and must rely on the most superficial and quickest of responses, which are not always the best or truest. His participation in the work becomes less an imaginative, reflective act than a passive, reflexive one, like a leg jerking when a doctor taps the knee.

"Immediate" means without mediation, without any barriers between subject and object, statement and response, action and reader. If the present tense, for my students, produces immediacy, then the past tense presumably acts as an intermediary. That is, no matter how intense an event or episode may have been, by virtue of being past it is less crucial and cannot have as forceful an impact. In short, the choice of the present tense implies a specific and curious value judgment that raises questions of what fiction is all about.

A belief in living in the moment, without the native hue of resolution sicklied o'er with the pale cast of thought, is more salutary for real life than for fiction. Because life is chaotic, constantly recreating and rearranging itself, the past can be a constraint: we need to be free, available, and spontaneous enough to seize what comes our way. Fiction, on the contrary, presents made-up people whose stories are told precisely because they have more than ephemeral import. Fiction is an artifice giving coherence and boundaries to arbitrary swatches of life. To understand a character we need to see the trajectory of his or her experience: fiction *is* the trajectory—the shape of the fiction is. The present tense can be a way of evading scrutiny of that trajectory, evading the obligation of applying sensibility and evaluation. Thus after reading some present-tense fiction we may be left with no more sense of what the characters' lives have been about, or mean, than we have of the lives of strangers glimpsed on the street. The implication is that all we can ever understand is what can be understood from a glimpse.

It might be argued that if art imitates life, what better way to do so than to seize this very means—the fleeting glimpse? Surely that is a bit facile. If art imitates life, perhaps photography, of all the arts, can be made to give the most accurate picture. But photographs have a frame; most photographers arrange their subjects and do not snap at random. And even so, the result is a photograph and not a painting. (Those who study the subtle aesthetics of photography might argue that it is as "invented" as painting, but we will leave them aside for the moment.) The difference between the fiction in question and the more durable kind is like the difference between a photograph and a painting, one a copy of life and the other a copy of a vision of life, which is why some fiction is reminiscent of photo-realism. As far as art imitating life: while its subject matter resembles that of life, its procedures are quite the opposite.

The fashionableness of the present tense is linked to several adverse and well-known cultural developments. Naturally if we feel we have no long-range future to speak of, we may come to feel we have had no past, or that we might as well behave as though we hadn't. The decline of a sense of history is exacerbated by a narrowing of the scope of education; what is taught appears increasingly to be determined by what students are willing to learn, and the sense of history is not, regrettably, an innate craving. But since the past is undeniably there, regardless of nuclear or ecological threats, the young as well as the old would do well to be aware of what it consists of, to acknowledge continuity. The present tense, in fiction, seems to come out of nowhere; the experiences of reader and writer are not connected by a common past nor by a past elucidated and made common in the work, but by the use of brand names known to all. Thus consumerism rather than the continuity of the human spirit informs our fiction. Thus we have stories where we know what brand of shaving cream or cereal a character uses but not if he ever had a mother or father or what part of the world he grew up in. The shaving cream is taken to be more indicative than the father or mother.

The use of the present tense derives equally from another notoriously anti-historical phenomenon. For a long time, much new fiction reminded me of something familiar, so familiar that I could not place it right away. John goes to the window; he parts the curtains and looks out. He sees his neighbor, etc. What does this sound like? Exactly what you might get when a person describes to someone in the next room what is happening on a screen. A television screen. Instead of being more immediate, the experience is twice removed.

Through the ubiquity of television, the present tense is linked to the way current history is made—similarly removed, carefully selected, and displayed to us on a screen. Consider an event that can easily be made to sound like the fiction in fashion: The President is standing in the open car waving to the onlookers. His wife is beside him, smiling, wearing a pink suit. The President is falling. It appears he has been shot. Blood streams, etc. A blank space on the page denotes the passage of time and a new scene. Lee Harvey Oswald is walking down a corridor with a guard on either side. A man appears at the end of the corridor, holding a gun. . . .

The space shuttle disaster of 1986, as transmitted on television, sounded very much like that. Inevitably—it was taking place live. The television newsman cannot interpret; he has neither the time nor the responsibility and must simply report what he sees. The artist has the time and the privilege of reflection and moreover is in control of the material. One has to wonder why he or she declines to use it and assumes instead the persona of a TV newscaster.

One reason may be that in a visually oriented age, visible action is accorded high value. Fiction is rooted not in action but in character and destiny. Its major events are often spiritual or emotional journeys impossible to illustrate by physical gestures—which may be why novels like *Mrs. Dalloway* or *Middlemarch* do not find their way to the big screen. The present tense has the questionable facility of suggesting ac-

tion when nothing visibly significant is taking place, witness the example of John's looking out the window and seeing his neighbor's car,
then hearing his wife announce her intention to go to the store. While
the action described is devoid of interest, the real action may be taking
place inside the character—if, for instance, John, a suspicious person, is
shaken by the coincidence (?) of his wife and the neighbor going out at
the same moment. The writer has offered the visible, however boring,
and left us to infer the rest, like a host who serves his guests tunafish
and lets them smell the hidden caviar.

In sum, if the present tense makes things immediate, the critical issue
remains: what aspect of the character's experience is being made immediate?

The use of the present tense to give the illusion of significance might
be tested by transforming a passage into the past tense and seeing how
viable it is. The following—with the tense changed for illustration—is
from "Three Thousand Dollars," by David Lipsky, in the November 11,
1985, issue of the New Yorker. The narrator is a young man of nineteen
on the subject of his mother.

She taught art at a grammar school a few blocks up from our house, and the walls
of our apartment were covered with her drawings. That's the way she taught. She
stood over these kids while she had them drawing a still-life or a portrait or something, and if they were having trouble she sat down next to them to show them
what to do, and usually she ended up liking her own work so much that she
brought it home with her. We had all these candlesticks and clay flowerpots that
she made during class.

The half-affectionate, half-contemptuous attitude toward the mother,
making her into a "cute" character, substitutes for the adolescent's complex feelings: in the course of the story he lies to her about money, driving her into misery and confusion. A little further on, the narrator makes
a critical mistake, "forgetting" that through his own perverseness he
hasn't the money to return to college after the summer.

I got a job working at a B. Dalton bookstore. The manager had to fill out some
forms, and when he asked me how long I would be working—for the whole year
or just for the summer—I said, "Just for the summer," without thinking, and by
the time I realized, he had already written it down and it didn't seem worth the
trouble of making him go back and change it. Still, I went through the rest of the
day with the feeling that I'd done something wrong.

So much for the crucial issue. In effect the reader is expected automatically to supply the requisite emotion.

I was sent to the main floor, to the middle register, where old women came in pairs and shuffled through the Romance section. I ate lunch in a little park a block from the store, where a man-made waterfall kept tumbling down and secretaries drank diet sodas. There was a cool breeze because of the water.

Admittedly, these sentences sounded more alive in the present tense. They sounded as though something, however amorphous, was being conveyed; thus we can agree that the writer made a wise choice of tense. Specifically, the novelty or "immediacy," if you will, of the present tense masked the poverty of diction and sensibility. But when we change the tense, what is left? Rather than substance, an intelligent technical choice, and avoidance of the task at hand.

Another example: the conclusion of "Pupil," a story by Frederick Barthelme in the August 5, 1985, *New Yorker*, written in the present tense, here transposed to the past. The narrator, a teacher, has invited an eighteen-year-old student over for dinner and, finding her unexpectedly baffling and shy, is ambivalent about whether to sleep with her.

I took the bowl and dumped the chicken into the paper bag under the kitchen sink. Then I got a plastic trash bag from the closet and put the paper bag in the plastic bag. I scraped the rest of the plates into the paper bag, and put the dishes in the sink, then turned on the tap full blast and used the built-in spray nozzle to rinse the plates and glasses and the silverware. Tracy was watching me do all this. I got some paper towels and wetted them, wiped the countertops and the top of the stove, then the dining table. I shook the placemats over the sink, rinsed everything again, then led her out of the kitchen, hitting the light switch as we went.

"So now we start stuff, right?" she said. She grinned after she said it, reaching for one of the buttons on her shirt.

She was so beautiful. Her braces were shining. On one of her front teeth there was a tiny reflection of me and of the living room behind me. I thought about touching the white down on her face. I moved her hand away from the button.

The reflection in the braces is a delicate touch, a little epiphany, unfortunately too small and too late to redeem the pages of preparatory banality. The domestic details are used to create a feeling of tension, of waiting for the sexual part, or the renunciation of sex, as it appears. But in the past tense, is there really emotional, psychological, and sexual tension, or is there a lesson in cleaning up?

The reason why contemporary writers abstain from reflection (and expression) is hardly a deep mystery. Received modernist wisdom has it that after the intellectual upheavals of Freud, Marx, and Darwin, after the theories of relativity and probability, the writer no longer feels she has a privileged position regarding the meaning or value of anything, not even, alas, her own fantasies. To be judgmental has become the sin of the artist, just as to be immoral or subversive was his sin in former ages. Values still exist, to be sure, but, no longer held in common, they jostle under siege. Somehow the result is not a free, sophisticated, happy state of moral relativism, but one of timidity, with writers prudently staking no claims. The credo seems to be the less said on such matters, the better, or safer. The present tense serves this timidity admirably, as the writer can pretend to be simply reporting observations—the Sorry Madam I only work here posture.

The predicament is not the same as an honestly amoral stance on the fiction writer's part, which would be: You can think whatever you like about what I am about to show you, I do not presume to tell you what to think. Such utter objectivity would be almost impossible in any event. The stance of the present tense is rather: You can think whatever you like about what I show you, I am not going to tell you what I think, though you can bet your life I think something. In other words, we are not dealing with freedom of thought but with hedging.

Yet here, too, the present tense is paradoxical. Indirectly, the writer must be telling what she thinks because the material is not there by chance, as in an amateur snapshot. Its choice is every bit as meticulous as in older-fashioned fiction. As with the mini-skirt, a sort of double message or challenge is operating. While the writer pretends to take no discernible stance, the reader is more constrained than usual, misled about the degree of manipulation exercised. Compare this to the tactics of, say, Dickens, who makes it abundantly clear what a reader is to think and feel. Anyone diverging from Dickens's viewpoint, in the more sentimental passages, for instance, is free to laugh and say, Come on, I don't feel that way at all. Thus Oscar Wilde could quip that anyone not laughing at the death of Little Nell could not have a heart. The reader does not have the same freedom of rejection with most fiction in the present tense, for the writer's attitude cannot be accurately located. The reader is less free under the guise of being more free—an Orwellian situation.

It seems to me, though I have not made a scientific study, which some Ph.D. candidate might eventually undertake, that stories written in the present tense tend to sound more like each other, that is, to speak in the same voice, than stories in the past tense. I suspect it has to do with syntax and sentence structure. The present tense (with notable exceptions) has a colloquial tone and does not lend itself easily to complex structures, which make it sound inflated and self-conscious. Also, the reflexive response sought can be more readily attained by simple prefabricated language of the kind cited earlier (catering, incidentally, to the limitations of today's readers).

The sentences of Proust, James, Faulkner or Woolf are complex because the shapes of their visions are complex—circular, convoluted, labyrinthine—as the world is complex; they use subordination, relative clauses, and other grammatical baggage to portray the emotional, psychological, or intellectual contours of what is being offered. The present tense is commonly employed in a linear way, suggesting that nothing in the work at hand is terribly complex and that understanding, such as it is, can be reached by naming objects or accumulating data. But in truth very little in fiction's realm is simple or linear; all events are interwoven and interdependent.

Some exceptions might reinforce the case. The following, from Russell Banks's story, "Firewood," in *Success Stories*, demonstrates that the present tense need not always be used in the service of a reductive worldview. The character described, Nelson Painter, is an alcoholic who has spent the morning, as well as his whole life, becoming progressively more drunk.

It's [the snow's] deeper than he expected, eight or ten inches already, and drifting, a heavy, wet snow driven by a hard northeast wind and sticking to every surface that faces it, trees, houses, barns, chimneys, and now Nelson Painter, working his way down his driveway from the huge open door of the barn, a man turning quickly white, so that by the time he reaches the woodpile he's completely white, even his face, though he's pulled his head down into his coat as far as he can and can barely see through the waves of wind-driven snow before him.

And at the close, trying to return to the barn:

It seems so far away, that dark opening in the white world, miles and years away from him, that he wonders if he will even get there, if he will spend years, an entire lifetime, out here in the snow slogging his way toward the silent, dark, ice-cold barn where he can set his three pieces of firewood down, lay one piece of wood on the floor snugly against the other, the start of a new row.

How often do we find the present tense so exhaustively exploited to render, verbally and rhythmically, the feel of a character's being-in-the-world? What Banks has done, and most present tense writers are loath to do, is absorb his character's experience and let it permeate his own voice.

Another exception is Alice Adams, who frequently writes in the present tense, yet whose voice is among the few today one immediately recognizes. Here is the opening of "New Best Friends," from *Return Trips*.

"The McElroys really don't care about seeing us anymore—aren't you aware of that?" Jonathan Ferris rhetorically and somewhat drunkenly demands of his wife, Sarah Stein.

Evenly she answers him, "Yes, I can see that."
But he stumbles on, insisting, "We're low, *very* low, on their priority list."
"I *know*."
Jonathan and Sarah are finishing dinner, and too much wine, on one of the hottest nights of August—in Hilton, a mid-Southern town, to which they moved (were relocated) six months ago; Jonathan works for a computer corporation. They bought this new fake-Colonial house, out in some scrubby pinewoods, where now, in the sultry, sulfurous paralyzing twilight no needle stirs, and only mosquitoes give evidence of life, buzz-diving against the window screens.

Adams is not reluctant to let her voice be heard, nor to use modifiers that convey an attitude toward the proceedings. Her story, "Sintra," opens:

In Lisbon, Portugal, on a brilliant October Sunday morning, an American woman, a tourist, experiences a sudden rush of happiness, as clear and pure as the sunshine that warms the small flowers near her feet. She is standing in the garden of the Castelo de Sao Jorge, and the view before her includes a great spread of the city: the river and its estuary, the shining new bridge; she can see for miles!

The voice is distinguishable by its intelligence and sensibility; it is keenly aware of location in time and space and on a spectrum of emotions. The sentences seem to have been born in the present tense, rather than cast there for fashion or convenience.

On the other hand it is doubtful whether the past masters of elaborate structure could have worked their complex spells in the present tense. We might experiment, begging their indulgence. Listen to Proust, in a passage from *The Captive*, transposed to the present tense:

As in the old days at Combray when my mother left me without soothing me with her kiss, I want to rush after Albertine, I feel that there will be no peace for me until I have seen her again, that this renewed encounter will turn into something tremendous which it has not been before. . . . I spring out of bed when she is already in the room, I pace up and down the corridor, hoping that she will come out of her room and call me; I stand stock still outside her door for fear of failing to hear some faint summons, I return for a moment to my own room to see whether she may not by some lucky chance have forgotten her handkerchief, her bag, something which I may appear to be afraid of her needing during the night, and which will give me an excuse for going to her room. No, there is nothing. I return to my station outside her door, but the crack beneath it no longer shows any light. Albertine has put out the light, she is in bed; I remain there motionless, hoping for some lucky accident which does not occur; and long afterwards, frozen, I return to bestow myself between my own sheets and cry for the rest of the night.

What happens, paradoxically, is that all immediacy is lost; the passage is cheapened and made melodramatic. It depends for its great effect—in the original past tense—on the narrator's relating a completed episode and reflecting upon its meaning as a station in the course of his developing obsession with Albertine. So that along with the charged emotional content, there is philosophical and intellectual content as well. The past tense delivers both, the present, only the emotional part.

Here is an example from Henry James, the famous passage somewhat past the middle of *The Portrait of a Lady*, where Isabel Archer reflects on how awful her marriage to Gilbert Osmond has turned out to be. As before, I have changed the original past tense to the present.

... her soul is haunted with terrors which crowd to the foreground of thought as quickly as a place is made for them. . . . Her short interview with Osmond half an hour ago is a striking example of his faculty for making everything wither that he touches, spoiling everything for her that he looks at. . . . It is as if he has the evil eye; as if his presence is a blight and his favour a misfortune . . . ; a gulf has opened between them over which they look at each other with eyes that are on either side a declaration of the deception suffered. . . . It is not her fault—she has practised no deception; she has only admired and believed. She has taken all the first steps in the purest confidence, and then she has suddenly found the infinite vista of a multiplied life to be a dark, narrow alley with a dead wall at the end. Instead of leading to the high places of happiness, from which the world seems to lie below one, so that one can look down with a sense of exaltation and advantage, and judge and choose and pity, it leads rather downward and earthward, into realms of restriction and depression, where the sound of other lives, easier and freer, is heard as from above, and where it serves to deepen the feeling of failure. It is her deep distrust of her husband—this is what darkens the world.

Oddly enough, it is not as bad as one might expect; apart from the awkwardness of transposition, the meaning and images are clear. But something is missing—the weight of James, the specific gravity. Above all, the sense of progression, the narrative's moving force, is lost in the present tense. The passage feels lightened and less consequential, while in the original it is heavy with foreboding: a life being assessed, on its path to tragic and universal conclusions. This is only possible when something is looked at from a distance, as Isabel looks at her life. In the present tense everything looms too close to focus clearly.

When syntax and sentence structure are limited, the opportunities for diversity in voice are reduced, so that works in the present tense will naturally resemble each other to some degree. And possibly that is what beginning writers want. Given the pressures of the marketplace and the difficulty of getting unconventional work published, talented young people may feel they have a greater chance of success as they see their contemporaries winning acclaim at embryonic stages of their careers. So their voices tend to merge the way voices on a telephone are less distinct and more alike than they are in real life, and reading work in the present tense, one has the sense of hearing a telephone voice—in the worst of cases, the computer voice that gives the number when you call Information, which has all the hallmarks of a real voice except the breath and inflections of life.

This is a sharp contrast to the situation of, say, fifty years ago, when writers prided themselves on distinctiveness of voice rather than uniformity. Frank O'Connor, I am told, said that what is absent from contemporary fiction is the sound of a human voice. Just as a speaker's voice shows her degree of attachment to the words, and a monotone empty of affect can deaden a listener, so the writer's voice shows whether his connection to the story is authentic and live, or dead and inconsequential. The widespread use of the present tense suggests that, in addition to following trends, writers are resisting, and perhaps even afraid of the sound of their own voices (the same point has been raised in an essay by Rosellen Brown in the *Boston Review*). To understand the reasons for this resistance to the human voice, we need to look beyond the deplorable state of publishing to the inner pressures assailing individuality.

Despite the recent wave of censorship, we in the West still—and now, happily, those in Eastern Europe too—possess the freedom to say safely in fiction almost anything about ourselves or our society; safely, meaning we will not be thrown in jail or be shunned by our neighbors, though we may be shunned by publishers and certain schools and libraries. We can speculate about the universe unhindered as well as write of the intimacies of private lives as we please. This should yield a gorgeous array of possibilities. How are writers using their freedom? Besides doing sexually explicit things on the page, contemporary characters tend toward a vague nihilism and lead passive, meaningless, or unexamined and unexamining lives. But this is hardly original. Bungled or wasted lives are among traditional fiction's most fertile and hallowed themes. Nor are they being handled with startling originality. The best novel about idleness and passivity remains Goncharov's *Oblomov*, written in the far more repressive society of nineteenth-century Russia, in the past tense; having read *Oblomov* one cannot be too unsettled or aroused by the work of Frederick Barthelme or Deborah Eisenberg.

More important, these passive characters' lives, these sexually explicit scenes, are presented over the telephone, as it were, and not face to face. Writers today may feel comfortable physically exposed, as the promotion of some books indicates, yet they seem diffident about their fantasies, about the contents of their minds. Rather than saying, the character I have invented *did* such and such, which means an accomplished act, they say, my character *does* such and such, a more tentative act always in the making, for which one need not take full responsibility, yet. Can it be that they wish to separate themselves from what they are writing, mumble or murmur or mask their voices, as we do when we are uncomfortable about our words and prefer not to be held accountable for them? Very likely, since there is nothing more revealing than the naked imagination and the naked sound of the intimate voice. In this aspect, earlier writers, even Victorians, even those living under repressive political systems, were more daring and courageous about showing themselves than we are.

Not the human body but the individual sensibility is the essence of identity: not our thoughts but how we think, not what we see but how we look at things, not what has happened to us but what our intimate responses have been, and what our assessments are. The sensibility, made audible in the voice, is what is inhibited in beginning writers today. And the inhibition is encouraged by the impersonal, generalized present tense.

As distinct from most present-tense fiction, the sensibility of the writer can be heard in the following examples.

Standing before the kitchen sink and regarding the bright brass faucets that gleamed so far away, each with a bead of water at its nose, slowly swelling, falling, David again became aware that this world had been created without thought of him. He was thirsty, but the iron hip of the sink rested on legs tall almost as his own body, and by no stretch of arm, no leap, could he ever reach the distant tap. Where did the water come from that lurked so secretly in the curve of the brass? Where did it go, gurgling in the drain? What a strange world must be hidden behind the walls of a house! But he was thirsty.

That is the opening of Book I of *Call It Sleep*, by Henry Roth. The viewpoint is a six-year-old's, the language an adult's. From so homely an object as a dripping faucet the mystery of the world is evoked. From the directness of tone, sensual detail, and precision of diction, a reader is convinced that Roth has inhabited his character, breathed spirit into him, and, in the writing, shared his place and destiny.

The German author Heinrich von Kleist wrote the novella, *Michael Kohlhaas*, in 1808; this is the opening:

Towards the middle of the sixteenth century, there lived on the banks of the Havel a horse dealer by the name of Michael Kohlhaas, the son of a schoolmaster, one of the most upright and at the same time one of the most terrible men of his day. Until his thirtieth year this extraordinary man would have been thought the very model of a good citizen. In a village that still bears his name, he owned a farm on which he quietly earned a living by his trade; the children with whom his wife presented him were brought up in the fear of God to be industrious and honest; there was not one of his neighbors who had not benefited from his benevolence or his fair-mindedness—the world, in short, would have had every reason to bless his memory, if he had not carried one virtue to excess. But his sense of justice turned him into a brigand and a murderer.

Kleist's voice does not shrink from stating the subject in authoritative terms. The rhythm is temperate and measured; not so what follows. The story becomes an obsessive, furious, and violent quest for retribution. Totally absorbing, it makes the reader, in imagination, into a brigand and murderer as well—*there* is real immediacy. While events move at a galvanized pace, the writing keeps the controlled quality till it sounds like a madman trying with all his might to appear sane, in the same way that a drunkard walks with exaggerated precision. Besides being tremendously exciting, the prose is an accurate picture of the mind of Kleist, in whom passion and a constraining, compulsive logic were at war. The voice is the writer revealed.

Finally, the voice of Cynthia Ozick, in the story called "Puttermesser and Xanthippe," from *Levitations*. The heroine has attained a high place in New York City's municipal bureaucracy.

The truth was that Puttermesser was now a fathomer; she had come to understand the recondite, dim, and secret journey of the city's money, the tunnels it rolled through, the transmutations, investments, multiplications, squeezings, fattenings and battenings it underwent. . . . Every day, inside the wide bleak corridors of the Municipal Building, Puttermesser dreamed an ideal Civil Service: devotion to polity, the citizen's sweet love of the citizenry, the light rule of reason and common sense, the City as a miniature country crowded with patriots—not fools and jingoists, but patriots true and serene; humorous affection for the idiosyncrasies of one's distinctive little homeland, each borough itself another little homeland, joy in the Bronx, elation in Queens, O happy Richmond! Children on rollerskates, and over the Brooklyn Bridge the long patchwork-colored line of joggers, breathing hard above the homeland-hugging green waters.

Ozick is one of our scarce visionaries, albeit here with tongue-in-cheek. Few attempt such flights nowadays, maybe because exuberance is often mistaken for naiveté. What is most winning, I think, is that she shows no diffidence about being a *writer*, having a vocabulary and an ear—the primitive writerly goods, after all—and using them.

However diverse, these three writers share an equanimity, even abandon, in revealing the paths and by-ways of their imaginations. Such revelation should not be confused with self-expression, which is merely the other face of self-concealment, neither producing memorable writing. Roth, Kleist, and Ozick labor instead to construct, to translate a vision of the world, using their sensibilities as instruments—without coyness, without arrogance.

The question of tense led to voice, and voice leads to the center of where fiction comes from. What is real immediacy? To begin with, it has little to do with whether a story purports to be happening in the past or the present and a great deal to do with the truthfulness of the emotion informing the work. If a writer does not appear to be invested in the fates of his characters, clearly no one else can be. I am not alluding to superficial "warmth" or "caring" of the kind one desires from a friend or relative. Successful writing can be "cold" and unsentimental—witness *Madame Bovary* or the works of Nabokov or Céline. But the characters' destinies must matter, must have a place in a scale of values—the writer's scale of values—where there is such a thing as better or worse, joy or misery, where the end may be ineluctable, like Oedipus's or Othello's, yet is not depreciated with a shrug.

I can anticipate austere postmodernists objecting that the writer's allowing her scale of values to be known—perhaps even having one—is somehow "interfering" with the reader's response. Since when is showing how you feel and where you stand interfering? Interfering, manipulating, is the opposite, concealing how you feel but prying a response out of others.

A writer needs to love his characters not with personal fondness but with the kind of love that is thorough comprehension. It is no wonder that sexual love is called carnal knowledge; it does not necessarily follow that the people love each other warmly or even care to meet for lunch. The writer's kind of love is spiritual knowledge, the non-physical equivalent. Ideally, after carnal knowledge (excluding rapists and sadists with mad agendas), whatever one feels for the other person, one acknowledges her particular way of being in the world, the unique style in which his spirit moves the flesh and occupies space. The writer needs to feel the same. He may (unlike a lover, one hopes) loathe his characters, scorn them, even ultimately kill them, but he loves them in an existential way, granting their position in the scheme of things. This is something a reader can tell instinctively; aside from the formal merits of a work, it is what binds a reader to a book.

Well, how does a writer get to this comprehensive love? What is behind it, what makes it possible? She reaches it, with difficulty, by thoroughly knowing why she has chosen the story she has, where exactly it comes from, what it is really *about*. Not necessarily at the start of a work, but eventually, and then there arrives a great feeling of transcendence. "The reward of art is not fame or success but intoxication," Cyril

Connolly wrote in *Palinurus*. When intoxicated, you feel like yourself enlarged, a better, more buoyant self, an enhanced, and, for the moment, fully realized self.

How to reach this secret, crucial knowledge? Joyce Carol Oates once said the prime trait a writer must possess is patience. Another well-known writer said perseverance. To these I would add nerve. Many writers have courage, many are intrepid; nerve is a bit different. There is a dashing, swift quality to it, to the word itself, a sense of peeking or lurching into something dangerous but thrilling, a cavalier, more than noble, quality. Nervy people are not so much brave as a little outrageous. A writer's nerve consists in serving as his own specimen of human nature and looking at the very things he would most like to overlook—not only the standard character flaws, but the secret wickednesses, the perversities of every kind, the meannesses and stupidities, the fears, obsessive mistakes, blindness and deafness, grossness, and the whole residue of infantile cravings. Not looking at them with a view to correct or ameliorate, as one might do for therapeutic or practical purposes, but with a view to comprehend. And comprehending, to bring to light. These qualities need never explicitly appear as the writer's own nor attached to any invented character (that is, need not produce confessional writing—a term, by the way, usually applied to women's subjective fiction and rarely to men's). Simply the awareness of them, the appropriate ones for the story, must radiate from the words like an aura. The aura of knowledge and acceptance is what gives great works their magic and lucidity. The integrity of the work comes to reflect the integrity of the writer.

(Certainly the writer's awareness of human virtues may play a part as well. They need not be stressed since as a rule we tend not to overlook them as effectively as we do our flaws. As a matter of fact one sees the virtues of student writers poignantly and blatantly displayed—"look what a decent person I am"—to the detriment of objective truth as well as fiction.)

The present tense is ideally suited for writing from the core of this intimate comprehension of the work. Because of the requirements of narrative, few works can take place there all the time. But when one has gotten as close to the bone as one is going to get, the present tense does indeed give immediacy. A good contemporary example is Graham Swift's novel, *Waterland*, where the present and past tenses' interweaving is beautifully appropriate to display the simultaneity of past, present and future in human destiny. The stories of Alice Munro too are firmly grounded in history: their protagonists have fully documented pasts, yet commit anomalous acts springing from obscure sources. For this kind of mystery, the juxtaposition of present and past tense serves well. J. M. Coetzee's superb novel, *Waiting for the Barbarians*, is written almost entirely in the present tense, and almost all of it takes place in the marrow of the spirit.

A final example from Proust—undoctored this time—demonstrates a potent, and once obvious, use of the present tense. Again, from the narrator's musings and frettings about Albertine:

As soon as Albertine had gone out, I felt how exhausting was her perpetual presence, insatiable in its restless animation, which disturbed my sleep with its movements, made me live in a perpetual chill by her habit of leaving doors open, and forced me—in order to find excuses that would justify my not accompanying her, without, however, appearing too unwell, and at the same time seeing that she was not unaccompanied—to display every day greater ingenuity than Sheherezade. Unfortunately, if by a similar ingenuity the Persian storyteller postponed her own death, I was hastening mine. There are thus in life certain situations . . . in which . . . the problem of whether to continue a shared life or to return to the separate existence of the past poses itself almost in medical terms: to which of the two sorts of repose ought we to sacrifice ourselves (by continuing the daily strain, or by returning to the agonies of separation)—to that of the head or that of the heart?

About halfway through the passage Proust makes a switch, from the past tense in discussing a specific instance, to the present for a general comment about such quandaries. This was at one time a natural use of the present tense—for stating truths we all participate in, brought into high relief by the fictional situation. It is no longer fashionable to state such truths; there is implied doubt that they exist at all, and if they do, the reader is supposed to deduce them on her own. But given the force and reverberation—and wit—of Proust's paragraph, perhaps we might reconsider how the two tenses could work together to reaffirm the commonality of human experience and to link not only past and present, but specific and general, action and effect, character and reader: the world of the story and the world outside.

On Tone

I had intended, for months, to write about clarity—as a first principle, as a life's goal. I had even set aside a clutch of my favorite poems as illustration and working text—poems that were resonant, complex, and yet clear. Then the mail brought in a bulletin, a newsletter, some of whose news was a symposium on Emily Dickinson, one of the poets in my clarity file. With more than a mild interest I turned to the appropriate pages and fixed especially on the treatment of "My Life Had Stood—A Loaded Gun."

> My Life had stood—a Loaded Gun
> In Corners—till a Day
> The Owner passed—identified—
> And carried me away—
>
> And now We roam in Sovereign Woods—
> And now We hunt the Doe—
> And every time I speak for Him—
> The mountains straight reply—
>
> And do I smile, such cordial light
> Upon the Valley glow—
> It is as a Vesuvian face
> Had let its pleasure through—
>
> And when at Night—Our good Day done—
> I guard My Master's Head—
> 'Tis better than the Eider-Duck's
> Deep Pillow—to have shared—
>
> To foe of his—I'm deadly foe—
> None stir the second time—
> On whom I lay a Yellow Eye—
> Or an emphatic Thumb—

Though I than He—may longer live
He longer must—than I
For I have but the power to kill,
Without—the power to die—

Despite the hitch in the syntax in the last stanza (it takes a while to understand the panicked insistence of *must*), this had always seemed so available to me—dominant and recessive traits managed perfectly through six stanzas and gradually shifting in weight: the dependent speaker's almost ecstatic gratitude for rescue, for usefulness, is increasingly undermined ("speak for Him," "Vesuvian face") as she puts on knowledge with power—power first seen as His, then recognized as her own, but no sooner claimed (she lays the "emphatic thumb" on the enemy in stanza 5) than recognized as a powerlessness worse than before. And the terms of both the power and the dependency of the weapon, the tool, the partner, become more and more precise, more and more clear, until the reader recognizes that the speaker has inched so far out onto the ledge, nose to the ground, that there is no more solid ground beneath her, and we plummet, as we so often do in Dickinson, to a reversal.

But the symposium commentators seemed not to find it clear. Or rather, if each read it clearly, each read a different poem. "My Life Had Stood—A Loaded Gun"—wasn't this, one asserted, a reference to armies, specifically the Civil War, evidence of a socially conscious Dickinson? Or, another insisted, since the gun's owner hunts a female animal, since the speaker wishes to share the pillow, there must be a subtext of gender politics. And how about the "Sovereign" woods, the reverence for the "Master"—another of her religious poems? Impasse. Awkwardness. General agreement that the poem is thorny, difficult.

And so I passed on to my second example, a poem by John Berryman, one without the immediate blunt metaphor:

There sat down, once, a thing on Henry's heart
so heavy, if he had a hundred years
& more, & weeping, sleepless, in all them time
Henry could not make good.
Starts against always in Henry's ears
The little cough somewhere, an odour, a chime.
And there is another thing he has in mind
like a grave Sienese face a thousand years
would fail to blur the still profiled reproach of. Ghastly,
with open eyes, he attends, blind.
All the bells say: too late. This is not for tears;
thinking.

But never did Henry, as he thought he did,
end anyone and hacks her body up
and hid the pieces, where they may be found.
He knows: he went over everyone, & nobody's missing.
Often he reckons, in the dawn, them up.
Nobody is ever missing.

What would the symposium think of this one? The surface of the poem lacks even the textual cleanness of the Dickinson—the syntax is anything but straightforward, is in fact deliberately contorted, delayed, elided, inverted, reeling from grammatical violation to sophisticated median appositives, as the diction likewise reels from burlesque blackface to sonorous allusion. And the plot—can there be a narrative when nothing happens?

But, despite the absence of landmarks, there is, for me, something immediate—a path, a lantern, that either passes for clarity or else gives me the patience or the willingness to make my way through the underbrush. Essentially, that "something" in this Berryman Dreamsong is a structure that inverts the Dickinson. In her poem, the initial concept is developed logically, relentlessly, example after example: it is the tone, which is to say the implications suggested by the examples, that shifts. In the Berryman, our initial assumption of Henry's guilt—the probable cause of something heavy on Henry's heart—is increasingly undercut, reversed, more and more frantically, down through the poem: why, he's never murdered anyone. Meanwhile, the tone, beneath the manic energy of the surface, is unwavering, the self-recrimination increasing as convincing hard evidence for it dissipates. Whatever Henry has done to, or felt about, women, he might as well have hacked one up and hid the pieces. Such is the nature of self-loathing.

In other words, what I had meant by *clarity* had to do with *tone*, with a clarity of purpose and inference more than with the discursive prose elements.

But what exactly is tone? While crucial to the making of and reading of poems, it seems nearly impossible to define. Thrall, Hibbard, and Holman, in their *Handbook to Literature*, drawing directly on I. A. Richards, call it "a term designating the attitudes toward the subject and towards the audience implied in a literary work" (p. 444). But this seems helpful in understanding neither the Dickinson nor the Berryman poem. *The Princeton Encyclopedia of Poetry and Poetics*, which has its own problems with tone, gives a fuller entry:

Traditionally, tone has denoted an intangible quality, frequently an affective one, which is metaphorically predicated of a literary work or of some part of it such as its style. It is said to pervade and "color" the whole, like a mood in a human being, and in various ways to contribute to the aesthetic excellence of the work. . . . In *Practical Criticism*, I. A. Richards compared tone to social manners and defined it as the reflection in a discourse of the author's attitude towards his audience. (p. 856)

This is not promising. Yet most of us can identify tone in *life*—and depend on it for meaning. When you're in your bed, at the verge of sleep, and you hear voices in the next apartment, what you register is tone. The actual words don't pass through the wall, but from the volume, pitch, relative stress, pacing, and rhythmic pattern of the speech you reconstruct the emotional content of the conversation. It's what the dog registers when you talk to him sternly or playfully—the form of the emotion behind or within the words. It's also what can allow an obscenity to pass for an endearment, or a term of affection to become suddenly an insult.

In life, what we depend on is inflection—exactly what is missing when the robot speaks. Consider this little dialogue:

—Where did you get those pants?
—On sale at Sims.
—I should have known.
—They're very comfortable.
—I'm sure they are.

On the page, this exchange is what we would call "flat"—mostly monosyllabic words, of seemingly equal importance, and foreshortened syntax, which deprives us of both the relativity of subordination and the arc, or rhythmic shape, of the sentence. It might help if I provide a context—some discursive information that would encourage a reader to infer inflection. This is a technique used by fiction writers, particularly those writers of the "minimalist" school. In this case, let's say the pants in question are ones I'm wearing, a bright plaid in loose folds, and that the first voice is my older sister, a plausible substitute for my mother. That at least poses several options for tone. One might be solicitude alternating with resentment:

(inquiringly)—Where did you get those pants?
(brusquely)—On sale at Sims.
(ruefully)—I should have known.
(aggressively)—They're *very* comfortable.
(agreeably)—Oh, I'm sure they are.

Another is disapproval and meek acknowledgment:

—*Where* did you *get those pants?*
—On sale at Sims.

—I *should* have known.
—They're very comfortable (?)
—*Oh* I'm *sure* they *are*.

Which is how I remember it.

The point is that the exchange, the actual language, needs a context in order for its meaning to be clear, and while a dramatic or narrative (that is, discursive) context may allow us to infer tone, inflection—a context of sound—is more dependable. So it is, I will try to argue, with poetry as well: no matter how many discursive meanings a poem may partake of, its central meaning, or purpose, or identity derives from its tone. For a primary text, I want to use a Kunitz poem that may be more immediately accessible than either the Dickinson or the Berryman.

> *My Sisters*
>
> *Who whispered, souls have shapes?*
> *So has the wind, I say,*
> *But I don't know,*
> *I only feel things blow.*
>
> I had two sisters once
> with long black hair
> who walked apart from me
> and wrote the history of tears.
> Their story's faded with their names,
> but the candlelight they carried,
> like dancers in a dream,
> still flickers on their gowns
> as they bend over me
> to comfort my night-fears.
>
> Let nothing grieve you,
> Sarah and Sophia.
> Shush, shush, my dears,
> now and forever.

Admittedly, the immediate discursive context for the poem is a little shaky. In that opening stanza, we don't know who is speaking; there seems to be no dramatic location, no event to fasten on. And yet, the poem draws us in: the tentativeness inherent in all nonrhetorical questions lets us recognize immediately an internalized argument with the self. Somebody—the speaker won't or can't say who—believes in ghosts. First he dismisses the notion (could be the wind); then he disavows a position one way or the other ("But I don't know") while immediately (spliced into the sentence with a comma) allowing its continued possibility ("feel things blow"). Meanwhile, this ambivalence sets us on edge, alerts us; we know how to feel: not terrified but uneasy.

As the poem proceeds to the next stanza, we're on firmer ground. There is a self-proclaimed speaker, an I; the syntax is straightforward, full declarative sentences with obvious subjects and verbs, modifying phrases used sparingly and more or less predictably. The diction, too, poses no threat of difficulty; the words are idiomatic, familiar. The structure is not conventional but still seems accessible. The initial voice from the ditch has been italicized and thus set aside as prologue, having raised the essential premise of the poem: do ghosts exist or not? Next we are given the barest bones of a narrative. The speaker tells us he had two sisters, that they were unhappy, that they are dead, that their spirits come to comfort him. The third stanza shifts again—this time to direct address, the speaker now comforting the dead sisters.

None of this "information," however, addresses the power or the effectiveness of the poem, because none of it conveys the emotional content. What does address this content is *tone*, which I would also argue is the source of the poem's clarity. Even in the opening question, there is more challenge than request ("who whispered," who claimed such a thing), and that is followed by a noticeable defensiveness ("So has the wind, I say"), concomitant with the lines' disturbing, almost violent sibilance. Nine of the first eleven words share initial consonantal sounds that are full of air: *wh, w, sah, sh,* and *hah,* underscored by the medial and final *s* sounds in "whispered," "souls," "shapes," and "has." These vigorous consonants are contained, as it were, by the open long *a* vowel placed in matching stressed syllables (*shapes/say*) at the ends of the end-stopped trimeter lines. And there is also a breathiness, and a serious, halting pace, introduced into the regularized meter: Kunitz puts an immediate caesura after the first foot of the poem, which reinforces the hovering possibility of an initial stress ("Who whispered"—compare that to "who whispered to me"). This potential initial stress is made authoritative in the next line ("So has the wind"), but there the caesura is delayed: thus our metered 3-foot couplet is varied (1—2, 3; 1, 2—3): "Who whispered, souls have shapes? / So has the wind, I say." Then the speaker retreats a bit from his initial dismissal retreat with the shortened flat line, "But I don't know—." This line is held in tonal abeyance as the expectation of another 3-beat unit is thwarted: delayed though just for a moment, until the next line restores trimeter in liquid *l*'s (*only, feel, blow*) as the rhymes (the loudest sounds) shift down into the closed long *o*: "I only feel things blow."

Such a weak part of speech, that adverb "only," so undeserving of metrical stress, but here so sly, working in the sentence as a musical transition in its two vowels, the *o* of "know," the *e* of "feel"—and a slightly smug, slightly stubborn "I know what I know" creeps into the tone to complicate, if not contradict, the statement.

The edgy ambivalence of the opening stanza is relieved somewhat in stanza 2 as the voice takes up its brief weary narrative. Gone are the trimeter couplets (gone too the caesuras). But music doesn't require meter and rhyme. The *s* in "souls" in the first line carries forward to the now limited category of souls, "sisters once," and the *l* that closed the stanza recurs in their "long black" hair as, in lines of increasing length, the specific dead are identified. The suggestion of rhyme scheme—an identifiable pattern or structure of sound—remains in *tears, fears,* words which end and end-stop the two complete sentences of the stanza, and in the carefully placed *me, dream, me*—as though the earlier closed couplets had been stretched open, must as the sentences and lines lengthen and relax, bulge the stanza out at the center, then return more or less to the trimeter.

Certainly, nothing in the narrative information of the second stanza (the speaker's own approaching death is the gradually emerging conflict here), nothing in the prose context, nothing discursive anticipates the final shift, the role reversal in the final stanza. When the speaker turns to comfort the ghosts (who, after all, may or may not exist), he does so with a direct address, and his shift to imperative syntax and more formal diction signals the extent to which the initial question has been mooted as the speaker is overwhelmed by tenderness: "Let nothing grieve you." Whether or not the reader's analytical brain recognizes it, some primitive reptilian brain does: this is dimeter, the two-beat unit that surprised us earlier—"But I don't know"—and recurred in stanza 2—"With long black hair." Here, the duple unit uses the same iambic opening but is softened by an extra unstressed syllable. So with this subtle repetition, and a variation even more subtle, the poem displaces the earlier coy disavowal first with a formal, then immediately an intimate, address: "Sarah and Sophia." Meanwhile, the poem prepares us for closure with a four-line stanza again, to balance against the initial halting four lines of the poem. This quatrain neatly divides into syntactical, if not rhymed, couplets—four lines that return us to the initial sibilance, but this time with all the threat gone: "Sarah and Sophia, / Shush, shush, my dears . . . ," maternal, compassionate, one's own pain or fear eclipsed, turned outward.

It is tone that marks the striking difference between the last four lines

of the poem and the first four. Earlier, we had a stanza of a folk song—
its set pattern of 3-beats, its single duple variant, its rising rhythm and
its masculine rhyme. For closure we have four end-stopped lines in
which the initial variation (two-beats) becomes the pattern—"But I
don't know" resonating in rhythm no longer ironic, protective, but as
dilemma: I don't know whether you're even there or not, but I bless you
anyway.

Whereas the opening lines considered initial stress and then gave way
to regular iambs with masculine line-endings, this stanza pulls us back
from that movement with strong initial stresses in the final three lines
(*Sarah, shush, now*) and feminine endings (*grieve you, Sophia, forever*).
Because of the similarity of the broad strokes (stanzaic arrangement, recognizable meter), we are made to catch the difference in the smaller
strokes (an extra syllable, a change in diction, a move from interrogative
to imperative) and thereby register the shift in tone. The stanza's falling
rhythm not only departs from the predominant rising inflection of the
poem, but in the last line recalls a sound pattern from outside the poem
by duplicating, after dimeter prolonged by spondee and caesuras ("Shush,
shush, my dears"), the cadence and language of prayer:

> Now and forever
> [World without end].

The last word of the poem—*forever*, which is in fact the source of the
threat in the idea of death—here is converted, by the context of the
sound, to a source of promise.

It is this "plot line"—attention focused by formal arrangement onto
the complex emotional field—that *is* the poem. It is immediately accessible—we can follow it, are engaged in it, because we *hear* it, in the
music. Even before we have any notion of the submerged narrative, we
register the tonality, provided by the sounds in the diction, syntax, pronouns, formal manipulation of rhythm, arrangement of vowels and consonants—*simultaneous with* the denotative verbal information and the
visual cues.

Simultaneous: any single element contributory to tone, that is, does
not contain it. In the exchange about the pants, it would help to see the
pants. When one talks to the dog, he also registers the familiar or unfamiliar face and smell, voice and body language. Likewise, through the
wall we are building a supposed context—whether it is a man or a
woman or a child in the next apartment, whether we recognize the
bitchy landlord or someone drunk, whether we should call the cops or
go on to sleep. What's important is the combination of elements. This

is a well-known aspect of "tonality" in music. A single note can not truly be said to have any emotional content at all. Even two notes in conjunction only barely suggest one—a major third, for instance, A to C-sharp, could be part of the tonic in A major or of the sixth chord, an F-sharp minor. It's only with the third tone, E or F-sharp, that a key or tonality is established, and with it some specific color or character that makes the song different in different keys.

So any analysis of tone must include elements in conjunction with one another, and, crucially, the simultaneity of those elements—voice, face, smell, body language. This is the primary distinction that Susanne Langer makes in *Philosophy in a New Key* between discursive and presentational modes of logic or apprehension. Discursive logic is always linear. This is, of course, true of language itself. "Man bites dog" as a unit of syntax gives us three ideas or propositions or symbols in succession. Language can only be linear; therefore, it makes itself available to rules (syntax), to a lexicon (we can make a dictionary of fixed denotation—meaning that does not change), and to translation. Here's Langer's phrasing:

Language in the strict sense is essentially discursive; it has permanent units of meaning which are combinable into larger units; it has fixed equivalences that make definition and translation possible; its connotations are general, so that it requires non-verbal acts, like pointing, looking, or emphatic voice-inflections. . . .   (p. 78)

Much of what we apprehend in the world, however, is not linear—one item at a time—but simultaneous, and this is what Langer calls presentational. The senses function that way. When we witness a painting, or a man biting a dog, the elements of the visual image impress themselves simultaneously; it is only the need to verbalize them that makes them linear.

[A non-discursive symbol] is composed of elements that represent various respective constituents in the object; but these elements are not units with independent meanings. The areas of light and shade that constitute a portrait have no significance by themselves. In isolation we would consider them simply blotches. Yet they are faithful representatives of visual elements composing the visual object. . . . We may well pick out some line, say a certain curve, in a picture, which serves to represent one nameable item; but in another place the same curve would have an entirely different meaning. It has no fixed meaning apart from its context.   (pp. 76–77)

Surely we're not interested in poems that content themselves with only discursive experience for the reader. To a large extent, even though poems must, as language objects, release themselves discursively, and even though some of them undertake the discursive tasks of narrative or argument, history or philosophy, the best poems of any mode become nondiscursive symbols. That is, syntax and diction work not only to convey discursive information, not only as "rules" and denotative items from the lexicon, but also to duplicate, with their sounds, something of the inflection we respond to, in life, nondiscursively. Isn't this what we're after:

[V]erbal symbolism . . . has primarily a general reference. . . . In the non-discursive mode that speaks directly to sense, however, there is no intrinsic generality. It is first and foremost a direct presentation of an individual object.   (Langer, p. 78)

If the "object" is experience rendered by the poem, then all the sounds of the poem—and in particular patterns of sound, since they impress themselves more indelibly on the ear—work as a unified or common context (tonality) *against* the necessarily linear movement of word after word after word.

The meanings given through language are successively understood, and gathered into a whole by the process called discourse; the meanings of all other symbolic elements that compose a larger articulate symbol are understood only through the meaning of the whole, through their relations within the total structure. Their very functioning . . . depends on the fact that they are involved in a simultaneous, integral presentation.   (Langer, pp. 78–79)

In order for a poem to become such a "larger articulate symbol," context is crucial. There is no fixed emotional equivalent of any particular vowel sound, no matter its high or low "frequency" (*pace* J. F. Nims), nor any given metrical pattern (*pace* Alexander Pope), nor any particular syntactical arrangement (compare Plath's assaultive questions to Hopkins's plaintive ones). A fast song is not necessarily happier than a slow one. If anapests seem to murmur, it's because the statement as well as the sound of the statement suggests it. And when we hear tenderness in Kunitz's address, it comes from the sound as applied to the information already released—our knowledge that Sarah and Sophia are the speaker's sisters, and long dead. At the same time, it does seem true that context in a poem is built less often from narrative or expository elements, which are required by the nature of language to be linear or discursive, and more often, more easily, more effectively from those elements in a poem which appeal most directly to the senses, those instruments for gathering presentational information. Poetry derives, that is, from music and from imagery.

In much of her discussion, Langer relies on painting, on the visual and nonverbal, to develop her distinction between discursive and presentational apprehension, and one thinks as well of the sensory power of images in a poem. Certainly, Kunitz's visual cues do establish context, reinforce the tone: the long dark hair, the candlelight flickering, the bending figures are of a piece with the suggestion of something extraordinary in the heightened folk music of the opening, the initial question and consequent evocation of the elements, the broad strokes of the narrative, even the abstract central phrase, "history of tears." But I wonder if they are sufficient, without the supporting score, to establish tone— if, in fact, they aren't rather predictable pictures of ghosts, which, when isolated, might evoke either a sentimental or a cynical response.

There may be other poems that depend more heavily on imagery than this one—one thinks in particular of poetry in translation, Follian, for example, where the images seem to function as, say, a narrative or dramatic context might function, absorbing some of the contribution usually made by inflection. But the case of Sylvia Plath and her indelible imagery seems to suggest otherwise. Diary entries recording the death and funeral of a neighbor in June, 1962, rely on observed visual details that turn up again in subsequent poems—but with markedly different tonal implications. Even the difference between the diary entry and its appropriation into "Berck-Plage" is itself instructive—the tonal difference, that is, between the prose excerpt with its discursive context and reductive exposition (*it made me sick, it was a horror*), and the poem with its musical context and tonal complexity, its sense of exhilarating release and fascination.

Percy lay back on a heap of white pillows in his striped pajamas, his face already passed from humanity, the nose a spiraling, fleshless beak in thin air, the chin fallen in a point from it, like an opposite pole, and the mouth like an inverted black heart stamped into the yellow flesh between a great raucous breath coming and going there with great effort like an awful bird. . . . His eyes showed through partly open lids like dissolved soaps or a clotted pus. I was very sick at this and had a bad migraine over my left eye for the rest of the day. The end, even of so marginal a man, a horror. . . . When I went down they had just brought the coffin and put him in. The living room where he had lain was in an upheaval—bed rolled from the wall, mattresses on the lawn, sheets and pillows washed and airing. He lay in the sewing room, or parlor, in a long coffin of orangey soap-colored oak . . . the lid propped against the wall at his head with a silver scroll: Percy B, Died June 25, 1962. The raw date a shock. A sheet covered the coffin. Rose lifted it. A pale white, beaked face, as of paper, rose under the veil that covered the hole out in the glued white cloth cover. The mouth looked glued, the face powdered.   (*Johnny Panic and the Bible of Dreams*, pp. 76–77)

(II)

This black boot has no mercy for anybody.
Why should it, it is the hearse of a dead foot,

The high, dead, toeless foot of this priest . . .

(IV)

A wedding-cake face in a paper frill.
How superior he is now.

. . . The bed is rolled from the wall.

This is what it is to be complete. It is horrible.
Is he wearing pajamas or an evening suit

Under the glued sheet from which his powdery beak
Rises so whitely unbuffeted? . . .

Now the washed sheets fly in the sun,
The pillow cases are sweetening.

It is a blessing, it is a blessing:
The long coffin of soap-coloured oak,

The curious bearers and the raw date
Engraving itself in silver with marvellous calm

(VI)

The voice of the priest, in thin air,
Meets the corpse at the gate,

Addressing it, while the hills roll the notes of the dead bell;
A glitter of wheat and crude earth.   (from "Berck-Plage," June 30, 1962)

If the same image can command different emotional implications,
then images are not a dependable source of tone in a poem. Perhaps this
is because we receive them through the linear arrangement of language,
as though given first a swatch of red, then a straight black line, which
we must piece together to recreate the painting. Most probably, we are
responding as much to an abstraction of, or symbolic quality within, the
object as to some actual visualization of that object. Sound, on the other
hand, provides the simultaneity that Langer stresses. Alter the sounds
even slightly in the Kunitz poems—make it read *Shush, my dears,* or
Hush, hush, my dears—and the tone wobbles. Thus, despite the importance of each of the elements contributing to the overall "tonality" of a
poem, I have come to believe that the best poems build their tonal context—even discursive poems such as narrative and argument—primarily
through their sounds.

Let me stop to summarize. In a poem, an event or idea has been verbalized—cast into discursive logic—and we respond also with a discursive linear logic to the statements made. But we are also responding to, registering, the combined and simultaneous effect of those presentational elements that produce a "tonality" or key. It is this simultaneity that makes it so difficult to isolate the source of tone in a poem—that, and the need to break down the presentational apprehension of it into the linear or discursive logic of language when we try to talk about it. Nonetheless, I am making a case that tone is located, most often, most dependably, in sound, a nondiscursive context apart from, though simultaneous with, the discursive information provided. I say *apart from* because we can hear it when the two are in conflict or opposition, and call it irony.

Thus, I might formulate the following hypothesis:

—that the best poems also function as nondiscursive symbols, in addition to their discursive purposes;
—that the nondiscursive logic operates through tone;
—that tone itself is primarily lodged in and conveyed by the sounds of the poem, both gross motor (pattern and repetition, sentence and line) and fine motor (syllable, vowel, and consonant);
—that disregard of the music of the poem, or application of only its technical apparatus, particularly in poems already heavily discursive in mode (i.e., narrative or argument), leads to a loss or disturbance of tone, and with that loss comes a loss of clarity;
—and, conversely, if the tone is so entirely expected, or conventional, that it admits no friction between subject and the sensibility perceiving it, the poem is diminished.

"The sensibility perceiving it": are we back to the old dichotomy of thought vs. feeling? Not according to Langer:

A subject which has emotional meaning for the artist may thereby rivet his attention and cause him to see its form with a discerning, active eye, and to keep that form present in his excited imagination until its highest reaches of significance are evident to him; then he will have, and will paint, a deep and original conception of it.   (p. 203)

The presentational logic of the poem, it should be stressed, is not so much self-expression of emotions felt by the artist as it is his or her grasp of the form of the emotion: "not 'self-expression' but exposition of feelings . . . expressing primarily the artist's knowledge of human feeling, not how or when that knowledge was acquired" (Langer, p. 179). The form of the emotion, which in turn must be embodied in the formal expression or arrangement that is the text where, as Kunitz has put it elsewhere, "line-by-line progression of subtle harmonies and discords [correspond] with variable states of feeling . . ." (*Next-to-Last Things*, p. 121).

It is my purpose here to contradict the *Princeton Encyclopedia* in its use of Richards to claim that tone emanates from the poet's "attitude toward the audience"—a matter that seems to me more an element of style than of tone. Essentially, attitude toward audience is part of the fixed persona of the poet—fixed, that is, within an aesthetic position that may (indeed, must) shift over time but contains or reflects overall self-presentation. In a single volume of poems, we find an identifiable "style" that is applied to various subjects. Thus it emanates from the poet rather than from the material or subject. Sufficiently consistent through a lifetime, it becomes the thumbprint of the writer. And sometimes the style is sufficiently idiosyncratic, or sufficiently concomitant with inherent personality, so that a characteristic tone becomes a part of that style. In Elizabeth Bishop, for instance, the caution, the decorum, betrayed by her hesitancy, exactness of detail, understatement, and parenthetical syntax within a rough trimeter call to mind "Bishop" as much as hearing a familiar voice would. This seems the set of manners toward one's audience Richards must have had in mind.

But I would argue there is no necessary connection between style and tone. We can compare, for instance, several of the *Ariel* poems written in the last weeks of Plath's life, treating the same subject: her past suicide attempt and the increasing attractiveness of death as a renewed option. The style of these poems is remarkably unified—the exaggerated comparisons, the severe enjambment of sonorous passages, the punchy declarative sentences, yoked by commas or fully end-stopped as the pitch of the frenzy requires, and the dramatic description. Many of the same images recur, the boot, the toe, the bell, the beak, the lifted linen seen first in the diary entries and poem ("Berck-Plage," June 30, 1962) about the death of a neighbor. Nevertheless, the tone is remarkably different in "Daddy" (October 12), "Lady Lazarus" (October 21), "Ariel" (October 27), "Death & Co." (November 14), and "The Edge" (February 4), moving respectively from hysterical rage to puerile revenge to ecstatic escape to cool resignation to—finally—a kind of sympathy or forgiveness toward the self, now as distanced as the unaffiliated corpse in "Berck-Plage."

The source of these differences in tone seems not the poet's "attitude toward her audience" but her *apprehension of the subject*. Apprehension: no neat little division between the hard empirical fact of the subject and the warm runny ooze of the poet's "feelings." Rather, subject as perceived, and then rendered, presentationally, the form of emotion in its own logic. And a resulting tension is provided to the poem in part by the discrepancy between unchallenged (i.e., conventional) and creative understanding of the subject, that "deep and original perception of it."

I'd like then to offer a rough substitute for the Princeton definition, by way of Langer: Tone in a poem expresses the form of the emotion in that poem, and is lodged primarily in the poem's nondiscursive elements, especially in its music. Music is meant here to include both the broad units of repetition, sentence structure and lineation, and the small units of syllable, vowel, and consonant. As with "tonality" in a composition, tone organizes the attention of, first, the poet, then the reader, through a context of sounds working either with or against the discursive elements of the poem, and may itself be an element of either unity or energy (plot) within the piece.

The discursive possibilities in poetry are what currently most absorb contemporary poets, whether we are writers engaged in personal or historical narrative, neoformalists (who most often yoke the technical apparatus of verse to narrative and argument), or even "language poets" (who celebrate radically the sequential or linear nature of language by exaggerating the synapse from unit to unit). With Pound's dictum reverberating through hundreds of workshops (to make the poem "at least as good as good prose"), with theorists making a living by separating reference from its tonal context, and with our own natural aversion to the extremity of the subjective we saw in Plath and Berryman, our perception of a diminishing or alienated audience, our discomfort over the reductiveness of the domestic or personal *I*, and our wish for a greater capaciousness, poets are eager to redefine the nature of poetry. But a redefinition toward the linear risks the loss not only of power but of clarity. Langer is firm:

The logical structures underlying all semantic functions . . . suggest a general principle of division. . . . [D]iscursive and presentational patterns show a formal difference.   (p. 83)

Or, as W. B. Yeats put it in an essay of 1906, in the afternoon of another Discursive Age:

Art bids us touch and taste and hear and see the world, and shrinks from what Blake calls mathematic form, from every abstract thing, from all that is of the brain only, from all that is not a fountain jetting from the entire hopes, memories, and sensations of the body.

Close Encounters of the Story Kind

Once upon a time an editor, knowing my fascination with angels, invited me to write a story about one, and I thought, "Here's an assignment after my own heart," and I said yes. Then I panicked.

What did I know about angels?

The first angel I saw had a chipped nose. It was blond, male, and lived in a clock, which hung in the parlor of the apartment Mrs. Lear rented in my grandmother's house in Owosso, Michigan. When the hour struck, two doors opened at the top and a tiny platform revolved, bearing the archangel Michael from one door to the next. Such dignity, such beauty—he was a procession of one. Mrs. Lear's husband had fought in the First World War and brought it from Germany, along with a Luger and some empty shells. A local jeweler who repaired it told him that it must have once held other figures, probably Adam and Eve being driven from the garden. Time had taken the archangel's sword, the fugitives, and the tip of his holy nose. Nevertheless, when I knew the hour was preparing to strike, I would knock on Mrs. Lear's door and ask to see the angel, moving from darkness into darkness. When the novelty wore off and I no longer asked, Mrs. Lear would knock on my grandmother's apartment to announce the angel was marching and did I want to watch it?

An angel marching from darkness into darkness—such an event should not go unnoticed.

The second angel I saw was a picture from an old insurance calendar that my grandmother had saved long after the year was out. A young woman in a white nightgown is standing with arms outstretched over two children playing at the edge of a cliff. There is a large asterisk of apple butter on her wings, as if someone had hurled a full jar during an argument, and the angel had taken a blow intended for someone else.

The calendar hung in my grandfather's treatment room, where patients with rheumatism and asthma came to avail themselves of the wonders of osteopathy. Only the angel and our family knew that the treatment room had once been a pantry and the waiting room doubled as the doctor's bedroom; my grandfather unfolded the sofa at night to sleep and in the morning folded it up again before the office opened. Grandmother, who managed the renting of the other rooms, had her own quarters off the kitchen.

Though I have seen many pictures of angels since these two, they seem the real ones, the standard by which all others should be measured.

Two days after I'd agreed to write a book about angels, my sister, Kirsten, called from Ann Arbor with bad news.

"Mother fell and broke her hip," she said, "so I grabbed the first plane out of Pittsburgh last night. The doctor said he wants to give her a new one."

"A new hip? At eighty-seven?"

"He said it's her only chance of walking. And it's man-made, so it's even better than her old one. It will last forever."

"Is she conscious?"

"She's right here. I'll put her on the phone."

I pressed my ear to the receiver and heard nothing.

"Mother? How are you feeling?"

She did not answer for a long time, and when she did, she sounded far off, as if she were speaking from a different room.

"Isn't it the limit I should have to go through this?" she whispered.

A long silence, broken by Kirsten's voice.

"I found Mother's purse. It's been missing for two months. And now we can't find her teeth. They've simply vanished for good and all."

"How long will she be in the hospital?"

"A week. They like to get you out early here. But we'll need round-the-clock care when she moves home."

"What about bringing her to Shady Park?" I asked. "Can they keep her?"

From the house she'd lived in for fifty years my mother moved to a single large room in Shady Park Manor, a convalescent home in Pittsburgh five blocks from my sister and her husband. She had a room of her own. Kirsten made sure of that. On its bare surfaces my sister put spindles of snapshots; on its white walls she hung the brass filigree frames that kept us all in line: me in my cap and gown standing beside Daddy in the cap and gown he only wore when pressed into marching at Commencement; my sister in her wedding dress, rising from a swirl of lace; the grandchildren, who had long ago outgrown their school portraits; Mother's diploma from Michigan, its blue and gold ribbon faded but intact. The bureau held her lavender underwear, her nylons, her purple shoes. The closet held all ten of her best purple dresses.

This was the room I saw when I arrived from New York. My classes at Vassar were finished, Kirsten and John would be gone for two weeks. The note in the kitchen laid out my duties.

"Please take in the mail, water the plants in the dining room, and feed the tortoise. He only eats scraped carrots. Scraper is on sink. Please take Mother's dresses to the laundromat and wash them on DELICATE. They wash everything in hot water at the home."

Every morning I walked the five blocks to Shady Park. Past the Fourth Presbyterian Church and the synagogue, past the Greek restaurant, the Cafe del Sol, the Korean grocer who hangs strings of jade beads in the window among the melons. Past Eat'n Park, where families carry heaping plates from the salad bar and single men sit at the counter, drinking coffee and smoking. Past Jacov's Vegetarian Deli and Tucker's Secondhand Books.

Shady Park Manor stands over all, at the top of a steep hill. I hurry through the lobby, beautifully decorated in silver and blue wallpaper, up the stairs past the nurse's station. When I arrive at my mother's room she is sitting up in her chair, asleep, belted in, like a passenger in a plane about to land—but somewhere deep in the body of the plane, the fatigued metal has given way and sent this one woman, still strapped to her seat, hurtling through space.

Over my mother's bed, someone has taped a list of instructions.

7:30: Get Mrs W. up to eat breakfast. Be sure dentures are in with fast-teeth powder.

8:00–2:00: Keep Mrs W. up once she is in chair. She will fight to go back to bed, but she needs to be kept active.

"Mom," I say, "wake up!"

She opens her eyes.

"What is this place?"

"A condominium," I lie. "Come on, Ma, let's get the wheelchair and go for a spin around the block."

"Why can't I walk? What's the matter with me?"

"You broke your hip."

I unfold the wheelchair and lift her into it. She is staring at my feet.

"You need new shoes," she says.

We both gaze down at my scuffed loafers. Miles of pavement have pared the heels away and loosened the stitching.

"Promise me you'll buy a new pair. Take some money from my purse. Where is my purse?"

I hand it to her. She opens it and peers in and twitches up a five dollar bill.

"Didn't I have more money than this when I started?"

"Oh, Mother, you don't need any money here."

"Is this an old people's home?"

"It's a condominium, Ma."

"It's a home. I never thought my children would put me in a home."

"Ma, you need twenty-four-hour care."

"What did people do in the old days?"

What *did* they do? Dutiful daughters struggled with lifting, feeding, and changing their aged parents. I thought of my mother under the stress of caring for her own mother, who lived with us when I was growing up. Does my mother remember the night she got up to go to the bathroom and passed out from exhaustion? She landed against the radiator. Now, at the edge of her short sleeve I can see the long scar on my mother's arm, deep as a knife wound, where the flesh burned slowly away as she lay, numb to the pain. These dutiful women—caregivers, is the current term for them—did not go off to jobs in the morning. And they certainly were not writers.

We pass the nurse's station and the board that lists the day's activities. Talking Book Club, Pet Therapy, Monday Night Movie, Bingo, Current Events, Sensory Stimulation, this month's birthdays. In the all-purpose room, the physical therapist is tossing a beach ball to a group of men and women in wheelchairs. None of them raise their arms. As I wheel Mother outside into the sunshine, she raises a pleading face to mine.

"Can't you find a little corner in your house for me?"

In the evening, when I unlock the door of my sister's house, the tortoise creeps out of his shell and crosses the kitchen floor to meet me. His ancient eyes blink when I scrape his carrots, letting the shavings pile up on the plate like golden pages. Outside in the shimmering heat, children play hide-and-seek and call to each other. The bedroom is suffocating. I carry my sheet and pillow downstairs and make a bed on the living room floor. I read another chapter in John Gardner's *The Art of Fiction* and underline a sentence that sounds like good advice, if only I knew how to follow it: "Fiction does its work by creating a dream in the reader's mind." The last sound I hear before falling asleep is the tortoise taking his constitutional, the faint scraping of his claws along the floor.

Have I told you everything? No. I have not told you how every evening I sat down at my brother-in-law's electric portable and worked on my story. A story about an angel.

The hardest part about writing a story or a novel is beginning it. A letter that arrived recently from a friend of mine whose first novel got rave reviews opens with these words: "So painful coming into possession of a new novel. There is a deep agenda, and I sometimes think I haven't the faintest clue what it is. Still, every day, here I am, at my table, facing it and struggling with lethargy." The material of a story offers itself to the writer like a house in which all the doors and windows are locked. Whose story is it? Whose voice does it belong to? The opening sentence is the key, the way into the house. It may let you in at the front door like a homeowner or at the window like a thief, but it lets you in.

For my angel story, I had no opening sentence. But I had a great many notes on angels, particularly those I deemed useful to writers. Uriel the angel of poetry and Raphael the angel of healing led the list. And how many angels there are, for every problem and purpose! There is an angel who presides over memory and an angel who presides over time, even an angel who presides over Monday. There is an angel for small birds and an angel for tame beasts, an angel for solitude and an angel for patience and an angel for hope. The angel who watches over footstools can offer you a pillar of light to support you, a gift that Hemingway and Virginia Woolf would have appreciated since both wrote standing up.

I also noted the angels who presided over conditions that writers pray to be spared. Barakiel is the angel of chance, Michael the angel of chaos and insomnia, Harbonah the angel of annihilation, and Abaddon the angel of the abyss.

But among the angels, who can really tell which are for us and which against us? There is an angel who presides over hidden things. Forgotten names, lost notes, misplaced drafts—does he hide them or find them? There is an angel of odd events. Are they gifts or griefs, lucky accidents or lost opportunities?

Notice, I didn't say I wrote my story. I said, *worked on it*. What did I really know about angels? How do we come to know things as a writer? I looked at my notes but no story came. What was I looking for? I made tea. I thought of how other writers prepared to face the blank page. Balzac drank fifty cups of coffee a day, till it killed him, Disraeli put on evening clothes, George Cohan rented a Pullman car drawing room and traveled till he was done with the book or story. Emerson took walks. Colette's husband locked her in her room, and Victor Hugo gave his clothes to his servant with instructions to return them when he was done.

After struggling with the story for three days, I understood the problem. This story had the shape of the one I'd just finished writing. What we've just written lays its shadow on the next work, and it can happen with any length, any genre. A friend who was working on her second novel told me, "It took me two years to break the spell of my first book when I started my second. I kept wanting to repeat what had worked so well. Combinations of characters. Scenes." Writing is like panning for gold. You put your pan down close to the mother lode and scoop up a handful of gravel. You know the grains of ore are sparkling in front of you, if only you could see them. Knowing this, even when you find nothing but broken stones it's hard to throw them away.

So I wrote a story about angels. I wrote badly. I was on the wrong track, but I didn't have the courage to throw those pages away, for then I'd have nothing. Keats was right. All writing is a form of prayer. Was anybody out there listening?

Let me say right now that I don't think anyone can command the angel to come, though I've known at least one person to try, a nun who told her first graders about the guardian angels they'd received at baptism and then said, "I want you all to move over and make room for your angel." Twenty-five first graders shifted to the right and made room for the incorporeal and the invisible. *That* is perfect faith. The nephew who told me the story takes a more skeptical view of angels now.

None of this would be worth telling if I hadn't promised my sister that I'd wash Mother's clothes at the laundromat, and what shouldn't happen did happen. I had a simple plan. I would sit with Mother till noon. While she ate her lunch in the dining room, I would carry the laundry basket over to the Laundry Bored and read *The Art of Fiction* and work on my story while the clothes were spinning. And maybe I could take lunch down the street at Jacov's Vegetarian Deli. It had been closed all week but a sign promised it would be open on Monday.

I arrived at Shady Park around eleven and headed for Mother's room. A thin white-haired woman was walking toward me on crutches, leaning heavily on stout Miss Davidson, the physical therapist. Miss Davidson beckoned me over.

"I've been trying to get your mom to walk. She doesn't try. She won't even stand up for me. See if you can get her to make an effort."

"I'll do my best," I said.

"Now Beulah here is doing fine," said Miss Davidson.

The woman on crutches nodded.

"I walk every chance I get," she said. "Miss Davidson says, 'Well, how about heading back to your room now?' and I say, 'It hurts, but let's go just once more, up and down the corridor.' I can't wait to go home."

Miss Davidson frowned at me.

"Medicare won't pay for your mother's room if she's not taking part in the physical therapy program."

"Is she doing any activities?" I asked hopefully.

"She likes the crafts," said Miss Davidson. "She made a purple flyswatter out of felt yesterday. And she had the kitten on her lap the whole day."

"What kitten?" I asked.

"Pet therapy," said Beulah. "Your mother wouldn't let anyone else have it. Kept it on her lap the whole time."

When I walked into her room, Mother was asleep in her chair.

"Ma," I said, "I hear you had a kitten."

She opened her eyes.

"What kitten?" she said.

"She forgot already," said Beulah, leaning in the doorway. Mother turned to her.

"My husband taught for forty-seven years at the University of Michigan. We have a total of twenty-two degrees in our family, all from Michigan."

"Isn't that nice," said Beulah. "Now me, I never went to college. My papa worked in the steel mill, and so did my husband till it shut down. I'm going downstairs in the wheelchair. They have Kool-Aid on the terrace."

We heard her thumping back to her room. Mother gave me an odd look.

"Why are you carrying a box of soap?" she asked.

"I'm going to wash your clothes."

And I heaved the laundry basket onto one hip. Lavender plastic; my sister had picked it especially for her.

"You're a good girl," she said and smiled. "Lord, I'm just an ordinary mother. How did I get two such wonderful daughters?"

I wheeled her downstairs, and we sat on the terrace with Beulah till lunch time. The only other patient was a thin silent man in a wheelchair and a young woman who sat beside him asking,

"Grandpa, can you talk? Can you talk, Grandpa?"

"That's Mr. Levine," said Beulah. "He's a hundred and two. The president sent him a telegram." She leaned forward and whispered in my ear,

"You ask him how old he is and he shouts 'A hundred and two.' There's not much else he knows. He has Alzheimer's. And he still has a full head of hair."

"What disease do I have?" asked Mother.

"You broke your hip," I said.

"I've had lots of broken bones," said Beulah. "Last year I broke my arm."

Mother stared down at her own arm, the scarred one, as if it had just been brought for her approval.

"How old it looks," she said softly.

The Laundry Bored was nearly empty. A woman was sitting under the lone hairdryer, reading a magazine from which the cover had been ripped away. I threw Mother's clothes in the machine, dialed it to *warm*, and poured in the soap. I put *The Art of Fiction* and my box of Tide in the laundry basket and strolled half a block to Jacov's Vegetarian Deli.

The restaurant was tiny—no more than five tables. A sign on the wall read "TEL AVIV, Jerusalem, Ben Gurion Airport. Discover your Roots!" Only one other customer, an elderly man in a black suit, was waiting at the take-out counter for his order. The two cooks wore yarmulkahs, yet how different the same garment looked on each of them. The older man was clean-shaven and middle-aged. When he chopped the onions, he seemed to be murdering them. He poured coffee as if it were poison, he shoved a plate of dumplings at the elderly man like a punishment. The younger cook had a thick blond beard, kindly blue eyes, and he loped from the stove to the ice box to the counter as if he had not a care in the world.

The menu over the counter listed vegetable soup and vegetarian pizza.

"I'll have soup," I said. "What kind of dumplings did you just give that man?"

"You won't like them," said the sour cook.

"I'll have them anyway," I said.

"Try one first," said the young cook, "and if you like it, I'll give you a plateful."

He handed me a dumpling on a paper plate. It tasted like nothing I'd ever eaten before or would want to eat again. I ordered a plate of them, to spite the sour cook. The elderly gentleman took his paper plate, paused at a small rack on the wall from which he plucked a greasy page. Out of curiosity, I took one also and found it was a page from the Jewish prayer book, Hebrew on one side, English on the other. There was also a pamphlet, *Thought for the Week*, so I took that as well and read it as I munched my dumplings:

A Thought for the Week: Love your fellow Jew as you love yourself.

Alas, I was not a Jew. They would feed me here but they would not love me. I read on:

Sidra Vayeishev. It is different at home (Part II). Last week we learned that our forefather Jacob did not feel "at home" in the world of material possessions. Knowing that he was only a temporary resident in this physical world he felt that his true "home" was in matters of the Neshama, in Torah and Mitzvos. The world with all its comforts, its palaces and mansions, is nothing more than a tent, erected during the journey of life to sleep over for a night, or rest for a day or two. And on a journey, after all, only the bare necessities of eating and sleeping are required; but when the journey is over and one comes home . . . well, at home it's different.

When I'd finished the last greasy bite, I put the pamphlet and the prayer sheet in the rack and returned to the laundromat. The lights on the machine were off. The clothes were clean. So was the top of the machine.

The clothesbasket, along with *The Art of Fiction* and my manuscript, had vanished.

Though the day was hot, I felt as cold as if I wore the wind for a cloak. A terrible calm washed over me, leaving me lightheaded. Loss had numbed my capacity to rage.

Suddenly, among the *Reader's Digests* on the folding table, I spied *The Art of Fiction*. I snatched it up. With shaking fingers I rifled through all the other magazines, shook them, and waited for my manuscript to come out of hiding, like a mischievous child.

Nothing. On this occasion the angel who presides over hidden things was not on my side.

What else was there to do but walk across the street and sit on the bench at the bus stop and consider my life? When the elderly gentleman from Jacov's Deli sat next to me, I was scarcely aware of him till he began to edge closer.

"I notice the subject of your book," he said. "It is a subject dear to my heart. Are you a writer?"

"Yes," I said.

"Stories? You write stories?"

"Stories, a novel, poems," I said.

"I too wrote stories once," he said, "though I am not a writer now. I am a teacher. A teacher of American literature. But I have written stories."

My heart sank. He saw in me a kindred soul. Soon he would press his manuscript upon me. Yet he had used the past tense; perhaps he wrote stories no more. Had his inspiration run dry? Had he lost his memory?

"What kind of stories do you write?" he asked, "if I may ask?"

"Short stories," I said.

"Forgive me," he said. "It's like asking the birds what kind of eggs they lay. Blue? Speckled? Large? Small?"

"Look," I said, "I can't really talk about my stories just now. Somebody just stole the only copy of the story I've been working on for weeks."

"You are sure somebody stole it?" he asked, as if such things did not happen in this world.

"I left it in the laundromat while I was eating lunch. And when I came back—"

"Excuse me," he interrupted, "but may I tell you a story? Long ago there lived in a north province in China a man good at interpreting events. This man had a son, and one day the son's best mare ran away and was taken by the nomads across the border. The son was distraught, but his father said, "What makes you think this isn't a blessing?" Many months later, the horse returned, bringing with her a magnificent stallion. The son was delighted and mounted the horse, but had scarcely set out for a ride when he fell and broke his hip. Again he was distraught, and again his father said, "What makes you think this isn't a blessing?" Two years later the nomads invaded and every able-bodied man marched to battle. All were lost. Only the lame son and the elderly father survived. What is blessing and what is disaster?"

"Somebody stole my story. That's a disaster," I said.

Two young women joined us on the bench till one murmured to the other, "I can't stand this heat. I'm going to the drugstore."

"What you need in the drugstore?" said the other.

"Nothing. It's air-conditioned," said the first. "We can look at magazines."

I was about to follow them when the elderly gentleman said,

"Steinbeck's dog chewed the first half of the draft of Mice and Men. And Steinbeck forgave him, saying, 'I'm not sure Toby didn't know what he was doing when he ate that first draft. I have promoted Toby-dog to be lieutenant-colonel in charge of literature.' You know, I used to write stories. And I almost wrote a novel. I had three hundred pages written in a big notebook. And then the war came. During the war I lost everything."

"How terrible to lose a novel!" I cried. I meant to say, how terrible to lose everything.

He shook his head.

"Really, in my case, it was a blessing. I wanted to write a family history, a *Bildungsroman*. Thomas Mann was my hero. I had notes, a family tree, plans, hundreds of plans. But in my heart of hearts I knew my novel sounded wooden. A wise man said, "A writer with a fixed idea is like a goose trying to hatch a stone." In 1940, I was sent to Ravensbrück. All my life my teachers told me not to daydream. Now it was my salvation. Can you outline a dream? Would it be worth dreaming if you could? In that terrible place I let my mind wander, and my characters came back to me, not as I saw them in my notes and plans but as they saw themselves, full of memories and longings. I understood their real story at last. I turned no one away. Does the sea refuse a single river? Have you heard of Van Der Post and his explorations of Africa?"

"No," I said. "Sorry."

"Never mind. He tells of the time he traveled to a village where a great hunter lived. When he arrived, he found the hunter sitting motionless. And the villagers said, 'Don't interrupt him. He is doing work of the utmost importance. He is making clouds.'"

"Did you finish your novel?" I asked. I have a weakness for happy endings.

"How could I finish it? We had no paper. No pens. But we had tongues. So I became a storyteller instead of a writer. I no longer thought of plots, only of voice. Of whose story I was telling. When I hear the voice, I know the story will find me. Storytellers do not lose their stories, except when they die. I like to start my stories in the old style, *once upon a time.* Once upon a time is a promise, a promise of a story, and I try to keep my promises. Of course not everyone agrees with me about these methods. My son, for example. He's a TV writer. Weekends, he wants to write the great American novel, but he doesn't know how to get started. One day he calls me from New York, all excited. 'I've just signed a contract to write the bible!' Naturally I'm interested. He goes on to say that this bible is not from God, of course. This is the book TV script writers use when they're doing a new series of shows. It describes characters, it describes place, it describes adventures.

"'And for what show are you writing a bible?' I ask my son.

"'It's a mini-series,' he says. 'It's called *The Further Adventures of Alice in Wonderland.'*

"'How can that be?' I say. 'There is only one Lewis Carroll.'

" 'Yes, papa, but there are five script writers. They'll make up the other adventures. But they can write only about what they know. I'm going to write them a detailed description of Wonderland and the characters.' What do you think, fellow-scribbler? Is it a good idea, the further adventures of *Alice in Wonderland*?"

"I don't know," I said. "What happened to your son?"

"My son read the Alice books carefully. He mapped the terrain, noted the architecture, the dangers, the geography, the birds and animals. He wrote out character studies of everyone mentioned in the books. And he got paid well. And suddenly a brilliant idea struck him. Why not write a bible for his great unwritten American novel? How much easier it would be to start his novel if he had a detailed knowledge of his characters. Hadn't his English teachers always said, 'Write about what you know'?"

"My teachers said the same thing," I laughed.

"They all say it," said the elderly gentleman. "I even said it to my students. But I didn't mean my students should write such a bible. If you take everyone's advice, you'll build a crazy house. My son wrote descriptions of all his characters and their locale. Then he wrote the first two chapters and showed them to me. 'Aaron,' I said, 'how can I tell you? This is from your head, not your heart. It's predictable. No surprises. Even God is surprised by the actions of his creatures.'

" 'I've put a lot of time into this,' he said.

" 'The nest is done but the bird is dead,' I told him. 'You should take a lesson from your Lewis Carroll. He was a storyteller. I know for a fact that when he sent his Alice down the rabbit hole, he didn't know what would happen next. That white rabbit was a gift from Providence! We should follow Providence, not force it.' He's intelligent, my Aaron, but he thinks too much. He needs intelligence to keep him from hindering himself so he is free to do amazing things. I tell him to watch Charlie Chaplin. You have seen his great film, *Modern Times*?"

"A long time ago," I said, hoping he wouldn't quiz me on it.

"Maybe you remember, near the end, Charlie has to go on the stage and sing a song. And now he can't remember the words! So Paulette Goddard writes the words on his cuff. He goes onstage, he tries to read them, he's hopeless. Not a sound out of him. He's paralyzed. And then Paulette Goddard calls out, 'Never mind the words. Just sing.' "

"I think that kind of thing happens only when you tell stories," I said, "not when you write them."

"It can also happen when you write them," he said. "You have two choices. You can arrange the material, with outlines. Or you can arrange yourself. I see you looking at the laundromat. You have business there?"

"I forgot to put my mom's clothes in the dryer."

"And you want to see if the thief returned your manuscript," he added.

"Yes," I agreed.

Suddenly I remembered my promise.

"Excuse me," I said, rising. "Do you know a good shoe store?"

"From writing to shoes!" he said, and laughed.

"I have to run. I promised my mother I'd buy some new shoes."

"Are you in such a hurry?" he exclaimed. "Let me tell you about a man who set out to buy himself shoes. He measured his foot and put the measurements away. When he got to the market, he found he'd left the measurements at home. He chose a pair of shoes and hurried home for the measurements, but when he returned the market was closed. He never got the shoes, of course. And that night he dreamed his feet asked him, 'Why didn't you trust us? Why did you trust the measurements more than your own feet?"

We stood up in unison.

"There's a department store one street over," he said. "But all shoe stores are good if you need shoes."

I didn't go shopping for shoes, and I didn't find my manuscript. When I arrived at Shady Park, Mother was not in her room. She had been wheeled into the TV room. She was asleep, her head nearly on her chest; she had been left at a long empty table with her back to the TV. Probably she had told the attendant that she didn't like television. The other chairs were all facing the set, as if their occupants were worshipping it.

I rushed in and turned her chair around.

"Wake up, Ma. We're going back to your room."

But Mr. Levine's chair was stuck in the doorway, blocking it. He was making helpless swoops with his hands, trying to move the wheels.

"Let me help you," I said, and pushed him through.

Instantly a ripple of movement started behind me, as if I had waked the very walls.

"Lady, can you help me?"

"Miss, can you get me out of here? Miss!"

Heads lifted, hands waved.

"Miss!"

I can't help them all, I thought.

"Mother, do you want to look at the box of photographs with me?"

"I want to lie down," she said.

What angel was present in the room with us on that evening? The angel of chance or the angel of memory? The angel of time or the angel of hidden things? After I'd put away her dresses, clean but rumpled from being carried in my arms, I sat on the edge of her bed and flipped through the box of snapshots. Tucked in among the pictures were Christmas cards. Mother never threw away a Christmas card that had a photograph on it. I held up a picture of an elderly couple standing in front of the Taj Mahal.

"Who in thunder are they?" exclaimed Mother.

"I don't know," I said. "Let me read you the writing on the back. 'We visited fourteen countries and had a wonderful time. Love, Dorothy and Jack.'"

"Are both my parents dead?" asked Mother.

"Oh, Ma, you know they died a long time ago. If they were alive, they'd be a hundred and twenty."

I pulled out another picture and held it up. It showed a middle-aged woman standing on what appeared to be a cistern and smiling. I turned the photograph over and read the scrawled inscription.

"This is your old Aunt Velda standing by the well. Clark covered it over for me and put in running water, hot and cold. He also made the driveway you see behind me, to the left."

Mother's face brightened.

"I remember that well," she said. "There was a pump on Grandpa's farm in Iowa. Oh, he had acres and acres of the best farmland in the county. And when the men were working in the fields, Grandma would fill a bucket of water from that pump. And she'd send me out with the bucket and dipper to give the men a drink. And it seemed like such a long walk coming and going, I was dying of thirst by the time I got back to the house. And Grandma wouldn't let me pour myself a drink from the pump right off. No. She made me hold my wrists under the spout, and she'd pump and pump the water over them. To cool my blood, she said, so the cold drink wouldn't give me a stomachache. Lord, how good that cold water felt. And how good it tasted."

I'd never heard her tell this story. How many other stories lay hidden in her heart, waiting for a listener to wake them?

Suddenly I understood my real task. I would lay my angel story aside and forget about it for a while. Tomorrow I would bring a notebook and start writing down her memories. I would have to be patient. Memory has nothing to do with outlines and everything to do with accidents.

On my way home I stopped once more at the Laundry Bored and couldn't believe my eyes. There on top of the fateful washing machine stood the clothes basket. And safe in its plastic lavender embrace nestled my story.

I pulled it out and turned the pages, checking them for bruises. I counted the pages. I pulled up a chair and reread them. Was the angel of hope responsible for what happened next?

I threw the entire manuscript in the wastebasket. I would take Rilke's advice: "If the angel deigns to come, it will be because you have convinced him, not by tears, but by your horrible resolve to be a begginner."

Voices. Voices. That night, before I fell asleep, I heard the voices of my characters, though faintly, like a conversation accidentally picked up on a long distance line. I did not let them know I was listening.

The next morning I set out for Shady Park Manor with a light heart and was pleasantly surprised to meet my storyteller coming out of the synagogue at the end of the block.

"You are going to visit your mother? May I walk with you as far as Jerry's Good and Used?"

"What's Jerry's Good and Used?"

"Jerry has this and that of everything. His specialty is baseball cards. He calls last night and says, 'I have a treasure. Something you want very much, a card of the great Japanese ballplayer, Sadaharu Oh.' He asks me why I want a card of Sadaharu Oh. I tell him that I want a picture of the man who wrote in his autobiography not about winning but about waiting. Waiting, he says in that book, is the most active state of all. It is the beginning of all action. Did you find your manuscript?"

"I found it. And I threw it away. I'm starting over. This time I'll wait for the story to find me. Like you said yesterday."

I expected my new acquaintance to offer his congratulations, but he did not.

"The freedom of the dream doesn't mean doing nothing. You still have to sit down every day and write. What if the angel came and you were out shopping for shoes? God helps the drowning sailor, but he must row. You have a long journey ahead of you. And it starts with one footstep."

"It feels more like an ending than a beginning," I said.

"Endings and beginnings—are they so far from each other? When I was in Ravensbrück I was chosen to die. Only because someone among the killers recognized me was I saved. Now when I tell my stories, I remember that moment. It makes the telling more urgent. How is your mother?"

"Fine, I guess. Just very tired."

"You know, when I was little, my mother would put me to sleep by describing rooms in all the houses she'd lived in. And so many things happened in those rooms. Now you can hardly find a house in which someone has died or been born. It all happens away from us, in big hospitals."

"My mother told me a story yesterday," I said. And I described to him my mother's journey to the harvest fields with the bucket of water, and the journey back to the well, and the cold water on her wrists.

He was silent for so long that I felt I had said something foolish.

"The cold water—it's such an unimportant detail," I remarked.

"Unimportant?" he exclaimed. "That is why it's worth remembering. When I was young I fell in love with a girl named Hilda who happened to be a twin. I asked her to go out with me. She agreed to go, but only if I could tell her apart from her sister. I studied her face for several minutes. Then she ran and got her twin. Hilda had a blue vein on the bridge of her nose. Unimportant, a blue vein, but when I spied it, I knew I was saved."

"I'll save that detail about the cold water for my next story," I assured him.

He wagged a finger at me.

"Don't save it. Use it, use it now. You just threw out your life savings. This is no time for prudence."

We passed Jerry's Good and Used. My storyteller did not go in. Instead he kept pace with me, up the hill to Shady Park Manor.

"May I tell you a story as we take this little walk together? Long ago, when wizards still walked the length and breadth of the earth, there arrived in the world of the dead a great magician.

" 'Why have you come here?' asked the Mistress of the Dead.

The magician explained that when he was building his boat he found he could not finish it without four magic words, and that he had not been able to find them, however far he traveled.

" 'The Lord of the Dead will never teach you his spells,' answered the Mistress of the Dead.

But the magician would not give up the task of finishing his boat. He wandered here and there until one day he met a shepherd who told him to seek out the giant.

" 'In his vast mouth there are a hundred magic words. You will have to go down into his enormous belly and there you will learn marvels. But it's not easy to get there. You must go along a path leaping on the points of women's needles, and over a cross-road paved with sharp swords, and down a third road made of the blades of heroes' axes.'

But the magician was determined to try it. He would do anything to find those four words and finish his boat. Four words! Marvelous words! Would you believe I once bought a photography book because of a single sentence? I was standing in Tucker's—it's a block down the street from us—and I opened up a book and read the epigraph on the first page. It was the beginning and the ending of *Finnegans Wake.*

> A way a lone a last a loved
> along the riverrun,
> past Eve and Adam's

Right away I wanted to read *Finnegans Wake.* But Tucker's didn't have it. And the library was closed for a week. But how could I live without those words? So I bought the photography book. I bought it for those words."

We arrived at Shady Park.

"It is good you are listening to your mother."

"I'm going to write her memories down. I don't want to forget them."

"If you forget a few, don't worry. What you need will come back to you. We don't really understand something until we have forgotten it. Live in your roots, not in your branches."

I took the elevator to the second floor. When I stepped out a nurse hurried up to me.

"Your mother had a seizure last night. We phoned for the ambulance just an hour ago. Call Dr. Rubin right away—you can use the phone at the nurse's station."

The voice of medical authority at the other end of the phone named the problem: staxis epilepsicus. Dr. Rubin explained he had given her Valium and phenobarbital.

"It took us over an hour to stop her seizures. Now she's asleep."

"Did she have a stroke?"

"This morning I thought yes. When I looked at the CAT scan, I thought no. Her brain is shrunken, and there's an abnormal pattern of electric ions. It's probably caused by the little strokes she's had earlier."

"I'll be right over."

I hung up and the nurse touched my arm.

"I'm so sorry," she said. "Let me call you a cab."

I waited downstairs for the cab. The receptionist was changing the bulletin board, posting the new activities. Bingo, Sensory Stimulation, Current Events, Patio Outing.

A way a lone a last a loved along the riverrun.

Dr. Rubin and I are standing by my mother's bed in the intensive care section. Mother is sleeping under the watchful gaze of the IV and the blood pressure basket hanging over her bead, its black tubes coiled into a nest. Over the basket a large plastic bottle bubbles and quakes. This is not the first time I have seen Mother in intensive care.

"When do you think she'll wake up?" I ask.

The doctor shrugs.

"Who knows? It could be tomorrow. It could be in ten minutes. Or it could be never."

I reach out and touch her hair, still soft and wavy, and the translucent skin on her temple: pale freckled silk. The doctor pulls away the plastic respirator that covers the center of her face with a clear green beak, and her sunken cheeks flutter in and out like the throat of a frightened bird. A tube snakes out of her nose, ready for her next feeding. Her mouth is a small black hole. The doctor leans close to her face, as if he might kiss her. Then he pries open her eyelids and looks deeply into her pupils and calls,

"Mrs Williams! Mrs. Williams!"

Two green-gray coins stare back at him, as cold and indifferent as the eyes of a fish. I feel my knees growing weak and I sit down fast on the edge of her bed.

"Can she hear us now?"

"Possibly. There's no way of knowing for sure."

When he leaves us alone together, I take her hand, frail as the claw of a wren. The IV has left a deep bruise on her arm. How old it looks, this arm, limp when I lift it, a mottled mineral brown, across which white scars move like the shapes of ancient beasts.

I know I will never see her alive again. I do not know if she can hear. I put my mouth close to her ear and tell her I love her. I thank her for telling me about the cold water. I tell that I lost my story in Pittsburgh, a story about angels. I lost it at the laundromat, and I met a man who told me how to find it again. Maybe he wasn't a man at all, maybe he was the story angel? He did not have wings but who needs wings in Pittsburgh? Though my mouth is touching her ear, I feel my mother going farther and farther away. I want to talk to her till she is out of earshot. Though she is traveling with empty hands, I do not want my mother, who has given me so much, to leave with an empty heart. I give her an angel, a daughter, and herself. And I give her my promise to save them: *once upon a time.*

Twenty Questions

Movie stars are always asked what seem like extremely nosy and extraneous questions. "What do you wear to bed?" is probably the most famous of them all, and the most famous answer, usually attributed to Marilyn Monroe, is, simply, "Chanel No. 5." Very entertaining, but is it *useful* information? That depends on who's trying to use it. For the movie fan who longs to escape his own drab existence, it can provide visual and olfactory aid. For the aspiring starlet, there's a hint in Monroe's answer of how to distinguish yourself through naked lies and outrageous truths.

The following twenty questions are among those most frequently asked of writers, especially by students in workshops and audiences after readings. Many of them have always seemed pretty silly to me—who really cares whether you use a word processor or not? And does it matter if Hemingway stood or sat at his desk? What does any of that tell you about the *craft* of writing? But inquiring minds persistently want to know, so I've decided to reconsider the questions and see if there are, after all, some practical answers.

1. Do you use a word processor? Yes, I do, and Jane Austen probably used a quill, and Hemingway stood at a kind of bookcase-lectern and wrote with a pencil, one of twenty he's said to have sharpened every morning. Robert Frost would write almost anywhere except at a desk, even on the sole of his shoe. John Cheever once considered writing a novel on the plaster cast on his broken leg, starting at the toes and working upward, and Georges Simenon expressed a desire to carve one of his novels in a piece of wood. What I'm trying to convey is that like all magicians, we look for the sleight of hand that will fool not only our

audience but ourselves. Each of us develops particular rituals of work that get us going, that keep us going. These rituals *are* essential, and even sacred, but finally, it is not really the method that matters so much as the madness that impels it.

Still, I wish I could say that *I* use a quill—that kind of purity, so late in the twentieth century, would have a certain panache. But I'm too lazy and impatient—even a self-correcting Selectric seems sluggish and uncooperative lately. Like many writers, I've always been afraid of disturbing my sacred rituals by changing my tools. What I've learned is that the rituals can usually be safely transferred to a new instrument. Once I wrote stories on a manual typewriter at the kitchen table, facing my husband, who was typing psychological reports on his own little Remington Standard. We were like Ferrante and Teicher at their twin pianos. But now, after years of mulish, superstitious resistance, I have fallen headlong into technology. Even the technological language, with its vaguely sexual overtones—hardware, software, user-friendly, mode commands—fascinates as it repels. I was especially struck by the computer salesman saying, "Memory is getting cheaper every day." Tell that to Proust, I thought.

Louis Simpson advises against the use of word processors for poets because, he says, it makes rewriting too easy and "destroys the sense of urgency that is the very life of the poem." The poets will have to address Mr. Simpson's findings. But for novelists and other writers of long prose pieces, I think a word processor is invaluable. Not, alas, that characters and ideas develop independently behind the darkened screen while you sleep. But you do save the time and energy that retyping, cutting, and pasting all take. Graham Greene, who uses a pencil himself and never even learned to type, says, "There's a little bit of computer in everyone's head." But I find, lately, that the machine's memory (cheap or not) is more reliable than mine, and its electric hum and Martian-green light beckon me to work when I'd much rather play. I wouldn't advise trying to learn to use a word processor in the middle of a writing project, though. That would be something like dieting and quitting smoking at the same time. And beware—reading the work on the page and on the screen is subtly, but significantly, different. I still print out pages each day that I can carry around and compulsively scribble on. Those scribbles seem reassuringly human. They prove that the final, clean manuscript falling from the printer comes out of the old struggles of labor and revision, and not from some easy mechanical process. Remember, the book that appears to have written itself may have to read itself. That's all I care to say on the subject—the dangers of using a word processor are nothing compared to the dangers of talking about it. At lunch today, see if you hear more people discussing their programs or their prosody.

2. Where do you get your ideas? I don't. I get characters, and my characters get ideas.

3. Where do you get your characters? Are they based on people you know? If I knew where I got my characters, I'd go right back for a fresh batch. At the risk of sounding like Joan of Arc, I can only say that their voices invade my consciousness, and start to tell me their story. If I'm interested enough to become a co-conspirator, a novel is begun. I suppose we're all influenced by actual people (beginning with ourselves and our families), their mannerisms and physical features and bits of overheard dialogue. But George Sand argued convincingly that she did not paint portraits, and Turgenev was haunted by figures that appeared to him from out of the blue. Joseph Conrad said, "And what is a novel if not a conviction of our fellow-man's existence strong enough to take upon itself a form of imagined life clearer than reality. . . ." That seems a perfect goal for a fiction writer: to achieve "a form of imagined life clearer than reality."

Although *elements* of real people sometimes show up in my own work, I like to think that my characters don't really live anywhere but on the crowded page. Inventing your own people stretches the imagination and protects you from libel lawsuits. Still, it is hard not to make *some* use of a mother like mine, who's capable of such malapropisms as: "He dropped her like a baked potato," and "A girl in hand is worth two in a bush."

4. What are you working on now? If your editor or your agent asks this question, the answer, of course, is "the great American novel." But it's a particularly disturbing question if you're suffering from writer's block at the time. You can always say, "It's none of your business," or that you're superstitious and don't like to talk about your work until it's finished. The thing is, you probably really *are* writing, even when you're not committing anything to the page or the disk. Simple observation is a stage of writing, and so is dreaming about what you've observed. Just as everyone has private rituals of work, we all have mysterious and individual periods of gestation and birth, followed by equally mysterious periods of rest and replenishment. Or at least that's what I tell my editors and creditors. Remember, when you truly do have something in progress, there *is* a definite risk in talking about it in any detail, the risk of expending the material and your creative energy in the telling, instead of in the writing. So, what am I working on now? None of your business.

5. Who are your favorite writers? You would think that by now I'd have a list prepared, or that I'd be able to just reel off the names of best-loved books and their authors. But either the list keeps changing or I need an expanded memory system. Still, this is a provocative question, one that invariably reminds us of literary influence and its attendant advantages and anxieties. During a workshop I taught in Iowa in the late seventies, several of my students were reading John Irving. Their own manuscripts teemed with bears, castrations, and unheralded deaths. This kind of imitation is okay in the earliest stages of learning, when it's a natural part of the apprenticeship. But after a while, if those bears are still around, they'd better be doing new tricks. Some writers I know don't read at all while their own work is shaping itself, for fear that someone else's prose will be incorporated into their own. This is a legitimate fear. Before I begin a new project, though, I almost *have* to reread a few favorite authors, as if to relearn how to write.

But, in case you hadn't noticed, I still haven't answered the original question. Among my favorites, to whom I can assign influence, are Jane Austen, for her wit and expansiveness on such a small canvas; Henry Green, for believing that everything matters, if it happens; John Updike, for his sentences; J. D. Salinger, for his risk of sentimentality; Emily Dickinson for telling the truth "slant"; Nathanael West, for his dark yet redemptive vision.

6. Why do you write? That's easy—because I can't tap-dance. But of course that's a facetious answer. I think I began writing, as a middle child in a middle-class family, to get attention from my parents. And I continue to write now because I feel compelled to do so. The poet, Donald Hall, quotes Milton—"Fame is the spur, that last infirmity of noble minds," and then goes on to say, "The notion of fame embarrasses us because we confuse it with *mere* vanity, like preening before a mirror. Or we confuse it with celebrity, as if Milton had been confessing his desire to become Johnny Carson. Fame is a word for the love that everyone wants, impersonal love, love from strangers for what we are, what we do or make."

Vengeance can be another spur. Dan Wakefield once confessed here at Bread Loaf that he became a writer so that the girls who wouldn't date him in high school would be sorry. But sometimes the need is for the work itself. Keats wrote, in a letter to a friend, "I find that I cannot exist without poetry. . . . I had become all in a tremble from not having written anything of late." And sometimes the motivation is more ambiguous. V. S. Naipaul said he began writing, when he was a youngster, simply because he thought it would be nice to be a writer. "I had nothing to say," he added. Tim O'Brien would surely advise you to wait until you do. But often you don't *know* precisely what it is you want to say until you start putting it all down. The process itself provides revelation, a bit of thrifty autoanalysis. Only then do you understand not only what it is you want to say, but also why you're moved to say it. Searching for a moral imperative to write, *before* the fact, can inhibit you into absolute silence. Don't worry, if your motives are corrupt the work will reflect that, and be meretricious and dull.

7. Are you married? This may seem like the most inane of all questions, but in fact it isn't. Being married, or just living intimately with someone, can surely affect your working habits, and even your writing style. Look what it does to the rest of your life. If you're lucky, you'll find someone literate and intelligent and honest, who's also amenable to reading first drafts, and will be generally tolerant and protective of the creative process. Colette had her Willy, who locked her in her workroom; Tolstoy had Sophie to abuse; Scott had Zelda for their mutual torment; and Virginia Woolf had the incomparable Leonard. Cynthia Ozick sees Leonard Woolf's function as nurse to his wife's threatened genius. And Virginia Woolf's madness, Ozick tells us, fed her husband's genius for responsibility.

Some of us believe that we need heroic nursing, too, and, despite the obvious sacrifices, others seem to need to be the nurse-saviour. But even in more conventional and equitable arrangements, in which one partner happens to be a writer, there are risks to both parties. The obsessive attention that writing demands can exclude and offend those around you. Whenever I drift off, during a conversation, into what John Gardner called the "fictional dream," I seem to come to about every fifth sentence or so. Even worse, the conversation can then, inadvertently, become part of the work, a true invasion of someone else's privacy. Resentment is inevitable. The former wife of a well-known writer once confided that she always told her husband she loved his new chapter when she had to read it at bedtime. If her admiration was at all qualified, he would become so upset they'd never get to sleep.

On the other hand, it's pretty hard to convince anyone, except maybe another writer, that you're actually *working* in that fugue state, especially if you haven't published anything yet. Writing seems more like a hobby to nonwriters (not to mention to the IRS) when it doesn't have the authority of print and remuneration. My husband, who kindly supported me during the years preceding publication, still asks if I'm going to be *typing* on a given day. So marry if you must, but not out of editorial necessity.

An appropriate additional question to the one about marriage, especially (but not exclusively) for women, would be: Do you have any children? Jane Austen, Virginia Woolf, Willa Cather, the Brontë sisters, Eudora Welty, and George Eliot (among many others) did not. I started writing pretty late, and I think it's hardly a coincidence that I wrote my first short story soon after my younger child started school. It's also no coincidence that the story was rife with domestic references. My first novel was published when I was forty-four. That younger child's first novel was published when she was an unencumbered undergraduate of twenty-two, the age I was when I married. The family joke is that my mother has until she's eighty-eight.

8. Do you have a writing schedule, and a special place to work? Schedules make me think of trains and buses, not writers. But that's because I'm dilatory and wait for what I call, for want of a better word, "inspiration." Once I really get going, though, I work nonstop until I get hungry or the Board of Health orders me to take a bath. Inspiration is that voice in my head that keeps talking. Sometimes, because I'm busy doing something else, or because I'm testing the validity of the inner voice, I'll keep lines and lines of prose in my head, and when I can't contain them any longer, rush to get them down. John Irving, by the way, does the same thing and refers to it as the "enema syndrome." Maybe more meticulous toilet training leads other writers to more conventional and tidier work habits, but I'm heartened by Tolstoy who said, "One ought only to write when one leaves a piece of one's flesh in the ink-pot each time one dips one's pen."

As far as place goes, that seems to be part of the necessary ritual for many of us. Proust, of course, had his famous cork-lined room, and Jane Austen sat down at a simple pine table. Almost everyone agrees on the agreeability of quiet. Dickens was once so disturbed by the incessant barking of some neighborhood dogs that he threatened to shoot them. Privacy is another essential, especially if you have ever heard someone else clear his throat of your next line. In her famous essay, "A Room of One's Own," Virginia Woolf wrote, "A woman must have money and a room of her own if she's to write fiction." About five years after our older daughter left for college, I realized that I didn't have to maintain her room as a shrine to her adolescence, but could use it, in her absence, as a study. My ideal writing environment, though, is a place called Yaddo, the artist's colony in upstate New York, where I have had that room of my own—without a telephone—a room in which no one hums or whistles or cracks her knuckles but me. A room in which the ghosts of its previous tenants have left their benevolent shadows.

But I know writers who can work while they're driving a car, who keep a notepad handy on the sun visor, to scribble madly on at stoplights. Auden said, "My poetry doesn't change from place to place; it changes with the years." And the volumes of work that have come from political prisoners during their imprisonment and from the writers of the Holocaust remind us that a particular, sanctified place for writing is truly more of a luxury and a privilege than a necessity.

9. What advice do you have for young writers? Oh, the usual stuff about reading, and about committing yourself—body and soul—to your work. Henry James's dictum to be someone on whom nothing is lost remains sound, and so does that old chestnut about less being more. I'd also echo the poet who advised his students to "get a trade." Face it— Meryl Streep is unlikely to take an option on your latest sestina. And when the story collection you've been working on these last several years is finally published, the advance will hardly cover that week's groceries. Calvin Trillin once asked his publisher, pleadingly, at lunch, if his next advance could possibly exceed the lunch tab, and was advised not to be ridiculous.

Aside from the obvious monetary gain, working at something besides writing enriches your writing by expanding your experience of the world. Dickens worked in a blacking factory. William Carlos Williams, Céline, and Chekhov were all doctors. Wallace Stevens worked in insurance and Kafka, to his great despair, did, too. (Read *The Metamorphosis* for what is probably the most desperately creative reason for not showing up at the office.) I've worked at several odd jobs over the years, from operating a bookkeeping machine to renting beach chairs and umbrellas under the boardwalk at Coney Island. I haven't written *directly* about these experiences, but they've surely given me a new perspective on human events. My most recent extracurricular work and the most common supplemental job for writers is teaching writing, or encouraging others to do what you can't earn a living at yourself. The ironies abound. Which brings me to the next question.

10. Can writing be taught? The argument over this one continues even as writing programs proliferate all over the country. My answer is qualified—yes, writing can be taught, but only to writers (a paraphrase, I guess of William Stegner's two-part answer: 1. It can be done. 2. It can't be done to everybody). By writers, I mean anyone simultaneously seized

by the senses and by the possibilities of language. A writer may or may not have a formal education, and certainly not necessarily one in "creative writing," whatever that is. So what can all those well-intentioned and well-promoted programs do? Well, for one thing, they can provide a respite from solitude (remember, it's not loneliness, really, just solitude), and give you admission to a community of your peers. John Ciardi, who was the previous director of this conference, reminds us that there was no writer of any consequence in history who was not at some time a member of a group, from the Greek agora, to the Roman bath, to the French café, to the English university.

This community of your fellows will offer encouragement in your struggle, which might turn out to be a mixed blessing. Do you know the road signs as you approach campus, something like "Caution, students ahead"? Well, Theodore Morrison, another former director of the Bread Loaf Writers' Conference, once suggested there be one that says, "Encouragement ahead, pass at your own risk," an indication of the dangers of workshop praise, when it's unleavened by honesty.

A new writer of heart and originality can learn to hone and polish his work. A writer of polish alone can be made to recognize the absence of heart and originality. Writing programs also furnish an audience for your work, that entity we all fear and desire with equal intensity. You will probably learn something about criticism, of your own writing and of others'. And a talented writing teacher can help you discover the most important thing of all—what *you* do well, where your natural strengths are, and how to develop them. I hasten to add that you can, of course, become a writer without any of these advantages.

11. Aside from teaching, what do you do when you're not writing? Much of that time is spent in longing to write. During the rest of the time, I live my real, frequently unexamined life and I read, the two greatest sources of refreshment and replenishment I know. The fear, I think, for some writers, including myself, is that you no longer are one when you're not actually doing it. The other fear is that this pause you're experiencing now is a true, and perhaps terminal, block. Hardy wrote, after thirty proseless years, "Less and less shrink the visions then vast in me." I don't know any magic formula to release you from the agony of writer's block, except to keep believing that all sorts of wonderful ideas are swimming around down there, just below the level of consciousness, and will rise to the surface at precisely the right moment.

12. Is an agent necessary? This is the question that Kurt Vonnegut, in his novel, *God Bless You, Mr. Rosewater*, has the imprisoned war

criminal, Adolf Eichmann, who's preparing his memoirs, ask a visiting writer. Of course you don't have to have an agent, Herr Eichmann. We all know at least one anecdote about someone now famous who was first discovered in the slush pile. An agent, to some minds, is only one more person, after your mother and your writing instructor, who can give your work some validation by praising it and pronouncing it marketable, and your mother doesn't charge you ten percent. But a gifted, dedicated agent is far more than that. He or she is the matchmaker between you and your potential editor, a business wizard who understands the nuances of contracts and royalty statements, a friend of the highest order. Now here's the catch: finding a reputable agent who'll represent an untried writer is almost as hard as finding a publisher. Offering a book-length manuscript, as opposed to individual stories, poems, or essays, will help, at least, to get you a reading. Look at one of two reference books, *Literary Marketplace* or *The Writer's Market* for suitable candidates. I'll let our visiting literary agents fill you in on the rest, and get back to our real purpose here, the pursuit of craft.

13. Do you revise? Is the sun going to set today? One of the great *pleasures* of writing is revision, the second and third and fourth chance you hardly ever get in any other area of your life. Look at the facsimile manuscript pages in the *Paris Review* interviews called "Writers at Work." Most of them look like fly paper, they're so speckled with changes. S. J. Perelman, in his interview, claimed to do thirty-seven drafts of each story. "I once tried doing thirty-three," he says, "but something was lacking, a certain—how shall I say—*je ne sais quoi.*"

If you think your work is perfect in the first draft, just read it aloud. Listen for the music of your language, and for the false notes and tiresome repetitions. Remember that every word of your fiction should either illuminate the characters or move the story forward. Try, as Grace Paley advises, to make it more *truthful.* You may find you've now reduced that four-generation saga to mere haiku, but that's the risk of revision for you. The skill I'm still trying to master is how to *stop* revising, to finally, completely let something go. I've discovered that bookstore managers frown on the writer who scribbles belated changes into bound books.

14. What is your response to reviews? I wish I could have the sang-froid of Philip Roth, who usually leaves the country before publication, or be as civilized and agreeable as Alain Robbe-Grillet, who says, "When the review is violently against, it's a stimulus. When the review is intelligent, it's a dialogue." But I'm afraid I run the hysterical gamut from

ecstasy to disbelief over the favorable reviews of my books, and from
suicidal to homicidal impulses over the unfavorable ones. Workshop
criticism prepares you in a way for the vagaries and harshness of professional criticism. In any event, writing well is the best defense, the only
revenge.

15. Do you keep a notebook? No, except in the loosest sense. I mean
that I sometimes make illegible notes on the margin of my newspaper
or in my checkbook and occasionally even on the palm of my hand. I've
bought perfectly nice notebooks and then forgotten to carry them, or I've
filled them with recipes copied from magazines at the dentist's. This is
merely an example of my own lack of discipline; I would recommend
notebook- or journal-keeping to others more organized than I am. My
novelist friends who faithfully keep them say that certain useful observations would be lost without an immediate record, and that writing
informally in a diary is a kind of ongoing training for the big event. I
would also recommend reading the collected diaries, memoirs, and/or
letters of writers one admires for further insights into the writing process. Among those I found especially interesting as well as useful are
Flaubert's, Katherine Mansfield's, Virginia Woolf's, Ford Madox Ford's,
and Flannery O'Connor's.

16. Do you write an outline before you begin a novel? Good heavens,
no! Then I would know what happens and I'd lose the sense of mystery
I always set out with when I start a novel, and that propels me toward
finishing it. It would be disingenuous to pretend I don't have *any* plans
for where it all might end. I do, but I'm not committed to a final shape
for the story or a final destination for my characters. During the process
of writing a book, I generally find out where it's really going.

John Gardner, on the other hand, hung butcher paper from one end of
his workroom to the other, and mapped out the entire plot structure
before he set down a word of prose. The danger of my method is to discover, after one or two hundred pages, that *nothing* is going to happen
in this story, and that the project must be abandoned. The danger in John
Gardner's method, at least for me, is of simply losing my curiosity, and
therefore my impetus to continue writing out a fictional life that's preor-
dained.

To keep a long project, like a novel, going, when it seems to lose steam,
you might try changing point of view, or moving out of the chronology.
Write the ending, for instance, and then drive ahead toward it.

17. How do you decide on the use of first or third person, present or
past tense? Sometimes, these seem less like choices than inevitabili-

ties—you just start writing and everything falls into place. But at other times, it's like choosing a dress. You try several of them on until something fits, something looks good. There are certain limitations to any form or style. The hot and compelling whisper of the first-person voice excludes the inner voices of the other characters. You worry about whether they've been given justice in this one-sided narration, and about the claustrophobic atmosphere inside only that one head. The omniscient third person overview seems fairer and more interesting in its variations, but loses the particular intimacy of that single voice. The present tense has immediacy, but, as we all know, it can become monotonous and precious. The past tense gives you the perspective of distance, but sometimes too much distance. As the bartender said, name your poison.

18. Do you write poetry? Not that anyone would know it. But I read it, and I think all prose writers should, especially for its lessons of economy and music. I'm sure the poets can learn something from us, too, but I don't know exactly what.

19. Do you think you would have continued to write if you hadn't been able to publish? Yes, I do, despite my conventional lust for fame and fortune. And I think my own history bears me out. The first thing I ever had published was a poem about winter in the *Junior Inspectors' Club Journal*, sponsored by the New York City Department of Sanitation, when I was ten. Aside from some appalling adolescent poetry accepted by my high school literary magazine, the next thing I published was a short story in the *Saturday Evening Post*, when I was thirty-five. So I'm able to be sustained, at least for a while, by the gratification of work. Of course, being published is *fun*. When my mother took me down to the Department of Sanitation to receive the certificate that went with my first poem's publication, the garbage trucks lining the street had all the majesty of royal guards. But writing, in case we ever forget it, is also a kind of perverse and agonizing fun.

20. What do you wear to bed? I confess that no one has actually ever asked me this question, but I want to answer it anyway. Sometimes, when I'm writing, I get into bed in the middle of the day. Usually, either the chill of discovery or failure is upon me and I just want to get warm. So I wear layers of sweaters and scarves over my nightgown or jeans, and heavy socks, and once, as I remember it, a pair of mittens. Maybe I'm charged by some of the electricity from my infamous word processor, because the sheets seem to crackle around me and the bedside lights flicker. The sexy perfume of ink pervades the room.

Are there any further questions?

CONTRIBUTORS

MARVIN BELL teaches at the University of Iowa and has published numerous books of poetry, including *New and Selected Poems* and *Iris of Creation*.

ROSELLEN BROWN has published numerous books, including *Tender Mercies* and *Civil Wars*.

NICHOLAS DELBANCO directs the graduate program in writing at the University of Michigan. His novels and stories have been widely published. Most recently, he published *Running in Place: Scene From the South of France*.

STANLEY ELKIN teaches at Washington University in St. Louis. His numerous books include *Searches and Seizures*, a collection of novellas, and *The Rabbi of Lud*, a novel.

RICHARD FORD is a novelist and short story writer whose books include *Wildlife, Rock Springs*, and *The Sportswriter*. He lives in Montana.

GAIL GODWIN is the author of many novels, including *The Finishing School* and *The Odd Woman*.

DAVID HUDDLE teaches at the University of Vermont. His books of short fiction include *The High Spirits* and *Only the Little Bone*.

T. R. HUMMER edits *New England Review* and teaches at Middlebury College. His books of poetry include *The 18,000-Ton Olympic Dream* and *Lower-Class Heresy*.

JOHN IRVING is the author of many novels, including *The Cider House Rules* and *A Prayer for Owen Meany*.

ERICA JONG most recently published *Any Woman's Blues*.

DONALD JUSTICE teaches at the University of Florida and has published numerous books of poetry, including his *Selected Poems*.

SYDNEY LEA is a poet and novelist; his books include *A Place in Mind*, a novel, and *Prayer for the Little City*, a book of poems. He was a founding editor of *New England Review*.

PHILIP LEVINE has published many volumes of poetry, including *Not This Pig*, *Sweet Will*, and *Selected Poems*.

WILLIAM MATTHEWS teaches at City College of the City University of New York. His numerous books of poetry include *Flood* and *Blues If You Want*.

PAUL MARIANI teaches at the University of Massachusetts in Amherst. His books include *Dream Song*, a biography of John Berryman, and *Salvage Operation*.

JOYCE CAROL OATES teaches at Princeton and most recently published a novel, *Because It Is Bitter and Because It Is My Heart*, and a collection of stories, *Heat*.

TIM O'BRIEN most recently published *The Nuclear Age*, a novel, and *The Things They Carried*, a collection of stories.

ROBERT PACK teaches at Middlebury College and has published many books of poetry and literary criticism. Most recently he published *Before It Vanishes*. *The Long View*, a collection of essays, is forthcoming.

JAY PARINI teaches at Middlebury College. He most recently published *Town Life*, a book of poems, and *The Last Station*, a novel.

LINDA PASTAN has published many books of poetry, including *The Imperfect Paradise* and *Heroes in Disguise*.

FRANCINE PROSE is the author of *Women and Children First, Hungry Heats*, and other books.

LYNNE SHARON SCHWARTZ has published novels and collections of short fiction, including *Acquainted with the Night* and *Disturbances in the Field*.

ELLEN BRYANT VOIGT lives in Vermont and has published many collections of poetry, including *Claiming Kin* and *The Forces of Plenty*.

NANCY WILLARD teaches at Vassar College and has published books for children, novels, stories, and poems, including *Things Invisible to See* and *Water Walker*.

HILMA WOLITZER is the author of novels and short stories. Her books include *In the Palomar Arms* and *Silver*. She lives in New York City.

ACKNOWLEDGMENTS

A number of the essays in this anthology appeared first in the periodicals listed below, sometimes in another version. To their editors, thanks are due.

"Don't Just Sit There: Writing as a Polymorphous Perverse Pleasure" by Rosellen Brown first appeared in *NER/BLQ.*

"What's in a Name?" by Stanley Elkin first appeared in *The Denver Quarterly.*

"Reading" by Richard Ford first appeared in *Antaeus.*

"A Diarist on Diarists" by Gail Godwin first appeared in *Antaeus.*

"Taking What You Need, Giving What You Can: The Writer as Student and Teacher" by David Huddle first appeared in *Writer's Craft, Teacher's Art,* edited by Mimi Schwartz (Boynton/Cook, 1991).

"Against Metaphor" by Terry Hummer first appeared in *New England Review.*

"Getting Started" by John Irving first appeared in *Publishers Weekly.*

"The Prose Sublime" by Donald Justice first appeared in *Michigan Quarterly Review.*

"Making a Case" by Sydney Lea first appeared in *NER/BLQ.*

"On Being Prolific" by Jay Parini first appeared in *The New York Times Book Review.*

"Remembrance of Tense Past" by Lynne Sharon Schwartz first appeared in *NER/BLQ.*

"On Tone" by Ellen Bryant Voigt first appeared in *NER/BLQ.*

UNIVERSITY PRESS OF NEW ENGLAND publishes books under its own imprint and is the publisher for Brandeis University Press, Brown University Press, Clark University Press, University of Connecticut, Dartmouth College, Middlebury College Press, University of New Hampshire, University of Rhode Island, Tufts University, University of Vermont, and Wesleyan University Press.

Library of Congress Cataloging-in-Publication Data

Writers on writing / Robert Pack, Jay Parini, editors.

   p.   cm.—(A Bread Loaf anthology)

ISBN 0–87451–559–9.—ISBN 0–87451–560–2 (pbk.)

    1. Authorship—Quotations, maxims, etc. 2. Authors—Quotations.

1. Pack, Robert, 1929– . II. Parini, Jay. III. Series.

PN165.W684 1991

808.88′2—dc20   91–50372